HOUSE
AND
SENATE

HOUSE
AND
SENATE

Ross K. Baker

THIRD EDITION

W·W·Norton & Company
New York·London

Copyright © 2001, 1995, 1989 by W. W. Norton & Company, Inc.

All rights reserved
Printed in the United States of America

The text of this book is composed in Times Roman
with the display set in TF Habitat Contour B-Bold
Composition by PennSet, Inc.
Manufacturing by The Courier Companies, Inc.
Book design by Marjorie J. Flock

Library of Congress Cataloging-in-Publication Data
Baker, Ross K.
    House and senate / Ross K. Baker.— 3rd ed.
      p. cm.
    Includes bibliographical references (p.   ) and index.
    ISBN 0-393-97611-4 (pbk.)
      1. United States. Congress. I. Title.

JK1061 .B33 2000
328.73'079—dc21

                              00-030557

ISBN 0-393-97611-4 (pbk.)

W.W. Norton & Company, Inc., 500 Fifth Avenue, New York, N.Y. 10110
www.wwnorton.com

W. W. Norton & Company Ltd., 10 Coptic Street, London WC1A 1PU
1 2 3 4 5 6 7 8 9 0

To my mother,
Augusta L. Baker, and to the memory of Maurice Baker,
wonderful parents and good friends.

Contents

Introduction

A SUSTAINED COMPARISON of the House and Senate is something that most people assume to exist. They are usually surprised to find that such a book is not to be found. Tantalizing parts of the drama have been written and there are even some summaries of House-Senate differences that are prized for their compactness.[1] I wanted to cover the difference in greater scope.

I realized that a book based on documentary sources alone might not provide enough richness of texture and detail to do justice to a relationship so multifaceted and subtle. I also was not certain that the House-Senate distinctions set forth in the literature constituted a complete inventory of differences. These concerns prompted me to interview people who could add to that category of differences or elaborate on those already recognized.

I conducted roughly 150 interviews for this book and its first two editions. The interviews took place over a seven-year period from 1986 to 1999. Those interviewed were incumbent senators and former senators who had first been elected to the House, journalists assigned to cover one or both houses of Congress, lobbyists who visit both House members and senators, and congressional staff who have served in both chambers.

The careers of the senators to whom I spoke spanned a large portion of recent American history. They ranged from Senator Margaret Chase Smith, the Maine Republican whose career began in the House before the United States entered World War II and ended in the Senate in 1972, to Michael D. Crapo, an Idaho Republican who was born in 1951, the year after Margaret Chase Smith delivered her "Declaration of Conscience" speech on the floor of the Senate denouncing the excesses of Senator Joseph R. McCarthy.

Among the past and present senators I interviewed were a former presidential candidate, George S. McGovern, the Democratic nominee in 1972, and a Democratic senator whose insurgent campaign brought down a Democratic president Lyndon B. Johnson, Senator Eugene McCarthy. Also in the group was the senator closest of all his Senate colleagues to John F. Kennedy, Senator George A. Smathers of Florida and the closest Senate friend of Ted Kennedy, Senator Chris Dodd of Connecticut.

Among the journalists I interviewed are people whose names are familiar to a daily newspaper reader, a subscriber to a news magazine, or a viewer of network and cable news programs. They include Cokie Roberts of ABC-TV news and National Public Radio, Dan Balz and Helen Dewar of the *Washington Post*, Adam Clymer of the *New York Times*, and Chris Matthews, host of the MSNBC and CNBC program *Hardball*, and Linda Wertheimer of National Public Radio.

Although the names of some of my most valuable informants are not widely known to the public, those familiar with the world of Washington will recognize Thomas A. Dine, currently president of Radio Free Europe and Radio Liberty, and Bertram D. Carp, former deputy director of the Domestic Council at the White House and currently with the law firm of Williams and Jensen. I would also like to acknowledge the help of Michael B. Levy, former Assistant Secretary of the Treasury.

Interviewing "elites," as these people are described by social scientists, entails a set of challenges different from those encountered during mass surveys of public opinion with thousands of anonymous respondents or even from in-depth surveys of ordinary citizens. Surveys are more structured and proceed according to a set of questions that look to a certain uniformity of response. Elite interviews are less manageable. Elite interviewees are often skilled, through years of practice, at side-stepping questions or even rephrasing questions to enable them to provide the answer they want to give you. Some of the interviews were invaluable; others were of limited use. In the aggregate, however, they paint a picture of two houses of Congress that have not merged into a single undifferentiated entity called "Congress."

Sometimes the differences between the House and the Senate are so obvious and overwhelming that the logic the framers of the Constitution expressed in a two-house national legislature is manifested with startling clarity; other differences are expressed with such fineness and subtlety that only the *cognoscenti* can savor them. From time to time an incident occurs that reminds people, in a dazzling symbolic fashion, just how different the two houses are from each other.

On March 20, 1999, a train carrying members of the U.S. House of Representatives left Union Station in Washington, D.C., for the town of Hershey, Pennsylvania. The purpose of the trip was for the members to attend a retreat for House Democrats and Republicans in the aftermath of the impeachment and trial of President Clinton.

The choice of Hershey was both practical and symbolic. Located only a few hours from the capital, it is also the home of the Hershey Company, the world's largest manufacturer of chocolate candy. The town advertises itself as "The Sweetest Place on Earth." In announcing the retreat and inviting colleagues to sign up for the weekend, Representative Christopher Cox, a California Republican, stood behind a podium festooned with Hershey's kisses. Sweetness was the order of the day.

The March 20, 1999, event was the second of these retreats. The first took place in 1997 and the purposes were the same: to instill in the House of Representatives a sense of bipartisan civility. The very fact that a second retreat was needed to diminish the bitter partisan rancor in the House might well raise in people's minds questions about how well the first one had succeeded in dampening the fires of partisan enmity.

But conditions had become even graver in the intervening two years. Impeachment proceedings had begun in the House. The election of 1998 took place and results shattered most historical precedents. Instead of the normal pattern of losses in a midterm election by a president's party, Bill Clinton's Democrats had actually gained seats. So stunning was this Republican loss and so narrow was the Republicans' new majority that Speaker Newt Gingrich resigned not only the speakership but also his seat as a representative from Georgia's 6th Congressional District. Representative Robert Livingston of Louisiana quickly gained the votes needed to claim the speakership, but before he could be sworn in, he too resigned his seat on December 19, the very day the House voted two articles of impeachment against President Clinton. Livingston had been revealed to have had an extramarital affair and he concluded that he could not serve as Speaker of the House. In an act that symbolized the harshness of partisan relationships in the House that day, many Democrats walked out of the House chamber after the failure of their motion to substitute a censure resolution for impeachment.

The speeches of both Democrats and Republicans dripped venom as the vote approached. California Democrat Barbara Lee and New York Democrat Jose E. Serrano accused the Republicans of staging a coup d'etat. In response, South Carolina Republican Lindsay O. Graham accused Clinton of committing crimes that cheated our legal system. Deputy Minority Leader David E. Bonior retorted that the Republicans were trying to "hijack an election and hound the President out of office against the will of the American people." Judiciary Committee Chairman Henry Hyde, an Illinois Republican, characterized Clinton as "a serial violator" of his oath of office.[2]

The House is usually a more partisan place than the Senate. The boundaries of House districts, in the majority of states whose populations entitle them to more than a single member, are subject to change after each census. The process of redistricting is one of the most political in all of American government. Wishing to confer political advantage on one party or the other, the state legislatures create districts that guarantee the election of either Democrats or Republicans depending on which party dominates the state legislature at the time of re-districting. New York Republican Peter King, in the aftermath of the House impeachment vote, estimated that as many as 180 of the 228 House Republicans represented districts in which the overwhelming number of voters were Republicans.[3]

Democratic state legislators are equally inclined to fashion safe seats for House Democrats. Most states are much less likely to be dominated by a single party even though they may be no more heterogeneous demographically in such things as race, income, or education than many House districts.[4]

The citizens most likely to care enough to vote in these strong party districts tend to be drawn from their party's base: very liberal Democrats and highly conservative Republicans. Getting elected and reelected means for members that they cannot alienate these highly partisan voters. In 1998 and 1999, this situation dictated to Republicans that they wage a relentless offensive to drive Bill Clinton from office, and to Democratic members that they mount a last-ditch stand to save him from impeachment.

It seemed beneficial, then, in the wake of the polarizing impeachment and trial to make a gesture of reconciliation. Representative David Bonior, the party's number two leader in the House, urged his fellow Democrats to attend, saying, "I believe this Congress faces no more important challenge than making democracy work again in a manner that is civil and respectful." Other Democrats were not so hopeful. Representative Eva Clayton of North Carolina derided the event as "kiss and make up." Another Democrat was even more blunt: "There's no reason to think, after what we just went through, with them trying to throw out the leader of our party, that we're all suddenly going to be buddies. That's absurd."[5]

And as it turned out, some of the most conspicuous absentees were those in the greatest need of healing. Of the House

Judiciary Committee that recommended the impeachment, only three members showed up, and one of them was Representative George Gekas (R-Pa.) in whose congressional district the town of Hershey is located. Absent were two of the president's most ardent defenders, Democrats Barney Frank of Massachusetts and Maxine Waters of California. Neither of Clinton's two most aggressive antagonists, Representative Bob Barr (R-Ga.) and Judiciary Chairman Henry Hyde, were to be found on the train to Hershey.[6]

Clearly the scars that had been inflicted by the clash over the impeachment in the House cold not be easily erased by a pleasant weekend in Pennsylvania nibbling chocolates and listening to actor Sam Waterston doing his flawless imitation of Abraham Lincoln.

When the dust from the impeachment trial settled in the Senate, there was also a call for bipartisan healing from Connecticut Democrat Joseph I. Lieberman and Kansas Republican Sam Brownback. The two senators invited their other ninety-eight colleagues to a gathering that featured clergy of all faiths. Those attending would be serenaded by a group of gospel singers to instill the proper feeling of forgiveness. Six senators showed up.

But far from being evidence of partisan estrangement, the low turnout was interpreted as a healthy sign. The Senate did not require a soothing poultice of chocolate and Lincolnesque oratory. Even one of the sponsors, Senator Lieberman, conceded, "This very divisive, troubling episode actually united us, as men and women, as individuals who happen to be senators." To this, Lieberman's Connecticut colleague Christopher Dodd added, "[I]t may be that many members felt they had already, in a sense, gone through a reconciliation with each other."[7]

To assert that important differences exist between the House and Senate is not a self-evident proposition. A respectable, indeed eminent, body of scholarly and official opinion holds that the differences between the House and the Senate have narrowed significantly. There is much to commend this "convergence theory," not the least of which is that many people believe it.[8]

No one would argue that the two houses are as distinct from each other, and in the same way, as they were in 1789. The ratification of the Seventeenth Amendment in 1913 made senators subject to popular election rather than election by the state legislatures, and this greatly narrowed the distance between the senators and the voters. The once-hierarchical House now resembles somewhat more closely the Senate where there are few gradations of power. The House has, on occasion, shown itself to be an estimable forum for debate on national issues, superseding a Senate once considered the preeminent forum for debating the great issues. Party-line voting in which all or most Democrats are arrayed against all or most Republicans is now almost as much a feature of the Senate as it is of the House. Some House members have broken free of the rigid division of labor that forced them to restrict their pronouncements to the subject matter within the jurisdiction of their principal committee assignments. Even the difference in length of term looks less imposing as House incumbents have shown themselves almost invulnerable to challenges.

While acknowledging this evidence of convergence, or even reversal or rearrangement of some traditional characteristics, this book seeks to persuade the reader that important House-Senate differences persist. I will try to make the case by pointing out that members of both chambers know it. Journalists who cover Congress know it. People who lobby Congress know it. Staff members who have worked on both sides of the Capitol know it. Members of Congress, above all, know it.

Not only are the houses different, they are also distant, mutually suspicious, and inordinately prideful and sensitive.

Christopher Matthews, host of the MSNBC and CNBC program *Hardball*, provided his impression of working in a building shared by the House and Senate.

There's kind of an invisible shield across the rotunda. Senators can be on Capitol Hill for years and never cross the Capitol except to hear a State of the Union Message.

There's no reason why somebody over there would disgrace himself by going over to the House side, and the House member, for fear of humiliation, would never risk going over there.

Matthews's comments suggest something more than innocent obliviousness of one house for another. Do they contain a hint of rancor and resentment? I think that the ensuing chapters will show that they do.

William S. White, the journalist who wrote on both the Senate and House in the 1950s, captured a feeling prevalent among House members in an anecdote about House Speaker Sam Rayburn, who served for almost twenty years in that post. Speaking to White about former House member Lyndon B. Johnson, who went on to become the most powerful leader of the Senate in modern times before being elected president, Rayburn said of his fellow Texan's shift to the Senate, "You know, Bill, it was a sad thing—no it was a terrible thing—when old Lyndon decided to leave here and go over yonder. If he had stayed on here he could have been quite a powerful figure—in a few more years."[9]

You get it from the other side as well. Former U.S. senator Joseph Sill Clark, a Pennsylvania Democrat and an aristocrat from Chestnut Hill, was asked some years ago if there existed in the Senate the kind of informal "sociolegislative" lunch groups and clubs that were so popular in the House. These groups have names like "Acorns" and "SOS" and combine serious discussion with good fellowship. Clark reacted with shock and disdain. "Oh, God, no! The other body was scorned. We'd never cavort like that."

Characteristically, Clark resorted to a euphemism—"the other body"—to refer to the House. The word "Senate" was actually ineffable in the House until a rules change took effect on January 6, 1987, that allowed House members to call the Senate by its proper name, rather than "the other body." Senators often use the more cumbersome phrase in a derisive manner.

If these incidents suggest that the two houses have nothing to do with each other unless compelled to do so by the constitutional requirement that no bill shall become law unless passed in identical form by both houses—a requirement necessitating House-Senate conference committees that force the two chambers to interact—it might overstate the case, but not by much. In the course of the research for this book, I was shocked at how little contact there is between the House and Senate under normal circumstances.

A Sketch of Contemporary Bicameralism

In the seven chapters that follow I give the reader a few clues to why the course of the impeachment in the House was so different in tone from the trial that took place in the Senate. The final chapter of the book will be devoted to looking at the impeachment process with an eye toward understanding House-Senate differences.

But before we reach that place, we need to take a brief historical excursion in Chapter 1 to probe the origins of these two distinct institutions that are collectively called "Congress." The fact that House and Senate are subsumed under that title leads casual observers to gloss over the differences between the two and thereby miss some important distinctions about what the framers of the Constitution bequeathed to us.

In Chapter 2, the case is made that the simplest and most obvious of all differences between the House and the Senate is the basis from which most other important differences derive. That basic difference is size.

In Chapter 3, we begin to explore one of the important differences that arise from the fundamental size distinction between the 435-member House and 100-member Senate. It is the difference in the intensity of partisanship—the force that played out so dramatically in the impeachment and trial of President Clinton and in many other areas as well.

A major influence on the degree of partisanship in both chambers is that House members represent much different kinds of constituencies from those of the senators. There are, moreover, important differences in the way House members and senators seek election and reelection. Those distinctions are made in Chapter 4.

Both House and Senate function in the larger context of the federal government and as the focal point of a complex network of interest groups. Congress is ever in the crosshairs of the national media. How lobbyists and journalists distinguish between House and Senate are addressed in Chapter 5.

In Chapter 6, we turn to the question of how permanent and enduring are these House-Senate differences. At times, it has seemed that the two chambers were converging. The case I set forth in this chapter is that, from time to time, it does appear that the shared characteristics of the two bodies seem magnified and the distinctions appear less pronounced, but that the two cannot overlap entirely. The size difference alone distinguishes the two houses so dramatically that even when an election produces a major infusion of ex-representatives into the membership of the Senate, they do not change the fundamental nature of the Senate.

Finally, in Chapter 7, we turn to the impeachment and trial of William Jefferson Clinton and present it as a case study in House-Senate differences. The evidence of the abiding and significant differences between the chambers is drawn not only from published accounts of the events but also from the direct testimony of U.S. senators who participated in the deliberations. A number of these senators are former members of the House and provide eloquent testimony to the differences between the chamber to which they were first elected and the one in which they now serve.

NOTES

1. See Roger H. Davidson and Walter J. Oleszek, *Congress and Its Members,* 2d ed. (Washington, D.C.: Congressional Quarterly Press, 1985), p. 216; Lewis A. Froman, Jr., *The Congressional Process* (Boston: Little, Brown, 1967), pp. 7–15; and David C. Kozak, "House-Senate Differences: A Test among Interview Data," in David C. Kozak and John D. McCarteney, eds., *Congress and Public Policy* (Chicago: Dorsey Press, 1987), pp. 79–94.
2. *New York Times,* December 20, 1999.
3. Adam Nagourney, "Behind the Urge to Impeach," *New York Times Week in Review,* December 20, 1998.
4. See Paul Gronke, *Settings, Institutions, Campaigns, and the Vote* (Ann Arbor, Mich.: University of Michigan Press, forthcoming).
5. Katherine Q. Seelye, "House, with Help, Starts Push to Find the Road to Peace," *New York Times,* February 25, 1999.
6. "Bitterness Melts at House Retreat," *Sunday Star-Ledger,* March 21, 1999.
7. "Low Turnout in Senate to a Reconciliation Call," *New York Times,* February 26, 1999.
8. See, for example, Norman J. Ornstein, "The New House and the New Senate," in Thomas E. Mann and Norman J. Ornstein, eds., *The New Congress* (Washington, D.C.: American Enterprise Institute, 1981), and John R. Alford and John R. Hibbing, "The Electorally Indistinct Senate," paper submitted for presentation at the Norman Thomas Conference on Senate Exceptionalism, Vanderbilt University, Nashville, Tennessee, October 21–23, 1999.
9. William S. White, *Homeplace* (Boston: Houghton Mifflin, 1965), p. 45.

Acknowledgments

THIS BOOK IS ABOUT the two houses of the U.S. Congress, their differences, their similarities, their relationships with each other, and the current status of American bicameralism. The word that comes to mind when describing such an approach is "institutional." It is a word that conjures up an image of forbidding marble buildings in which complex and mysterious civic rituals are acted out.

But my experience, both as a political scientist and a sometime staff member who has worked in both the House and Senate, tells me that the beginning of all wisdom on the subject of Congress is that people provide the key to understanding Congress. And in the two years it took to conduct the research and write this book, it was the willingness of helpful and generous people that enabled me to fulfill the goals of the project.

The list that follows contains many names. Others might have been added except for the fact that the frankness of their answers led them to request anonymity. In appreciation for their forthrightness, I have marked their interviews "not for attribution."

Others were willing either to go on the record or to facilitate the research in other ways. Their names appear below and with their mention goes my thanks.

Luke Albee, Chief of Staff, Senator Patrick J. Leahy

Donnald K. Anderson, former Clerk of the House of
        Representatives

Richard A. Baker, Historian of the U.S. Senate

Dan Balz, *The Washington Post*

Bill Cable, Timmons & Co., Washington, D.C.
Bert Carp, Williams and Jensen, Washington, D.C.
Philip Chartrand, Government Affairs Institute, Georgetown University
Adam Clymer, *New York Times*
Ann Compton, ABC News
Brad Davey, Office of Senator Patrick Leahy
Helen Dewar, *The Washington Post*
Thomas A. Dine, President, Radio Free Europe and Radio Liberty
Kenneth Duberstein, Timmons & Co., Washington, D.C.
Thomas Edsall, *The Washington Post*
Peter Fenn, Fenn & King Communications, Washington, D.C.
Richard F. Fenno, Jr., University of Rochester
Alvin From, Democratic Leadership Council
James Gerstenzang, *The Los Angeles Times*
Kenneth Gold, Government Affairs Institute, Georgetown University
Brenda Hart, Office of Senator Chuck Hagel (R-Neb.)
Greg Harness, Librarian of the U.S. Senate
James Hershman, Government Affairs Institute, Georgetown University
Janet Hook, *The Los Angeles Times*
Spencer Hsu, *The Washington Post*
Patti Iglarsh, LegisFellows Program, The Brookings Institution
Susan S. Lagon, Government Affairs Institute, Georgetown University
Bert Levine, Rutgers University
Eleanor G. Lewis, Washington, D.C.
E. Raymond Lewis, Washington, D.C.
Burdett Loomis, University of Kansas
Lawrence D. Longley, Lawrence University
William T. Lyons, William T. Lyons Associates, Washington, D.C.

Christopher Matthews, Washington Bureau Chief, *San Francisco Examiner* and host of the MSNBC and CNBC program *Hardball*

Tony Mauro, Law Correspondent, *Legal Times*

Harris Miller, Director, Information Technology Association of America

Larry Neal, Press Secretary to Senator Phil Gramm (R-Tex.)

Ilona Nickels, C-SPAN

Mildred A. Porter, Council on Competitiveness, Washington, D.C.

Leroy Rieselbach, University of Indiana

Donald A. Ritchie, Associate Historian of the U.S. Senate

Cokie Roberts, ABC News and National Public Radio

Janice Churchill Sadeghian, Government Affairs Institute, Georgetown University

Gene Smith, Chief of Staff, Office of Representative Howard L. Berman (D-Cal.)

Steven S. Smith, University of Minnesota

Howard Stevens, Government Affairs Institute, Georgetown University

Karen Tumulty, *Time* Magazine

Kathleen J. Tuttle, Office of the Los Angeles County District Attorney

Kirk Victor, *The National Journal*

Linda Wertheimer, National Public Radio

Patricia Dillon Woods, The Woods Institute, Washington, D.C.

Special thanks and appreciation go the following people who made the first two editions of *House and Senate* a success.

Professor and Academic Dean of Fairleigh Dickinson University, Barbara G. Salmore, who read the original manuscript with her trained social scientist's eye and made a number of important improvements.

Edith Sacks, who retired from the Eagleton Institute at Rutgers after a long and meritorious career. In the days before I had learned to use a computer, she did the typing chores and assisted in the preparation of the manuscript.

Alan Rosenthal, of the Eagleton Institute of Politics, who has been a wise and helpful colleague during my thirty years at Rutgers.

Frank Mackaman and John Kornacki at the Dirksen Congressional Institute in Pekin, Illinois, who have supported this and other projects of mine over the years.

Although I have previously acknowledged them, I owe a special debt of gratitude to the men and women who served on the staff of the U.S. Office of Personnel Management and especially to Howard Stevens. Their invitation to me to give a speech on House-Senate differences in 1983 was the real genesis of this book, and Howard has invited me back to speak many times in subsequent years. He and his colleagues are now at the Government Affairs Institute at Georgetown University. Their former colleague, Patty Iglarsh, runs the Legislative Fellows Program at the Brookings Institution.

Finally, my thanks go to Roby Harrington, director of the college department of W. W. Norton & Company, who agreed to publish *House and Senate* and to update it in 1995, and to Steve Dunn who has ably succeeded Roby as editor of this book.

It is the members of the U.S. Senate and the U.S. House of Representatives, past and present, living and dead, whose testimony is the very backbone of this book. Their willingness to take the time to talk to a political scientist whose work profits them very little has been for me a source of the greatest satisfaction:

Senator James G. Abourezk, Senator Wayne Allard, Senator Mark Andrews, Senator Max S. Baucus, Representative Richard Bolling, Senator Thad Cochran,

Senator Larry Craig, Senator Michael D. Crapo, Senator John C. Culver, Senator Christopher J. Dodd, Representative Floyd Fithian, Senator Wyche Fowler, Senator J. William Fulbright, Senator Phil Gramm, Senator Chuck Hagel, Senator William Hathaway, Senator Patrick J. Leahy, Senator Mike Mansfield, Senator Charles Mathias, Senator George S. McGovern, Senator Edmund S. Muskie, Senator Jack Reed, Senator Donald W. Riegle, Jr., Senator Abraham Ribicoff, Senator Warren B. Rudman, Senator Paul S. Sarbanes, Senator Richard S. Schweiker, Senator Hugh D. Scott, Senator George A. Smathers, Senator Margaret Chase Smith, Senator Robert A. Taft, Jr., Representative Frank Thompson, and Senator Timothy Wirth.

HOUSE
AND
SENATE

I

Two Sides of the Capitol
The Evolution of the House and Senate

REPRESENTATIVE CLARENCE CANNON (D-MO.) was a man described by one colleague as having "the air of a man smelling a rotten egg." Chairman of the House Appropriations Committee from 1949 until his death in 1964, Cannon's face—often described as "prunelike"—was seen by millions of Americans as they viewed the quadrennial Democratic Conventions, where he was a longtime parliamentarian. Once, when an opponent accused him of being two-faced, Cannon replied, "Don't you think if I had two faces I'd use the other one instead of this one?"[1]

In 1962, at the dignified age of eighty-three, Cannon became involved in an indecorous public spat with his Senate counterpart, Appropriations Committee chairman Carl Hayden (D-Ariz.), a man one year his senior who had represented his state from the very day it entered the Union in 1912. At the time of his squabble with Cannon, Hayden was also president *pro tem* of the Senate and third in line to succeed the president. Described as "quiet and manly,"[2] Hayden had the reputation for having "smiled more money through the Committee on Appropriations than any other senator has gotten by valid argument."[3]

Perhaps it was inevitable that two such different men in comparable positions in the House and Senate, and having shared custody of the spending of public funds, would ultimately clash. What was at stake in this unseemly quarrel was nothing less than the honor of the House and Senate. The event itself saw the breakdown of the appropriations process—the constitutional procedure whereby Congress provides money for the operation of the federal government.

The Bicameral Battle of the Titans

The origins of the 1962 appropriations war can be found in the bare language of Article I, Section 7, of the Constitution, which says, "All bills for raising revenue shall originate in the House of Representatives." That would seem to mean that only tax bills need originate there, but from the very earliest time the House took the institutional position that the phrase "raising revenue" should also include the making of appropriations. The reason for this position was that at the time of the writing of the U.S. Constitution the British House of Commons, upon which the U.S. House of Representatives was modeled, enjoyed the right to initiate all "money bills."[4]

At no time in history was there any question but that the Senate could freely amend any tax or spending bill when it arrived from the House, and while the Senate never challenged the House on the question of initiating tax measures, the right to move first on appropriations in the absence of House action was quite another matter.

The controversy over who got first shot at appropriations bills flared up occasionally during the nineteenth century because of the occasional failure of the House to act in a timely fashion on spending bills, with the Senate claiming the right to initiate appropriations when the House failed to take the initiative. By the end of the nineteenth century, the Senate accepted the general principle that the House would initiate the appropriations bills but reserved to itself the right to do so if the need arose. The House conceded to the Senate something that might have appeared purely symbolic but that in the delicate and subtle realm of bicameral relations was to prove important. Meetings of conference committees convened for the purpose of working out differences between House and Senate versions of the annual appropriations bills would be held on the Senate side of the Capitol and would be chaired by a senator.

A more direct influence on the struggle between the two chairmen was a practice that had grown up in Congress in the 1930s called "back-door spending," which enabled a federal agency to borrow money directly from the U.S. Treasury rather than seek a regular appropriation of Congress. Cannon regarded himself as a watchdog of the Treasury and detested the practice of back-door spending because it circumvented his committee and violated his notions of frugality. Accordingly, when the House adjourned in September 1961, one of its last acts was to pass an appropriations bill that eliminated back-door spending for four major programs.

By adjourning with the Senate still in session the House was in effect telling the Senate, "Take it or leave it." With the House in adjournment and its members back in their districts there would be no way for the Senate to get the appropriations back into the bill in a conference committee. If the Senate played hardball and took no action on the appropriations bill, the federal government would close down for lack of money, so the Senate acquiesced. "By its formal act of adjournment with so major a bill still unpassed and in disagreement, the House had profoundly insulted the Senate at one of its most sensitive points, its own prestige."[5]

But Cannon's seething resentment against the Senate was generated by more than back-door spending. There was the matter of the location of the appropriations conferences—which, for Cannon, and others of the House, symbolized the arrogance of the Senate. One senior Republican representative had complained, "The House members have to walk over to the Senate side. We don't like that at all. We've asked the Senators, "Why don't you come over here once in a while?' but they won't."[6]

While Cannon was personally irked at the inconvenience of having to scurry (if one of his age and distinction can be said to scurry) back from appropriations conferences on the Senate side when the buzzer for a roll-call vote on the House floor sounded, the pique was more institutional than personal. "The issue symbolized for House members the unfair domination exercised by senators in relations between the houses and also symbolized the prestige enjoyed by the upper house."[7]

Senator Joseph S. Clark, a Pennsylvania Democrat, saw in the assertiveness of the House members an effort to downgrade the Senate to the largely symbolic status of the British House of Lords. "Senate resentment at this desire," Clark observed, "is naturally fierce."[8]

The battle broke out dramatically when Congress returned for the 1962 session, with the House led by a new Speaker, John McCormick of Massachusetts. Chairman Cannon phoned Chairman Hayden to inform him that henceforth House-Senate conferences on appropriations bills would alternate in their meeting places between the House side of the Capitol and the Senate side and that the House Appropriations Committee had recently adopted a resolution to that effect.

The Senate retaliated swiftly. On February 9, Chairman Hayden called his committee into session and they voted to accept the arrangement for alternate meeting sites on the House and Senate sides provided that the House agree to allowing the Senate to originate half the appropriations bills taken up each year.[9]

The first actual test of wills took place on April 10 when a conference committee met on the Senate side under the chairmanship of a senator. At the conclusion of the meeting, House members announced that the next meeting would take place on the House side under a House chairman. The meeting broke up in angry disagreement, and for the next three months each house passed its own appropriations bills. But since the House and Senate chairmen could not agree on a mutually acceptable meeting site for the next conference, there was no way to work out the differences between the House and Senate versions of the appropriations bills and combine them into a single piece

of legislation to be sent to the president, as the Constitution requires. The two houses' versions of the same bill might be astonishingly close, but close is not good enough when a single
bill must be presented to the president for his approval or veto.

Throughout the spring of 1962 the differences between the
two chairmen went unresolved, but by the latter part of June
what had been an irritating but hardly dire situation grew more
ominous as the end of the fiscal year approached.

In those days, the federal government's fiscal year began on
July 1 instead of the current October 1. Any agency of the federal government without money appropriated for it after June
30 would have to begin closing down. Accordingly, a desper-
ate last-minute meeting was called by Carl Hayden, the Senate
appropriations chairman. The locale chosen for the meeting underscored the delicacy of the situation. Hayden asked Cannon
and his House colleagues to meet with their Senate counterparts
in the old Supreme Court chamber, which was located almost
precisely within the Capitol at the midpoint between the House
and Senate wings, but slightly over the line on Senate terrain.

After demanding that the chairmanship of the meeting be
divided between Hayden and himself, Cannon attacked the
Senate's appropriations bill as spendthrift, thereby injecting a
note of substance into what had thus far been a procedural and
symbolic tiff. Cannon saw himself and his committee as vigi-
lant guardians of the public's money, and the recommendations
of the Appropriations Committee to the House reflected that
frugality. The Senate Appropriations Committee, in contrast,
was viewed by Cannon as entirely too sympathetic to the pleas
of agencies of the executive branch for more funds and alto-
gether too open-handed in appropriating money for such
"frills" as foreign economic assistance and operating funds for
the State Department.

Given this set of underlying differences, based largely on
the peculiarities of the bicameral system, institutional positions
hardened. July 1 was approaching with the prospect that 2 million federal workers would go without pay. A very disquieting

plea was issued by Secret Service chief James Rowley to his
agents to agree to continue protecting President Kennedy despite the cutoff in their paychecks.[10]

In the last week of June a flurry of angry letters passed between the two chairmen. Cannon wrote to Hayden criticizing
the Senate for having "invariably increased every appropriations bill passed by the House." One of Hayden's colleagues
characterized Cannon's accusation as "unfair and vicious."
Senator A. Willis Robertson of Virginia (father of 1988 presidential hopeful Pat Robertson), who had spent seven terms in
the House before coming to the Senate, accused Cannon of "in-
sulting" the Senate by "subtly charging the Senate committee
with wasting public funds." But he went beyond the mere upholding of the Senate's honor by transgressing on one of the
most sensitive areas for House members. He said, "No sitting
member of the Senate ever ran for election to the House of
Representatives."[11]

Robertson had uttered the ineffable. His observation was
tantamount to mentioning rope in the house of a hanged man.
Senators might know, in their heart of hearts, that all House
members hankered to be senators, but one would never be so
bold as to proclaim it. The flames of intercameral warfare had
been fanned and the government teetered on the brink of in-
solvency as House members and senators upholding the honor
and dignity of their respective chambers slugged it out in
public.

But communication between the House and Senate was
never suspended and, despite the acerbity of their exchanges,
Cannon and Hayden, who were known to be on personally
friendly terms, continued to negotiate. The immediate problem
of a payless government was solved by a temporary "continuing resolution" to extend the funding of existing programs past
the July 1 deadline.

The more far-reaching constitutional crisis was solved in a
remarkably prosaic way on July 20, 1962, when House and
Senate conferees met to discuss a supplemental appropriations

bill. The first order of business was a coin toss. The winner was a House member, Albert Thomas (D-Tx), who took the chair, and for the first time in living memory a House member presided over an appropriations conference committee.[12]

While this episode with its display of unbridled power on the part of committee chairmen would be unlikely to be repeated today, the episode does tell us a good deal about these two great deliberative bodies. It tells us that they are very different institutions and although we refer to the two, collectively, as "Congress," the components are distinct.

We see chambers of dramatically different size in which there is a prestige differential that favors the smaller house, but this situation is accompanied by a sensitivity to slights on the part of the larger body that its prerogatives be properly venerated by the more elite chamber. The size difference also produces broader responsibilities for those in the smaller body, where there are but 100 members to do the legislative work that 435 members do in the larger house.

We see that although the lawmaking power vested by the Constitution in both houses is more or less the same, there are important differences, and these differences create two quite distinct institutional personalities. At the time it was fashionable for people to refer to the Senate as the more "liberal" of the two institutions based, in large measure, on its greater open-handedness on appropriations.

Underlying the more generous disposition of the Senate were the structural and functional characteristics that set it apart from the House. The most fundamental characteristic is that senators represent broader constituencies than do House members. Senators represent entire states whose interests and populations can be extraordinarily diverse, so the senator must pay heed to a bewildering variety of voices. "A House member, who represents only a segment of a state's population, can look out for his own constituents' needs and do the bidding of the small number of interests in his own territory. For all other groups, he need show no mercy. The senator, on the other hand

. . . must serve as caretaker of the interests of a wider variety
of groups."[13]

Another reason for the Senate committee's generosity came
from the fact that the Senate, with fewer members than the
House but the same legislative responsibilities, required senators to serve on several committees while House members usually had only one major committee assignment. Senators,
accordingly, might find themselves not only members of the
committee that provided the legal authorization for an agency
or program but members of the Appropriations Committee that
provided it with the money to operate. In a congressional system in which there are separate legislative cycles of authorization and appropriation, a senator could influence both the
operating authority of an agency and the amount of money it
received. "In the House, an Appropriations Committee member
has no other committee. Therefore there is no interlocking di-
rectorate—the man who appropriates cannot be the one who
has authorized. Therefore, slashes will be made more freely."[14]

Finally, there was the simple fact that the House acted first
on appropriations bills and the Senate had the final shot at
them. This made the Senate into the court of last resort for interest groups or officials of the executive branch who needed
more money for their agencies. An important factor in the Senate's "liberalness" was that it often had to offset the excessive
parsimony of Cannon. Over the years of Cannon's chairmanship of the House Appropriations Committee, senators had
come to expect appropriations bills from the House to be stingy
in the extreme. This stark structural difference no longer char-
acterizes the positions of the two houses on spending matters,
but at that time senators were prepared to add funds to their
own appropriations bills that were well beyond what Cannon
and his colleagues would consider prudent. The expectation on
both sides of the Hill, however, was that the dollar differences
would be worked out in the conference in which members of
both appropriations committees would predominate.[15] So the

liberal reputation enjoyed by the Senate on spending bills was largely a product of comparison to the frugal House.

We must also be mindful of the 173 years of House-Senate relationships that preceded the Cannon-Hayden showdown. Considerable historical baggage was carried into that controversy, characterized by fluctuations in the fortunes of both chambers and in the relations between them. The adoption of a bicameral form of national legislature was an obstacle to tyranny, but with it came a measure of jealousy and conflict for the two powerful and independent institutions charged jointly with making the nation's laws.

"The Remedy for This Inconveniency"

Bicameralism was not an American idea. It had its roots in the idea of mixed government that can be traced to Aristotle and his notion of a "golden mean"—a moderate middle course between extremes. Institutionally, this expressed itself in forms of government in which power was distributed rather than concentrated. The Roman philosopher Polybius brought the concept forward in the second century B.C. and it was advanced and refined in the Middle Ages by Marsilius of Padua (*c.* 1280–*c.* 1343), who argued that the power to legislate ought to reside in the people. In the period after the Glorious Revolution (1688–1689), John Locke styled a governmental system wherein power and functions were divided as "balanced government." But the most direct influence on the framers of the Constitution was the Frenchman Baron Montesquieu (1689–1755), who warned, in *The Spirit of the Laws* (1748), against concentrating legislative and executive power in a single pair of hands. He urged that legislative power be divided between two assemblies, one of which would represent the nobility and the other the people. This arrangement, of course, was the one that prevailed in Great Britain with a Parliament consisting of a House of Commons and a House of Lords.

But when the framers of the Constitution gathered in Philadelphia in 1787, they realized that Montesquieu's persuasive theory and Great Britain's admirable practice did not readily fit the American situation. Bicameralism in both was based upon representing the common people, which we had, and the aristocracy, which we did not have. Manufacturing an aristocracy in order to emulate British practice or Montesquieuan theory was not a serious possibility. Legislative power was greatly feared by these early framers because of their experience with a powerful British Parliament, but devising a basis for dividing legislative power between two chambers in a nation without a hereditary nobility was a test of the ingenuity of even this remarkable collection of men who participated in the constitutional debate. Indeed, the greatest single controversy at the Constitutional Convention took place over the composition and mode of selection of the second chamber. Should the upper chamber be selected by the lower? Should the people participate directly in the selection or election of senators? What role should the state legislatures play in the selection of senators?

The practice of the thirteen states and their own legislatures was even more compelling than the writings of Locke and Montesquieu or the example of the British Parliament. The constitutions of ten of the states had established bicameral legislatures, but neither the Continental Congress that had functioned during the War of Independence nor the Articles of the Confederation Congress that succeeded it had been bicameral. That seems, however, to have been considered a mistake, and there was little enthusiasm for a one-house legislature at the Constitutional Convention, except in the Pennsylvania delegation. The agenda-setting Virginia Plan put forth by Edmund Randolph called for two legislative houses. Randolph's plan, however, called for a lower house elected by the people which would, in turn, elect an upper house.

New Jersey's rejoinder on behalf of smaller and less populous states was that all states enjoy equality of representation in a single-house Congress that would choose the executive.

This proposal was rejected but the idea of having at least one house of Congress in which all states had the same number of seats was a rallying point for the smaller states and forced the Convention to appoint a committee to come up with a compromise. On July 16, 1787, by a one-vote margin, the Convention approved the committee's recommendation: In return for a Senate in which all states would have an equal vote, the House would be empowered to initiate revenue bills.[16]

So vitally important was the question of how representation would be determined in Congress that the Convention would probably have collapsed over failure to resolve it. Ratification, however, did not turn on the question; rather, the enduring concern of Americans was that Congress, as the branch of the national government with sweeping lawmaking powers, be deterred from using those powers for tyrannical ends. Bicameralism and a system of checks and balances made legislative despotism less likely. While required by the Constitution to co-operate in general legislation, each house was made—by reason of its diverse powers, different constituencies, and varying terms and methods of election—into a highly distinctive body. Just how distinctive was expressed by James Madison as he observed, "In republican government, the legislative authority necessarily predominates. The remedy for this inconveniency is, to divide the legislature into different branches; and to render them, by different modes of election, and different principles of action, as little connected with each other, as the nature of their common functions and their common dependence on the society, will admit."[17]

The device for dealing with this "inconveniency" was to produce two legislative bodies that differed starkly at their creation and had an enduring rivalry encoded in their constitutional makeup.

If the Constitution's framers looked warily on the institutions they had created, their greatest uneasiness concerned the House of Representatives. Elected by the people directly, it possessed a democratic legitimacy that was enjoyed neither by the presidency, which had the electoral college interposed between it and the citizens, nor by the Senate, whose members were chosen by the state legislatures. Anticipating a high turnover in House membership because of the briefness of these legislators' terms and the arduousness of travel to and from the seat of government, Madison concluded that the Speaker of the House would emerge as a formidable figure. He reasoned that with so few House members willing to "become members of long standing" and "masters of the public business," a resourceful Speaker would dominate a transient membership since few would ever learn enough about the institution to challenge him. Unlike the House, the Senate would have no powerful presiding officer. The vice-president designated by the Constitution to preside over the Senate would lack the legitimacy that came from direct election by the people. Accordingly, "the House seemed destined to be the most prestigious and powerful body because of its elective status, its preeminence in fiscal matters, and its presumed capacity to generate strong and forceful leadership."[18]

The Senate evolved from quite different institutional origins. It has been argued convincingly that what the framers intended in the Senate was the American equivalent of a House of Lords to act as a counterweight to what they saw as a House of Representatives that was excessively responsive to the popular will. The framers, however, were not forthright in their intentions during the campaign for ratification because, in that revolutionary age, they did not want to be seen as aping the aristocratic practices of the British. For a time after ratification, it does indeed appear that the Senate acted very like the lordly institution the framers planned but could not openly embrace.[19]

The accounts of the early nineteenth century reflect an image of a Senate as a kind of stuffy, somnolent, and semisecret society with little to do or say. A lugubrious entry in the diary of Senator John Quincy Adams for the last day of 1805 reflects the inactivity of life in the Senate: "The year which this day expires has been distinguished in the course of my life by its barrenness of events."[20]

Adams served only a single, unhappy term in the Senate. Entries in his diary suggest that he must have found debate in the House of Representatives more engrossing than that in his own chamber because he seems to have spent a good deal of time there. His Senate career ended abruptly and unpleasantly when the Massachusetts legislature chose his successor well in advance of the end of his term. It was a rebuke to Adams over his support of President Thomas Jefferson's foreign policy.

Adams went on to a career as a diplomat that culminated in his selection as Secretary of State. In 1824 he became president in an election so close it was decided in the House. Embittered at his failure to win a second term, Adams believed his public career had come to an end. But within six months of leaving the White House, Adams was visited by Representative Joseph Richardson, who represented the district in Massachusetts that included the ex-president's ancestral home. Richardson had decided not to seek another term in the House and urged Adams to run for his seat. Richardson told Adams that service "in the House of Representatives of an ex-president of the United States, instead of degrading the individual, would elevate the Representative character."[21] It is in some degree a measure of the prestige the House enjoyed that Adams agreed, saying, "I had no scruple whatever. No person could be degraded by serving the people as a Representative in Congress."[22]

It was in the House that Adams achieved his greatest distinction in public life. He had found the place where his talents could be expressed. He served just ten days short of seventeen years in the House, where he spoke out boldly against slavery. And it was on the floor of the House that Adams suffered the final paralytic stroke that ended his life.

Examining the political careers of some of the most notable figures of the first quarter of the nineteenth century one finds that they were as likely to leave the Senate for the House as they were to abandon the House for the Senate.

Henry Clay of Kentucky, one of Adams's rivals for the presidency in 1824 and founder and standard-bearer of the Whig Party, also moved from a seat in the Senate to one in the House, stating that he wished to be "an immediate representative of the people." In the House, Clay was elected Speaker in his freshman year in 1811 and became a leading "war hawk" in that chamber in urging hostilities against Great Britain.

The fact that Clay, a man known for his political astuteness, returned to the Senate in 1831 reveals much about the change in the status of the upper chamber. In the early years of the century when Monroe and Adams served there, senators were relatively inactive: They introduced less legislation than did House members, participated less in committee activities, and often did not even serve out a full six-year term. They were often under the thumbs of the legislatures that had elected them, and even the newspapers paid less attention to them than they did to members of the House. In 1805, for example, House activities accounted for 27 percent of newspaper space in a sample of papers of the day; Senate activities for the same period garnered only about 3 percent.[23] By 1830, however, the Senate was taking its place alongside the House as an equal partner and, in some estimations, was poised to surpass it.

The Rise of the Senate

The rise of the Senate was well under way by the middle of the 1820s. The great debate that culminated in the Missouri Compromise in 1820 was discussed as fully and as publicly in the Senate as it had been in the House, and the possibilities inherent in the six-year term began to be seen as political advantages in light of the balancing out of other differences. This change was first seen in the increased gravitation of promising national leaders like Clay to the Senate. By the 19th Congress (1825–1827), the Senate was full of future presidents: Andrew Jackson, Martin Van Buren, and William Henry Harrison were in the upper chamber along with such future notables as William R. King, who became vice-president in 1853, Robert V. Hayne, who would engage Daniel Webster in a classic set of Senate debates, and Thomas Hart Benton, whose influence would extend over an unprecedented thirty years of Senate service.

It was at about this time that Alexis de Tocqueville visited the United States and in the course of his extensive observations of the institutions and mores of America contrasted the House and Senate.

> On entering the House of Representatives of Washington one is struck by the vulgar demeanor of that great assembly. The eye frequently does not discover a man of celebrity within its walls . . .
>
> At a few yards' distance from this spot is the door of the Senate, which contains within a small space a large proportion of the most celebrated men of America. . . . The Senate is composed of eloquent advocates, distinguished generals, wise magistrates, and statesmen of note, whose language would at all times do honour to the most remarkable parliamentary debates of Europe.[24]

Tocqueville, with his dread of popular tyranny, could hardly be expected to embrace the House. He ascribed the superiority of the Senate to the election of its members by the state legislatures, which caused the Senate, in his estimation, "to represent the elevated thoughts which are current in the community . . . rather than the petty passions which disturb or the vices which disgrace it."[25] To Tocqueville, the House, with its direct election by the people, represented these "petty passions" and "vices."

But it was Tocqueville's characterizations of House members as "mostly village lawyers" and "people [who] do not always know how to read correctly" and his description of senators as enjoying "a monopoly of intelligence and of sound judgment" that occasioned a spirited rejoinder from Thomas Hart Benton, who recalled for the otherwise-opinioned French aristocrat something obvious that he had overlooked.

[Tocqueville] seems to look upon the members of the two Houses as different orders of beings—different classes—a higher and a lower class; the former placed in the Senate by the wisdom of state legislatures, the latter in the House of Representatives by the folly of the people—when the fact is that they are not only of the same order and class, but mainly the same individuals. The Senate is almost entirely made up of the House! and it is quite certain that every senator whom Mons. de Tocqueville had in his eye when he bestowed such encomium on that body had come from the House of Representatives![26]

That a thoughtful observer had placed the Senate above the House would have surprised the framers of the Constitution. Even Benton's vindication of the House might have struck them as a trifle defensive. What was happening was an equalizing of the statures that was not foreseen in 1787. Tocqueville was correct in his appraisal of the quality of senators, as was Benton in his rejoinder that "the Senate is in great part composed of the pick of the House, and therefore gains double—by brilliant accession to itself and abstraction from the other."[27]

It was, however, the playing out of the inevitable consequences of the greater formula for representation in the House that contributed most to the rise of the Senate. "While the large increase in the number of representatives had forced the adoption of rules that inhibited the role and opportunities for debate in the House, the growth of the Senate to a membership of almost fifty had worked to the contrary, making it a more lively and rewarding forum for those who wanted to lead and be heard. Moreover, the equality of state representation in the Senate, and the growing concern over divisions between the free and slave states that had been underscored by the Missouri controversy, heightened the Senate's importance as the arena in which southerners could block the action of an antagonistic House majority."[28]

At 183 members in the 17th Congress that convened after the census of 1820, the House had swelled to almost four times the size of the Senate, from less than three times its size in the 1st Congress (1789–1791). This growth in size was marked by a tightening of the rules of debate so that by 1841 House members were limited to one hour of debate and by 1847 a Five Minute Rule was imposed. Even the physical arrangements of the Senate chamber seemed to promote high-quality debate: "The small, semicircular Senate chamber, with plain walls and a domed roof, had excellent acoustics and was ideal for the ringing voices of eloquent men."[29]

The nature of American public policy was also changing in a way that favored the Senate over the House. So long as the United States was an isolated agricultural society preoccupied with domestic problems, the mainstream of policy consisted of the development of interstate commerce, internal improvements (such as roads and canals), and the revenues for defraying their cost. Foreign policy for a small and struggling nation was defined not in terms of grand alliances and broad diplomatic initiatives but rather in terms of trade and tariff policy—the domain of the House with its primacy in fiscal matters. Grand diplomatic strokes—the purchase of the Louisiana Territory from France and the proclamation of the Monroe Doctrine—were presidential in origin, infrequent, and not the subject of determined senatorial opposition. As mentioned, the Senate did emerge as the forum for debate on the question of slavery. At a political disadvantage in a House of Representatives where the more populous states dominated, the sparsely populated slave states chose the Senate with its equality of state representation as their first and last line of defense.[30]

The period of the Senate's rise to parity with the House extended through the Civil War and into the late nineteenth century. It was a period of dominance by the two chambers over the executive branch, "a golden era for the bicameral Congress. . . . Both the House and Senate possessed constitutional powers that were critical to national policymaking, and both were well organized. Each asserted its unique constitutional powers and played a clear role in making national policy."[31]

This period of bicameral parity was celebrated in 1885 by the young scholar Woodrow Wilson as an era of bicameral amity as well. "There is safety and ease," he wrote, "in the fact that the Senate never wishes to carry its resistance to the House to the point at which resistance must stay all progress in legislation; because there is really a 'latent unity' between the Senate and the House which makes continued antagonism between them next to impossible—certainly in the highest degree improbable."[32]

Wilson argued forcefully against the accusations of reformers that the Senate was a millionaire's club assembled by state legislatures that were, themselves, under the thumb of powerful economic interests. His defense was that of the classic pluralist: They may be millionaires but the interests they represent are so varied—and indeed often so antagonistic—that their wealth does not constitute a consistent upper-class interest. He assured his readers that "the Senate is quite as trustworthy in this regard as is the House of Representatives."[33]

It was during this period that the mode of electing senators came under attack by reformers who urged that popular election supplant selection by the state legislatures. The House had voted five times over a nine-year period, between 1893 and 1902, for a constitutional amendment requiring direct popular election of senators—twice by the constitutionally required two-thirds vote—but between 1902 and 1911 all such efforts ceased. The leadership of the House considered it a waste of time to persist in passing such amendments only to have them foiled in the Senate. But beginning with Oregon in 1901, states began to have nonbinding senatorial primaries that were, in effect, advice to state legislatures on who was the people's choice for the U.S. Senate. Finally, in 1911 under the leadership of Senator William Borah of Idaho the amendment passed the Senate by a two-thirds vote; it was quickly ratified by three-fourths of the states and went into effect on May 31, 1913, as the Seventeenth Amendment.[34]

The direct election of senators removed the one conspicuous disadvantage that had afflicted the Senate from its beginnings: lack of democratic legitimacy. The Senate retained its distinctive powers of advice and consent in treaties and presidential appointments and, above all, its compact size. At the time of ratification of the Seventeenth Amendment the number of House members had reached its present number of 435 while the size of the Senate was 96. Internal reforms in the House that had curbed the power of the Speaker made leadership of the larger body somewhat more uncertain. But it was a change in the content of American public policy in the World War I period that propelled the Senate ahead of the House.

The great national debates over American entry into World War I took place in the Senate. It was in the Senate that President Woodrow Wilson battled the "small group of willful men" who in 1917 opposed his plan to arm U.S. merchant vessels to protect them against German submarines. Only in the Senate could Wilson's opponents, through the use of the extreme form of extended debate, the filibuster, derail the armed-ship bill.

The Versailles Treaty was also fought on the floor of the Senate. The treaty, which would have provided for U.S. membership in the League of Nations, was defeated in large measure because of President Wilson's failure to consult the Senate adequately during his negotiations on the pact. The vote to reject the Versailles Treaty revealed more clearly than had any other vote the power of the Senate in foreign policy. The entry of the United States, albeit reluctantly, into the affairs of the world signaled a shift in public policy to an area where the Senate enjoyed special powers.

By the end of World War I, it was axiomatic that Senate service was to be preferred over House service. A third of the membership of the Senate had previously served in the House and even House Speaker Champ Clark, who wielded the gavel from 1911 to 1919, enumerated crisply the advantage of the Senate.

There are various reasons why Representatives desire translation to the Senate: First, the longer term; second, Senators being fewer, their votes are more important; third, patronage; fourth, participation in treaty-making; fifth, greater social recognition.[35]

When Lord Bryce evaluated the American institutions of government at roughly the same time, he gave a measured but unmistakable advantage to the Senate.

The Senate has been a stouter bulwark against agitation, not merely because a majority of the senators have always four years of membership before them, but also because the senators have been individually stronger men than the representatives. They are less democratic, not in opinion but in temper, because they are more self-confident, because they have more to lose, because experience has taught them how fleeting a thing popular sentiment is, and how useful a thing continuity in policy is. The Senate has therefore usually kept its head better than the House of Representatives. It has expressed more adequately the judgment, as contrasted with the emotion, of the nation.[36]

House reforms and the tendency of House members to make careers in that chamber tended to weaken the power of the leadership of the House. Senate reforms and careerism changed that body far less. The adoption of Senate Rule 22 did provide an easier mechanism to terminate excessive debate with a vote of cloture, but it proved so difficult to muster the required two-thirds majority needed to terminate debate that filibustering was not seriously hindered. Between 1917 and the beginning of the administration of Franklin D. Roosevelt in 1933, a mere eleven votes of cloture were taken. Of that eleven only four were successful in shutting off debate.[37]

The rise of radio as the first truly national medium, along with news magazines, was a development that enhanced the Senate more than the House. "These mass media were drawn to the Senate because of its small size, which allowed them to focus on individual senators, and because the senators' large constituencies and more national and international focus provided the media with a wider audience. Media attention made national personalities out of senators and a notable debating forum out of the Senate. Individual senators and the Senate as a body could convey their opinions to the public more easily than could the larger House and its more parochial and anonymous members."[38]

The leadership of the House was particularly hobbled by the consequences of some of the reforms of the Progressive Era. One important reform removed the Speaker from the chairmanship of the Rules Committee, which specifies the conditions under which all bills are debated and amended. Unlike the Senate system of unanimous consent, which involves consultation between the leaders and interested senators on the terms of debate and amendment, the House had formalized this crucial gatekeeping function in its Rules Committee. And it was mainly through this committee that such powerful Speakers as Thomas B. Reed, a Maine Republican (1889–1891 and 1895–1899), and Joseph G. Cannon, an Illinois Republican (1903–1911), established virtual dictatorships over the House. The separation of the leadership of the Rules Committee from the Speakership created the conditions for a powerful rival to the Speaker. But this did not occur immediately. During the period between 1937 and 1960, when conservative southern Democrats occupied the Rules chair, the committee and the party leadership of the House "operated independently and often at cross-purposes."[39]

The Senate has never vested great formal power in its leaders; even a Speakership reduced in prerogatives is more imposing an office than anything in the Senate. But the Senate, befitting the deference it pays to the individual, has yielded leadership to strong individuals only occasionally. The strength of this leadership, however, rests more on the force of personality and intellect than on legal authority. Perhaps the most powerful figure in the Senate in the early years of the twentieth century was Senator Nelson W. Aldrich (R-R.I.), whose highest formal post was chairman of the Finance Committee. Between Aldrich, who left the Senate in 1911, and Lyndon B. Johnson (D-Tex.), who became the Democrats' floor leader in 1953, there was no single individual who was able to amass

much more personal power. During this period, power sometimes resided in the hands of a few powerful committee chairmen. At other times, such as the early period of the New Deal
from 1933 until 1937, the influence of a president was greater
than that of any senator or group of senators. It was Johnson,
however, with his combination of political astuteness, utter
ruthlessness, luck, and hard work, who commanded the Senate
until he left to be John F. Kennedy's running mate in 1960.

Johnson's success was often attributed to the "treatment" he
visited upon senators who would not go along with the meticulously fashioned deals he would engineer, but the singularity
of his success had more to do with his deep understanding of
the Senate than of the forcefulness of his persuasion.

Johnson, a former member of the House, understood how
profoundly the Senate differs from the House. The House, for
all the years Johnson was there, was in the control of the Democrats. Indeed, when Johnson arrived in the House in 1937,
it was in the wake of the Democratic landslide in the 1936 presidential election, and the number of Republican members had
shrunk to 89 while the Democrats held 333 seats. Thirteen minor party members filled out the membership of the chamber.
Republican senators had dwindled to 17 in number. Nonetheless, Senate opponents of the efforts of Democratic president
Franklin D. Roosevelt to enlarge the Supreme Court to dilute
the power of conservative justices managed to defeat the president at the peak of his power and popularity.

Roosevelt was defeated not by the anemic ranks of the Republicans, but by a bipartisan coalition composed of conservative (typically southern) Democrats and Republicans. It was a
coalition that would persist until the early 1960s. Johnson understood that a bare majority of 218 votes would guarantee victory in the House, but in the Senate, with its filibuster that, at
the time, could be shut down only with a two-thirds vote, a different logic prevailed. Minorities, be they partisan or ideological, could stop the Senate in its tracks. Fashioning bipartisan
coalitions was Johnson's special skill and it was based on his

deep and subtle understanding of senators and how they differed from House members. As Johnson's longtime aide George Reedy recalled, "There are few issues that can command majorities in and of themselves. Bills become law because of delicate trades."[40] These trades, such as those fashioned by Johnson, were based upon "the art of pitting the left and right against each other and coming through the middle."[41] It is the fashioning of consensus by accommodating all interested senators and the concerns they represent. It is the senators as individuals rather than as partisans that is crucial in this process of adjustment and accommodation. It would seem axiomatic that a common sense of purpose befitting an arm of the national legislature would be lost in such a welter of special pleadings. But what might appear, at first blush, to be an adversary process can often act as a unifying force. The building of temporary majorities in the Senate is a process that is particular in form but, on many occasions, universal in result.

Jane Mansbridge uses the terms "adversary" and "unitary" to identify two models of democracy. The adversary expression of democracy is characterized by an emphasis on representing faithfully and meticulously the various interests in one's constituency. Unitary democracy, in contrast, emphasizes the overall good and the national welfare.[42] These models are closely related to the distinctions made by the eighteenth-century British philosopher Edmund Burke, who urged the electors of Bristol to look upon Parliament as "a deliberative assembly, one nation with one interest, that of the whole; where not local purposes, not local prejudices ought to guide, but the general good, resulting from the general reason of the whole."

Two Houses, Two Democracies

This book, in making the case that vital differences between the House and Senate persist, also suggests that the characteristics of adversary democracy are most commonly found in the House of Representatives and those of unitary democracy more typically in the Senate, and that both of these expressions of democracy are crucial to the survival of free government in America. Each model carries with it certain strengths and weaknesses, but these strengths and weaknesses are essentially complementary.

I attempt to present a picture of an astonishingly accessible House of Representatives in which members act to solve problems that are complex and daunting for the ordinary citizen and to defend vigilantly the interests of roughly 700,000 Americans. I also sketch a Senate in which representational concerns are increasing but which retains a more national perspective. While it is difficult to demonstrate that Senate legislation is somehow more "national" than House legislation, we see from the testimony of fourteen senators that most think the Senate, to use Burke's words, is more likely to reflect "the general reason of the whole." This broader worldview is, as I see it, the product of the ability of senators in the intimacy of a 100-member body to experience their colleagues as people rather than simply as partisans or brokers for interest groups.

House members, who lack statewide constituencies, often represent fewer interests and any given interest is likely to loom more imposingly in a House member's calculations than that of a single interest in a large complex state. House members may be said to reflect more directly the interests of their constituencies, and they provide an important link between citizens and their government that senators cannot provide. In a mass society where expanding governmental activity threatens to engulf citizens and render them helpless, the intimate relations between House members and the voters of these 435 manageable congressional districts serve to limit the estrangement suffered by people. The almost tactile sense of knowing what made their districts tick was a powerful memory in the minds of the senators I interviewed when they recalled their days in the House and may be an important force in limiting citizens' isolation from their government.

If senators and House members perceive and express these

differences between members of each house and their obligations to their constituencies and to the nation, so do Americans. Later in this book I make note of some recent public opinion results suggesting that citizens look upon senators and representatives as doing different things and being responsive to different constituencies.

The starting point in the examination of the differences between the House and Senate and of the meaning of those differences to American democracy begins with a very basic distinction: the number of members in each house.

NOTES

1. Richard Bolling, *House Out of Order* (New York: E.P. Dutton, 1965), p. 91.
2. Harry McPherson, *A Political Education* (Boston: Little, Brown, 1972), p. 36.
3. Warren Weaver, *Both Your Houses* (New York: Praeger, 1972), p. 33.
4. George Rothwell Brown, *The Leadership of Congress* (Indianapolis: Bobbs-Merrill, 1922), p. 238.
5. Neil MacNeil, *Forge of Democracy* (New York: David McKay, 1963), p. 397.
6. Richard F. Fenno, Jr., *The Power of the Purse* (Boston: Little, Brown, 1966), p. 637.
7. Jeffrey L. Pressman, *House vs. Senate* (New Haven, Conn.: Yale University Press, 1966), p. 83.
8. Joseph S. Clark, *Congress: The Sapless Branch,* rev. ed. (New York: Harper and Row, 1965), p. 136.
9. MacNeil, op. cit., p. 398.
10. Ibid., p. 399.
11. Ibid., p. 400.
12. Weaver, op. cit., p. 33.
13. Pressman, op. cit., p. 86.
14. Ibid., p. 87.
15. Ibid., p. 88.
16. *Origins and Development of Congress* (Washington, D.C.: Congressional Quarterly Press, 1976), pp. 32–35.
17. Federalist #51 in *The Federalist* (Washington, D.C.: Thompson and Homans, 1831), p. 224.
18. Edward G. Carmines and Lawrence C. Dodd, "Bicameralism in Congress: The Changing Partnership," in Lawrence C. Dodd and Bruce I. Oppenheimer, eds., *Congress Reconsidered,* 3d ed. (Washington, D.C.: CQ Press, 1985), p. 417.
19. See Elaine K. Swift, "The Making of an American House of Lords: The U.S. Senate in the Constitutional Convention of 1787," *Studies in American Political Development* 7 (Fall 1993):177–224.
20. Allan Nevins, ed., *The Diary of John Quincy Adams* (New York: Longmans, Green, 1928), p. 27.
21. Ibid., p. 405.

22. Ibid.
23. See Elaine K. Swift, *Reconstitutive Congressional Change: The Case of the United States Senate, 1789–1841,* unpublished doctoral thesis, Harvard University, 1989.
24. Alexis de Tocqueville, *Democracy in America,* v. 1, trans. by Henry Reeve (London: Longmans, Green, 1875), pp. 203–204.
25. Ibid.
26. Thomas Hart Benton, *Thirty Years' View,* v. 1 (New York: Appleton & Co., 1854), p. 206.
27. Ibid.
28. Alvin M. Josephy, Jr., *On the Hill: A History of the American Congress* (New York: Simon and Schuster, 1979), p. 159.
29. Ibid., p. 166.
30. Carmines and Dodd, op. cit., p. 419, and *Origins and Development of Congress,* p. 186.
31. Carmines and Dodd, op. cit., p. 420.
32. Woodrow Wilson, *Congressional Government* (Boston: Houghton Mifflin, 1885), p. 224.
33. Ibid.
34. George H. Haynes, *The Senate of the United States* (Boston: Houghton Mifflin, 1938), pp. 86–95.
35. Champ Clark, *My Quarter Century of American Politics,* v. 1 (New York: Harper & Bros., 1920), p. 219.
36. Viscount James Bryce, *The American Commonwealth,* v. 1 (New York: Macmillan, 1928), pp. 124–125.
37. *Origins and Development of Congress,* pp. 226–227.
38. Carmines and Dodd, op. cit., p. 423.
39. U.S. Congress, House, *A History of the Committee on Rules,* 97th Congress, 2d Session, 1983, p. 177.
40. George E. Reedy, *The U.S. Senate* (New York: Crown, 1986), p. 126.
41. Ibid., p. 205.
42. Jane J. Mansbridge, *Beyond Adversary Democracy* (Chicago: University of Chicago Press, 1983).

2

Politics of Scale
The Size Difference

W HEN ASKED WHAT SINGLE feature most clearly differentiates the Senate from the House, the twentynine* senators who had previously served in the House were overwhelmingly in agreement. Knowing that this group consisted of Democrats and Republicans, liberals and conservatives, prominent figures and those whose influence was fleeting, we might not expect such a resounding consensus. With only a handful of exceptions, however, it was the simple difference in size between the two chambers that was pointed to immediately by the vast majority. Even those who did not make size their first choice mentioned it prominently. Those who pointed first to other differentiating features mentioned such things as the senators' six-year term and those distinctive powers that the Senate enjoys exclusively such as confirmation of presidential nominations and the power to ratify treaties.

One does not need to be an expert in congressional politics to be struck by how fundamentally important size is in the manner in which institutions work. A large university is a very different kind of place from a small liberal arts college. Life is very different for a government worker in the Washington headquarters of the Department of the Interior than it is at the Craig Brook National Fish Hatchery in East Orland, Maine, which is under the jurisdiction of the Department of the Interior. The world of the army corps headquarters is unimaginably

*Twenty-nine former and currently-serving U.S. Senators were interviewed. All but two, Warren B. Rudman and Chuck Hagel, had previously served in the House.

different from that of a rifle squad. So while overall objectives of a very large and a very small organization may be education, the promotion of natural resources, or military success, the manner in which they pursue their goals, the procedures they follow, and the nature of the interaction among the people are all very different in the large and small group.

It is perhaps not totally surprising, after all, that the great majority of these twenty-nine people whose powers of observation are probably above average would seize upon the size difference as the most salient distinction between the large House and the small Senate.

For our purposes in examining these two legislative bodies, it is important to observe that the size difference is not one that is subject to change. What appear to be insurmountable barriers to one house of Congress transgressing on the constitutionally delineated turf of the other are less formidable than the probability that the House and Senate will ever be the same size. After all, the House gets involved in treaties if legislation is required to implement the agreement and the Senate, for all practical purposes in 1982, initiated a revenue bill. It is unimaginable, however, that the House and Senate would ever approximate each other in size. But is that which is permanent also important? This book tries to make the case that those House-Senate distinctions that flow from asymmetries of size are vital and important differences and in spite of some evidence in recent years that the two bodies are becoming more alike, they can never entirely converge.

The number of senators who said size, however, is less impressive than the categorical quality of their statements. For former senator John C. Culver, an Iowa Democrat, who spent ten years in the House and gained a reputation as a thoughtful and aggressive lawmaker in his one term in the Senate, his identification of the size factor was the most unequivocal:

I think the starting point of wisdom on comparing the House and Senate is frankly a very simple but, I believe, critical observation. That's the difference in size.

Size really explains so much else about those institutions in terms of their organization, in terms of their rules, in terms of the accessibility and participation of the members, the committees, the workloads and so forth.

More lyrical, perhaps, but no less emphatic, was the verdict of the late Senator Hugh D. Scott, a Pennsylvania Republican who spent sixteen years in the House and seventeen years in the Senate and who served as minority leader of the Senate. Scott observed:

The House is a massive creature. A huge overgrown elephant, but rarely turning into a rogue elephant. It's more lethargic, maybe more like a hippopotamus—a sort of hulking, sulking creature, barely showing its snout and only then when required for reasons of sustenance or curiosity.

Sustaining his zoological simile, Scott likened the Senate to

a group of people of various species like antelope or deer who leap with some grace from subject to subject, issue to issue. There is a great deal more grace of movement in a herd of antelope than in a group of hippopotamuses.

Size, as an element of House-Senate comparison, has many ramifications and implications. One obvious outgrowth of the difference in size is a stark difference in the rules that govern each chamber. A second is the degree of specialization that a senator or House member can achieve. Put another way, it means that the populous House and the tiny Senate must cover the same vast areas of public policy ranging from agriculture to space exploration. They must develop policy, legislate in identical areas, and oversee its implementation. But the House has 435 people to assign to the task and the Senate only 100. This results in vast disparities in the degree of expertise achievable between senators and members. The corollary is that there is also a vast disparity in the breadth and sweep of what senators and House members can authoritatively speak out on.

The relationship between leaders and followers in large and

small organizations is different. Large organizations tend to be hierarchical and efficient at processing routine tasks. Small groups tend toward more face-to-face contact between leaders and followers with individual expressions tolerated and even encouraged. Leadership in the small body becomes more problematical.

The starting point for the examination of the size question is to make a few observations about the places where the Senate and House conduct their business.

The Ecology of the House and Senate

The House chamber is not simply large, it is the largest parliamentary room in the world. It is three times larger than the British House of Commons upon which it was patterned.[1] Paneled in walnut and trimmed with marble, the room is dominated by the Speaker's desk atop a three-tiered dais. From his seat the Speaker looks out upon a chamber in which Republicans sit to his left, Democrats to his right. Aside from this demarcation, there are no other assigned places although the floor leaders of both parties address the House from behind tables on either side of the main aisle.

The House abandoned separate desks for each member in 1912 after the members from the newly admitted states of Arizona and New Mexico were sworn in and the chamber became too crowded. But the long, padded, curved benches are not simply filled randomly by whatever person happens in. A decade ago, the center rear of the chamber on the Democratic side was the favorite of conservative Democrats from the Sunbelt states, while the Pennsylvania delegation tended to congregate at the far right of the chamber.[2] More recently, however, members leave the chamber quickly after answering a quorum call or casting a vote.

The Senate chamber is much different. It is small (only 125 feet at its widest) and considerably more elegant. In amphitheater style, the floor steps down in five levels toward the front of the room where the floor leaders' desks are located. As in the House, the presiding officer faces Republicans on the left and Democrats on the right, but unlike the informal seating arrangement for members, senators are assigned particular seats based upon their seniority. For years, the general rule had been go for the "prime real estate"—seats located on either side of the center aisle, which is within the line of vision of the presiding officer. Senators located here can gain recognition to speak more easily than those located on the flanks or at the rear of the chamber.[3]

But little in the Senate is as straightforward as it appears, and many senators whose seniority would entitle them to claim "prime real estate" make individualistic—even quirky—decisions as to where they will sit. The introduction of television in 1986 seems to have altered the seating calculus for some senators. Given the steep camera angle, senators with bald spots are apt to avoid the front rows. The back row may well be the new "prime real estate" for media-minded senators. The dun-colored walls, which televised poorly, have been repainted a more soothing blue, and there is room for a senator to set up an easel with a display. The camera angle also favors certain locations in the back row.[4]

Sentiment, however, can play as important a role as telegenics. Senator Edward M. Kennedy sits in the seat occupied by his brother John F. Kennedy when the late president was a senator. Senator Thad Cochran occupies the seat once held by Jefferson Davis, president of the Confederacy who once represented Mississippi in the Senate. Senator Norris Cotton of New Hampshire went so far as to practice deception to claim for New Hampshire the desk of Daniel Webster, who was born in that state but represented Massachusetts in the Senate. When the two Massachusetts senators were absent one day in 1974, Cotton introduced Senate Resolution 467, 93rd Congress, 2d Session, which required that the Webster desk be forever assigned to a senator from New Hampshire, thus snatching it from the Massachusetts delegation.[5]

A great deal was once made of the Senate phenomenon of "seatmates"—such as the "fun bunch," consisting of, among others, Senators Donald W. Riegle, Jr. (D-Mich.), and Jim Sasser (D-Tenn.), who sought out adjoining seats because of their personal friendship. There was also a kind of inverse snobbery that had such influential senators as Ernest F. Hollings (D-S.C.) and Richard Lugar (R-Ind.) seated in the back rows of their respective sections. But friendship seems a less decisive factor than it once was.[6] A conclusion based on interviews with twenty-nine senators in the late 1970s would probably be reinforced by the advent of Senate television:

As is the case with so many things in the modern Senate, personal advantage and convenience rather than personal affection or even philosophical solidarity tend to provide better explanations for seat choice.[7]

One quaint Senate seating convention remains—the "candy desk," situated on the Republican side at the back of the chamber nearest the side door. The senator who occupies that seat (currently Rick Santorum of Pennsylvania) must keep the drawer stocked with candy for his colleagues. House impeachment managers commented sarcastically about the Senate goody trove during their visits to the Senate to make their case against President Clinton.

The distinctive, even privileged, status of senators in contrast with House members can also be seen in the places where Congress works as well as where they speak and vote. In the three House and three Senate office buildings are subtle and not-so-subtle indications of a differential in status based on numbers.

It is manifestly more difficult to find comfortable office space for 435 members than for 100 senators. Accordingly, no senator, however junior, suffers as many limitations on space and amenities as does the newly elected House member. For one thing, each senator receives a basic space allocation of 4,000 square feet. To this an amount of up to 900 additional square feet may be added to the suites of senators from the most populous states. A House member might find himself or herself with as little as 1,000 square feet, which amounts to two rooms, twenty-five by twenty feet each. The most spacious House office is 1,800 square feet. Greater disparities are found in the accommodations between the most senior and most junior members of the House rather than in the Senate.[8]

At the highest level, the difference in personal space between the senator and House member evens out somewhat with the addition of the so-called hideaway offices located in the Capitol building. These suites assigned to the most senior members of both chambers bring the formal leadership of the two bodies into rough equivalence. But there is an overall difference that cannot escape the discerning eye when it scans Capitol Hill. There is, for example, a huge difference in comforts and refinements between the newest House office building (Rayburn) and the oldest (Cannon). The least senior members face the unpleasant choice of an office on the fifth floor of Cannon or the sixth floor of the Longworth Building.

The Cannon quarters lack the good elevator service of the lower floors and resound with the noise of ventilating equipment. But these suites are often preferred to the smaller accommodations in Longworth that are also afflicted with the poorest views.

The largest suites in the Rayburn Building would not be scorned by the chief executive officer of a corporation. Those offices, 1,800 square feet, have the feel of a basketball court. The rooms, 2314 Rayburn and 2328 Rayburn, are now occupied by Representative David Obey (D-Wis.), ranking minority member of the Appropriations Committee, and John Dingell (D-Mich.), ranking minority member of the Commerce Committee. But, like so much in politics, Obey and Dingell were forced to make a trade-off in office amenities: The offices have a rather ordinary view of the "horsehoe"—the driveway on the east side of the building—instead of the more picturesque northern view dominated by the Capitol building.

When seniority entitles them to have some choice over where their office is located, House members tend to use the three criteria used by real estate agents: location, location, location. In practice, this usually means the office that is handiest to where they spend most of their time—their committee's hearing room and suite.

Where one chooses to put down roots on the Senate side is much more a matter of personal taste than of strict status. As in the House, selection is by lottery in seniority order, but a senator might well prefer to retain a suite in the ornate and stately beaux arts Russell Building (the oldest) than to opt for a glass-enclosed, starkly functional office in the Hart Building (the newest). Indeed, some of the most senior senators, such as Kennedy, Hollings, and Leahy, are located in the Russell Building while some of the newest senators are to be found in the Hart. The two largest suites in Hart are generally assigned to California's senators because of California's population.

Colleagues and Other Strangers

Even the total membership of one's own party caucus in the House is too large a number of people to permit recognition of all of them by an individual. Outsiders sometimes marvel at the ability of the presiding officer of the House to call upon "the gentleman from Maryland" or "the gentlelady from New York" with such apparent familiarity. In fact, certain members of the House staff who sit adjacent to the chair of the presiding officer are trained "member spotters" who whisper the relevant identifications to the chair.

The size of the House membership coupled with the shorter term and a fairly large number of voluntary departures or deaths in any given Congress produce a more changeable cast of characters. But even a House member whom an outsider would assume to be an intimate or at least a nodding acquaintance of another representative can often turn out to be a stranger. Sometimes an incident will illuminate for a House member the surprisingly distant relationships that can prevail in so large a body. An entry in the journal of a former House member portrays such a moment:

Back in Washington this evening, I learned that John C. Watts, a Democrat from Kentucky, had died of a heart attack. I remembered reading in the paper last week a small piece that pointed out that he was second-ranking Democrat on the Ways and Means Committee. Had Wilbur Mills left the Congress, Watts would have been chairman of that committee.

What struck me was the fact that I did not know John Watts. In almost five years here, I never had the occasion to meet or speak to him. Nor—until last week—had I read one line about him in print or heard anyone mention his name. A man can come here and serve many years. He can be very close to a position of real power, and at the same time, be virtually anonymous.[9]

One should never be surprised when even those House members with reason to know all their party members draw a blank on one of them. I was standing one day at the corner of New Jersey and Constitution avenues talking to a member of the House leadership when a fellow Democrat from a neighboring state walked by. The congressman chatted with us but as the conversation progressed, it became clear to me that the leader had no idea whom we were talking to. After the member left, the leader turned to me and said, "Who was that?" I replied, "That's X from the state of Y." "Oh," the leader said, "so that's X. I'd heard his name but can't honestly say I ever laid eyes on him."

While it is not the case that each senator knows every other senator, personally, the opportunity to interact with a larger percentage of the membership is an advantage that senators enjoy, and it contributes to the distinctive nature of the Senate.

Senator Wayne Allard (R-Col.) who came to the Senate from the House in 1997 reflected back on his time in the House by observing, "You've got 435 members over there and they just don't have the chance to get to know each other. Over here, I know all of the members of the opposite party by their first

names and they know me by my first name. Over in the House,
I couldn't say that."

In the Senate, personal interaction among members is more
important than it is in the House. Senators need to take the measure of a colleague as a person. The considerable personal influence of the individual senators and the ability that a single
senator has to influence the legislative process make knowing
what makes a colleague tick immensely important.

The Glittering Generalists and the Reluctant
Specialists: Congress in Committee

In terms of the legislative process that begins with the introduction of bills and culminates in their enactment, the roles
of House and Senate committees are identical. Both represent
the division of labor that enables institutions responsible for
lawmaking and oversight in diverse areas of public policy to
parcel out manageable portions of it to smaller groups. Both
groups specialize and develop expertise in particular areas.
Both hold hearings, write legislation, advocate the passage of
bills, and oversee their operation once the bills are law.

In terms of what meaning these committees have to individual senators or House members, there are substantial differences. Richard Fenno noted:

Senate committees are important as arenas in which decisions are
made. But they are not especially important as sources of individual
member influence—not when compared to House committees. That
is, a Senator's committee membership adds far less to his total potential for influence inside his chamber than a Representative's committee membership adds to his potential for influence in his
chamber.[10]

Fenno's point is that the House member is more a creature
of his committee assignment than is the senator. The life-and-

death nature of committee-assignment decisions in the House
has no parallel in the Senate. House members' identities are
wrapped up in their committees because these committees provide them with their platform, their ability to amplify their
voices, their campaign contributions, and almost their very
identity. For a House member to be assigned to one of the "exclusive" committees (Ways and Means, Appropriations, Rules)
that are considered so influential that service on another committee is prohibited is a towering accomplishment; a seat on the
House Commerce Committee ensures a generous supply of
campaign money from corporate political action committees
(PACs) because of the panel's broad jurisdiction. By way of
contrast, a senator will almost certainly get a seat on one of the
four choicest committees in his chamber: Appropriations,
Armed Services, Finance, and Foreign Relations. And it does
not end there for senators. They will also serve on three or four
other major committees because the Senate has fewer people to
cover the same policy turf as the House. Currently the average
senator serves on eleven committees and subcommittees, the
average House member on five. House members receive a slender slice of public policy and, in devouring it, get to know
every nut and raisin in the filling. Senators get multiple help-
ings from several pies, but they are not always certain whether
it is lemon meringue or mincemeat that they are eating at any
given time.

While each house has twenty standing committees, Senate
committees have fewer members. House Appropriations has
sixty-one members; its Senate counterpart, which is the Senate's largest, has only twenty-eight. Senate committees, typically, have fewer than twenty members. The only House
committees with twenty or fewer members are two that members struggle to avoid—House Administration and standards of
official conduct (ethics). House Administration deals with internal housekeeping matters such as office space and parking.
Members of Standards of Official Conduct investigate ethical

violations of their colleagues—not an enviable job. The only other committee with fewer than twenty members is the Select Intelligence Committee, which is not a standing (permanent) committee.

The individual senator looms even larger in the committee setting than in the chamber as a whole. Only one of the senators I interviewed declined to cite committee differences as a major distinction between the two houses. More typical was Larry Craig, an Idaho Republican who was elected to the Senate in 1990 after ten years in the House; he reflected on the difference in his own influence in the Senate as compared to the House.

I never—as a freshman, sophomore, or junior in the House—had ever been involved in a meeting in which the decisions that emerged were final. I was just an inputter into the process. I was not a decision-maker in the House. Only after being there ten years was I finally beginning to to get there. Seniority does become a factor in the House, especially for a minority member like me. Over here in the Senate, the power was immediate. I went to a meeting with some senators after I got here and we were sitting around talking about divvying up the pie and I could see they really meant it. I came back to my office and said to my staff, "Hey, we've really got some power."

The smaller size of the Senate committee obviously promotes a faster track to leadership of a committee in a system where seniority is the rule. It also fosters immediate influence for freshman senators because the multiple committee assignments often force senior members to be absent, particularly from subcommittee meetings, thus leaving only junior members to conduct business. Former senator John Culver recalls the dramatic change from his House experience.

One of the great shocks when I arrived in the Senate was that instead of being on a committee with forty members or whatever, you're suddenly on a subcommittee where you may be one of two people who show up and if you've got a couple of proxies [votes you can cast on behalf of absent senators] there's nothing you can't get passed. It's like taking candy from a baby in terms of the opportunities that there are to effectively influence and shape the course of a bill in committee.

The size difference and the overall contrast in the role of Senate and House committees were underscored with great directness by Senator Phil Gramm, a Texas Republican who served two terms in the House as a Democrat and one as a Republican.

I have been a little bit surprised at the Senate in that the committees are less important over here. First of all, subcommittees are almost meaningless over here. The committees are small enough that all the work is done in full committee. And a subcommittee chairmanship is of relatively little value.

And quite frankly, Senate committees don't do a whole lot. At least not in my two years here. Much of the work is done on the floor.

While no other senator minimized the role of the Senate committee quite to the extent that Senator Gramm did, all agreed that the committees just loom less large in the calculations of senators than of House members. This was discerned by congressional scholars Steven Smith and Christopher Deering, who noted that the objectives of senators in choosing one committee assignment over another are simply less differentiated than those of House members. While members tend to select the committee they want to serve on in terms of a number of calculations—such as whether or not the committee helps them gain reelection, rise in the House leadership, or shape policy—senators' decision rules seem less clear-cut. Whatever the senators' ultimate goals, publicity for their committee work seems to be a more dominant factor in what committee they choose than it is with House members.[11]

THE LIMITS OF EXPERTISE FOR HOUSE MEMBERS

Being assigned to three major committees may cause senators to be spread very thin and denies them the opportunity that

House members have to develop expertise in a single policy area. But few senators seem to think very highly of expertise—particularly if it is purchased at the price of being limited in what subjects they can speak out on. Multiple committee assignments are seen by senators as a kind of roving commission to speak authoritatively on a broad range of questions. The legislative director to a Midwestern Democrat commented the advantage that her boss saw in this arrangement. "From his perspective, there's much more of an ability to to assume leadership and get really involved in issues that fall outside the jurisdiction of his committees. When you've got five committees there really aren't many issues outside your committees' jurisdiction. There is that ability if you're not on Foreign Relations to still get involved in an international issue and even provide some leadership. In the House you are really constrained in terms of committee assignments and very, very rarely do you find people deviating and getting out of jurisdictional lines." What is particularly galling to House members is that they may have toiled on their subcommittee to build up expertise on an issue only to find that a senator has swooped down, seized the same issue, and is basking in the publicity to which the member thought his expertise entitled him.

Former senator John Culver saw this eclipsing of House members by senators as a general pattern that was demoralizing to the representatives.

The House members resent the fact, understandably, that they can work very hard in a public policy area and become genuine experts because of their association with their committee and its work and their forced concentration in the problem area, and yet the television news will be full of a senator who had been on the committee for a week and he's already a subcommittee chairman and he won't know one end from the other about the problem, but he's the one who will be quoted.

There he'll be popping off, and here is this highly informed, sophisticated, effective, eager House member who's going to die with the secret that he's the real expert. So it's not surprising that there's a lot of resentment.

UNDER THE DOME: HOUSE-SENATE CONFERENCES
AND WHO WINS THEM

If senators are better situated to win the battle of publicity and visibility, one might expect that House members would shine in those situations where substantive and concentrated expertise might show. The conference committee to reconcile differences over House and Senate versions of the same bill would seem to be one such example in which the House would consistently prevail. Seeing House members and senators in such close engagement might even reinforce the vision that the House gets its revenge in both substance and style. In fact, attempts to get a clear-cut idea of who wins in conference, that is, whose version of the bill is more likely to resemble the one signed by the president, have not been notably decisive.

The research over the past four decades as to who wins most often in conference ends up in an unsatisfying welter of qualifications, quibbles over what the word "win" means, and the ultimate retreat from a categorical answer: "It depends upon the circumstances."

Gilbert Steiner, in 1951, was the first to try to detect a pattern of House or Senate dominance in conference.[12] Steiner found a clear pattern of House dominance, especially in the areas of taxes, appropriations, and agricultural legislation.

Fifteen years later, Richard Fenno found that the Senate versions of bills in conference were the ones more often adopted because the Senate conferees (those chosen to represent the Senate in conferences) enjoyed greater support from the membership as a whole than did House members. Because of the decision-making structure of the Senate that emphasizes bipartisan consensus and House decisions that are frequently a reflection of the will of the dominant party, Senate conferees "not only represent the Senate—they are the Senate."[13]

But at the same time that the consensus seemed to be building on Senate dominance, John Manley put the case that the Senate's preeminence in conference was not so clear-cut. He found that in conferences between the House Ways and Means Committee and the Senate Finance Committee, House conferees seemed more influential in the final outcome of Social Security bills while senators seemed more influential on trade and revenue issues.[14]

Somewhat later another investigator came to a general conclusion that the Senate tended to prevail in conference. His figure, that about 65 percent of items in disagreement were resolved according to the Senate position, is remarkably close to that of Fenno.[15]

Why is the Senate so consistently the winner on disputed conference items? A pair of researchers attempted to answer this question and came up with the conclusion that the Senate wins because, on money bills at least, it gets the bill after the House. The constitutional requirement that the House originate tax bills and the convention that appropriations also begin in the House make the Senate the court of last resort. The Senate becomes the place where lobbyists who did not get what they wanted in the House can turn their political firepower. Even House members look to the Senate to preserve amendments that they have included. The two scholars make two additional points: (1) When the Senate is the chamber initiating the action, the House tends to prevail more often; (2) there is nothing inherently superior to the Senate's rules or procedures that translates into victory—it merely seems to be the case that the last-acting chamber becomes the focus of more outside support whether that chamber be the House or the Senate. What may be the ultimate vindication of the reluctant specialists in the House is that most of what is acted upon in general by both houses originates in the House.[16]

SENATORS' PERCEPTIONS OF CONFERENCE VICTORS

While the bulk of the scholarly literature points with some consistency to the Senate as the victor in conferences, senators themselves do not think so. Why do senators think that the House positions usually prevail over that of their own chamber? The answer has to do with the manner in which conferees are selected by the leadership to represent their respective houses in conference. Both senators and House members are usually chosen as conferees because they serve on the committee that had jurisdiction over the bill. They attended the hearings and helped write the committee report that urged its passage by the entire chamber. That committee, however, is likely to be the only one the House conferee serves on. Senators, with broader committee responsibilities, will serve on several panels and hence be unable to devote themselves as single-mindedly to the details of the bill as the more focused House members. This perception of greater expertise on the part of House conferees was uniform through the group of fourteen senators interviewed.

Senator Max S. Baucus, a Montana Democrat who spent two terms in the House, said categorically, "The senators are a lot less prepared than House members. They're spread thinner. And the consequence, in my judgment, is that House members tend to prevail in conference. When I'm at conference, I try to exercise every advantage I have to keep up with the House members because I am spread thin and have to rely much more on my staff."

Baucus's observation about senators' heavy reliance on staff in conference was echoed by others. His colleague, Georgia Democrat Wyche Fowler, recalled, "The House members would come in and know their stuff—no notes, no staff. The senators would have a trillion people standing around to answer their questions." A staff aide to a new senator who had recently come over from the House recollected her boss's amazement, "at how many senators didn't have a clue as to what was in the bill" and how "the only thing that saved the senators at the critical point was their staff people whispering in their ears." Perhaps the most damning verdict on the disparity between the knowledge brought to conference by House members and senators came from a currently serving House member who said, "I am frankly appalled at the number of times in conference that the dialogue doesn't go back and forth between House members and senators but between House members and Senate staff."

House members, for their part, believe the myth of their dominance. It seems to assuage the hurt of being considered so much less majestic than the Senate in other realms. Senator Richard S. Schweiker, a Pennsylvania Republican who spent four terms in the House before going on to the Senate and later serving in the Reagan Cabinet, recalled the malicious delight of House members in flaunting their mastery of the details in conference:

House guys have fewer committee responsibilities and know more of the substance on a particular subject. They make a fetish of one-upping the senators and proving that they've done their homework.

Also, because he's got so many committee obligations, a senator may be involved in two or three conferences at the same time, while the chances are that a congressman will be on only one or two at the most. So the House guy can sit there and methodically wait for the right time to put something through the conference.

Another reason that senators, in the face of some persuasive evidence to the contrary, believe that the House usually prevails in conference may be the product of the *noblesse oblige* that grants to the House a small advantage. Senators may also not be conscious of how powerful they actually are. Even though the pattern of Senate dominance is not uniform, most senators interviewed expressed surprise that the record of Senate success in conference might even be close to a draw. It is probably one of the few areas in which senators underestimate their influence.

The Role of Rules

It is difficult to overemphasize how profoundly the role of rules of procedure differs between the House and Senate. While the House member who wins a seat in the Senate is obviously more familiar with the legislative process than, let us say, a former governor or someone who operated a business, there are still major adjustments to be made.[17] Sometimes an event takes place early in the Senate career of a former House member that opens his or her eyes dramatically to the new system of rules. Hugh Scott had such an experience when he first came to the Senate after sixteen years in the House.

One of the philosophical gurus of the Senate at the time I was elected was John Williams from Delaware. I paid a courtesy call on him since he was one person I particularly wanted guidance from.

He said to me, "What do you want to know?" And I said that I'd been over on the Senate floor but I'd never studied the Senate rules. I asked him what I needed to do if I wanted to make a speech. He said, "You stand up." And I said: "What do I do then?" And he said, "The presiding officer recognizes you."

So I told him that in the House, [Speaker] Sam Rayburn didn't have to recognize me unless he wanted to. So Williams said that it's not that way in the Senate. "They've got to recognize you because your power to do mischief is too great if they don't."

Well, I thought about what John Williams said about mischief and about a month later I went to talk to [Majority Whip] Mike Mansfield. We didn't know each other very well and I said to him, "Senator, can I have a minute or two to talk on this bill?"

"Well," he replied, "I'm afraid you're too late. I don't think we have enough time left." So I said, "That's all right, I'll just ask for a quorum call, and that will take twice the amount of time I needed to say my piece."

So he said, "Well, I'll get you recognized," and he did it right away and from that time on we had the most cordial relationship.

By resorting to a rule that enables a senator to request a time-consuming quorum call, Scott was reminding Mansfield that it was better to comply with an untimely or even an unreasonable request than to risk tying up the Senate's business. If mischief making is what a senator wishes to pursue, the rules allow it. House rules do not confer this ability on members. As another former House member, John Culver, put it:

If you just want to be unpleasant and have a temper tantrum and if you just want to be excessively self-obsessed, you can have a field day in the Senate. You can break all the toys in the sandbox if that's what you want in order to get your way and you can pout with very great effect. You really can't do that the same way in the House. The rules of the Senate are congenial to permitting the least consequential member to shut the place down if he's smart enough or willful enough to do it. If you are one in a hundred, it really doesn't matter a lot how long you've been there. That gives any individual power—real power—in institutional terms. He just has to be dealt with.

RULES AND SIZE

Senate rules differ from House rules largely because the Senate is a quarter the size of the House. But beneath a Senate system of rules that magnifies the role of the individual senator and makes him or her so imposing, there lurks the constitutional principle of equal representation for all states. The smallness of the Senate and its different basis of representation seem inextricably linked in historical terms. So whether the individual's prerogatives were magnified because he or she was part of a small body or represented a whole state rather than merely a portion of one is difficult to sort out.

At the turn of the twentieth century Senator Henry Cabot Lodge, a Massachusetts Republican (and grandfather and namesake of the 1960 Republican vice-presidential candidate), wrote a series of articles on the Senate for *Scribner's Magazine*. In these articles he made the case for the constitutional superiority of the Senate, asserting that

in the formation of the Senate the States were retaining for themselves all the powers they believed needful for their safety, and as everything was theirs to give or withhold, they were naturally liberal in their endowment of the body which was to continue to represent them under a system where they necessarily parted with so much.[18]

At the same time that Lodge was exalting the Senate as a repository of state sovereignty, he also made the case that smallness was the reason for the simplicity of the Senate's rules. Writing about the first meeting of the Senate, which took place in Federal Hall in New York in April 1789 without the senators from North Carolina and Rhode Island, Lodge noted:

> These twenty-two gentlemen . . . sat together in one not very large room and talked matters over with an informality and familiarity which have never entirely departed from Senate debates. . . .
> This small body of men, sitting in this way in private, with comparatively little to do and with no record of the proceedings but the journal, did not require anything very elaborate in the way of rules. Business was largely transacted by general assent, and with much regard for the convenience of each Senator, habits which have survived unchanged to the present time.[19]

Smallness was also stressed as the defining character of the Senate by Woodrow Wilson:

> [The Senate] is small enough to make it safe to allow individual freedom to its members, and to have, at the same time, such order and sense of proportion in its proceedings as is characteristic of small bodies, like boards of college trustees or of commercial directors, who feel that their main object is business, not speechmaking, and so say all that is necessary without being tedious, and do what they are called upon to do without need of driving themselves with hurrying rules. Such rules, they seem to feel, are meant only for big assemblies which have no power of self-control.[20]

The rules of procedure that are promoted by the Senate's smallness magnify the influence of the individual by allowing a single senator to intervene—often decisively—in the legislative process. Power of this magnitude is accorded to only a handful of the top leaders in the House. This power when multiplied by 100 produces an institution far less predictable than the House.

What are these rules of procedure in the Senate that repose such great power in the hands of individuals? What gives them "the power to do mischief" or "to break all the toys in the sandbox"? And how do these powers differ from those available to House members? The two mentioned most frequently by the

fourteen senators were extended debate and the absence of a
general rule of germaneness.

EXTENDED DEBATE

Extended debate by a senator or group of senators, which
in its most extreme form is known as the filibuster, is one of
the most distinctive features of the Senate. Those intimately familiar with House rules find it hard to adjust to. Parliamentarian of the Senate, Floyd A. Riddick, whose career had begun
as an expert on House rules, found extended debate a major adjustment when moving from the House. This was apparent in a
1979 interview with Associate Senate Historian Donald A.
Ritchie.

After I got to the Senate I had to try to forget all of the rules of the
House because their rules are so different. The biggest contrast I'd
say is unlimited debate in the Senate as contrasted to very limited debate in the House. And the use of the previous question in the House
as contrasted to no limit on debate in the Senate.

Ritchie commented, "I suppose with the size of the House
there's almost no other way they could operate." Riddick
replied, "I think that's true, I think it's a problem of numbers."[21]
The history of extended debate in the Senate can be traced
to a revision of the Senate rules that took place in 1806 after
the Senate had been in operation for seventeen years. Until that
rules revision, Senate Rule 8 allowed debate to be terminated
by the calling for a vote on "the previous question." Such a motion was privileged: It could be moved and seconded at any
time and if passed by a majority vote debate would be terminated. That provision for closing debate was dropped in 1806,
and between that date and 1917 there was no way to terminate
debate in the Senate. Just a few years after the Senate instituted
unlimited debate the House limited it by adopting the previous
question rule. In 1811, the House made the motion for previous question nondebatable, thus precipitating an immediate
vote on whatever matter of business is pending.[22]

What caused the Senate to institute *cloture,* or limitation on debate, in 1917 was the inability of the Senate to vote on the armed-ship bill that had been favored by the Woodrow Wilson administration to protect U.S. merchant vessels from German submarines. Wilson used his constitutional authority to call a special session of the Senate. On March 8, 1917, the Senate adopted Rule 22 permitting a vote on cloture on the petition of sixteen senators. If two-thirds of the senators present and voting approved the termination of debate, cloture would be invoked. In 1975 Rule 22 was modified to allow cloture if supported by three-fifths of the entire membership (sixty senators).[23]

The history of closing off debate in the Senate has progressed from impossible (1806–1917) to almost impossible (1917–1975) to very difficult (1975–present).

But while the standards for cutting off debate have been eased, that is a far cry from saying that debate can be cut off readily. For example, even after cloture is voted, senators may continue to debate and offer time-consuming amendments for thirty hours. This led Senator Phil Gramm to conclude that the principle of extended debate stands virtually intact:

The rules of the Senate give tremendous power to the individual member if he feels strongly about something. He can literally stop the Senate. For example, in my two years in the Senate, we have never had a debate stopped. If an individual wanted to debate and wanted to prevent a vote from occurring, we have never in my experience taken action that stopped him. We had cloture motions adopted, but after cloture you've got 30 hours of debate. So if that one member really is opposed to something and is willing to stand up on the issue, it is very, very difficult to do anything.

Late in a congressional session when the Senate faces adjournment and time is running out to pass critical bills that must pass in order for the government to remain in operation, the filibuster (or even the threat of it) can be used to devastating effect as the Senate can conduct no other business on the floor so long as the debate continues. Recently, however, a "track system" has been used by Senate leaders to allow the Senate to conduct other business while a filibuster is going on.

This almost unlimited ability to block the Senate's schedule and the feeble claims of the House members to debate time summed up for former senator and House member Richard Schweiker the differences between the two bodies:

I was one of the real experts in the House on the all-volunteer army and the debate for the renewal of the draft came up in the House. But the most I could get was five minutes of speaking time in the House debates on that issue.

I got to the Senate and I was able to introduce an amendment even though the chairman of the Armed Services Committee was very much against the idea. So here I was a freshman Republican and even though I'd lost in committee I kept my pride and went to the floor and beat the chairman. So there it was: I'd gone from the House, barely able to speak three minutes on a major issue, to upsetting the chairman by making a case for it on the floor.

What enabled this senator to pull off such a feat was the unlimited debate in his new chamber. But there is another form of flexibility that works to the benefit of senators: the absence of a germaneness rule such as the one that prevails in the House.

THE GERMANENESS QUESTION

The absence of a general germaneness rule in the Senate was pointed to by most of the senators interviewed as the procedural difference between the House and Senate that most enhanced the power of senators. Put simply, the House rules require that amendments to a bill made on the floor must be germane, that is, relevant and pertinent, to the bill itself. With certain exceptions, senators can introduce floor amendments that have nothing at all to do with the bill as it comes to the floor from a committee.

The fact that the Senate lacks a germaneness rule and the House has one reflects the difference between the two houses in the importance of committees. What the germaneness rule in

the House really says is that, as a rule, the work of the committee shall not be tampered with on the floor. If a House committee has duly reported out a bill and its structure and
substance have been approved by the Rules Committee (a stop
that Senate bills do not have to make), there is a strong resistance to any amendment offered on the floor, particularly if it
comes from someone who is not a member of the bill-writing
committee.

Idaho Republican Larry Craig seized upon this difference
to provide an example of his own realization of the vastly
greater power accorded to senators by the more liberal amendment rules in the upper chamber.

The House Rules Committee is all-powerful in the way it structures
a bill on the floor of the House and what it will or will not allow in
debate on that bill or the offering of amendments on that bill. So a
powerful committee chairman, once he has worked a bill through that
committee can go to the Rules Committee and largely control it from
that point: either to allow perfecting amendments or to allow nothing. And he can get the support of the Rules Committee and usually
chairmen get that if they get the wink and the nod of the Speaker.

In the Senate, however, senior members like Ted Kennedy really
have to worry about junior members like Larry Craig because Larry
Craig can go to the floor and raise all kinds of havoc. And the senior
people know that they're going to have to be much more accommodating and much more willing to listen. If not, it brings about the ultimate political battle on the floor. That's a very powerful tool and it
was a tool I'd never had access to in the House. From the point of a
member of the minority in particular, it makes you feel like a full
partner in the legislative process.

There is no better example of the enormous policymaking
power vested in senators because they do not have to conform to the strictures of a germaneness rule than the Gramm-
Rudman-Hollings Act of 1986. This radical approach to
reducing the federal budget was offered as a nongermane
amendment to a bill extending the federal debt limit. The principal author of the amendment, Senator Phil Gramm, reflected

upon what he did and what he would have been unable to do as a House member.

In the House I would never have had the opportunity to offer Gramm-Rudman. I had to have a [legislative] vehicle that *had* to be adopted. The House rules are such that any change in the Budget Act had to go not to the Budget Committee but to the Rules Committee. The Speaker appoints the Rules Committee and there is no way in the world you're going to strengthen the budget process or impose any binding constraints through the committee process in the House.

So I had started really working on this idea that became Gramm-Rudman in 1982 when I was in the House. And when I got to the Senate I saw the vehicle I had been waiting for—the two trillion dollar debt ceiling. So I offered the Gramm-Rudman-Hollings law as an amendment to the debt ceiling extension, a bill that *has* to be passed on a timely basis for the government to continue to function.

Now I just could not have done that in the House. Because they would have ruled my amendment nongermane. In fact they would have ruled any amendment to the debt ceiling nongermane except maybe changing the numbers.

The implications of the germaneness differences go well beyond the substance of policy—they involve the political dynamics of the two bodies and the ability of senators and members to wound one another politically.

Because they are able to introduce amendments on the floor virtually at will, any senator can demand a recorded vote of his colleagues at almost any time. Going on record, particularly on controversial issues, is an act that most politicians would prefer to avoid.

A lobbyist for a major civil rights organization put the punitive aspects of the lack of germaneness requirements this way:

If a troublemaker like [Senator] Jesse Helms [R-N.C.] a month before the congressional elections wants a recorded vote on a school prayer, or a busing, or an abortion amendment, he can get it in most instances. At the very least, he can get a tabling motion which is a procedural vote, but understandably can be sold as a substantive vote also. It is much easier in the Senate to get a recorded vote and force someone to take a position.

Bert Carp, of the Washington law firm Williams and Jensen, who has lobbied Congress for almost three decades, notes the same destructive power but points out that senators use it sparingly.

Senators don't like to vote on controversial matters; they end up disappointing large numbers of people. It's this power to wound one another and to cause havoc. That's what causes it to be used so cautiously. But the institution does not lean so much on binding rules as it does on conventions of courtesy.

So while it is true that the sheer difference in volume between House rules and Senate rules (eleven volumes of House rules and precedents versus a single volume for Senate rules and precedents) is emblematic of the differences in complexity of procedure, the greatest differences are informal. Even if the Senate had a substantially larger body of regulations, the smallness of the Senate would permit the development of understandings among senators on a face-to-face basis that would not be possible for the larger House. What may exemplify best the difference between the formal and canonical House and the informal and subjective Senate is the phenomenon of the *unanimous consent agreement.*

While employed in both chambers to dispose of routine or noncontroversial business, the unanimous consent agreement in the Senate is an informal device that specifies the rules of debate on virtually every bill. The House requires the Rules Committee to issue a rule or special order after a bill leaves committee but before it reaches the floor as to what extent a bill can be amended and how much debate time will be accorded proponents and foes of the bill. The House version of the procedure is the subject of formal, public hearings by the Rules Committee; the Senate's version is formed by informal arrangements between party leaders. In the House, it is not even authentically unanimous because it is adopted by majority vote; in the Senate, every last senator must agree on the terms and conditions of the debate and vote.[24]

On the face of it, procedures that grant so much discretion to the individual would seem to promote an individualism so excessive that timely action would be virtually impossible. Indeed, where interests conflict, as they so often do in the Senate, the requirement for unanimity or near-unanimity on many matters has been seen as a prescription for anarchy. Senator Warren Rudman (R-N.H.), a man with a reputation for thoughtfulness, describes senators as "independent contractors" in their assertion of individual prerogatives and says, "We've got so many checks and balances around here, we're frozen." Then, he warns, "Either we make major changes or the House will become the dominant body."[25] The free rein given to individuals in the Senate also came under attack from political scientist Norman Ornstein, who complained, "It doesn't just bend over backwards to protect the intense feelings of its minorities, it lets individuals run roughshod over any semblance of institutional process."[26] The Senate has come under fire for allowing rules designed to protect minority interests to become subverted and used as devices for obstructionism and personal pique. One senator observed, "The rules around here are such that one determined member can wreak havoc with the schedule; even members who are generally disliked and who are notorious for being obnoxious and abusive, but people don't often call their hand because it's better to tolerate them than to screw around with the rules."

It would appear at first glance that obstructionism and the public interest are totally incompatible. But dismissing the hyperindividualism of the Senate as no more than a symptom of the fragmentation of American democracy would be a mistake. It would likewise be inappropriate to conclude that the absence of such strong checks on the will of the majority in the House necessarily promotes the public interest. It is more useful to see the operations of the two houses as promoting different kinds of democracy, both of which are essential. Consider the two models of democracy that have been referred to as "adversary democracy" and "unitary democracy."[27] Adversary democracy as it pertains to Congress refers to the faithful representation of the various interests of their states and districts by senators and House members and the practice of bargaining among members for benefits and protections for those constituencies. Unitary democracy, in contrast, involves the establishment of a consensus among legislators on what is the common or national interest.

The American legislative system is based on geographical representation and no member of Congress is elected by the nation as a whole. Only the voters in the 50 states or the 435 congressional districts have any direct control over the composition of Congress. With the fate of all senators and representatives in the hands of voters in these smaller geographical units, adversary democracy enjoys a built-in advantage in both chambers. Indeed, much legislation bears the unmistakable seams of having been assembled out of 535 components; it reflects a distributive strategy in which policy is subordinated to parochial considerations. Increasingly, moreover, American elections turn not on the major issues of the day but upon the sole question of who can deliver the best set of particularized benefits to a state or district. Adversary values clearly dominate the world of congressional elections.

Senators and House members come to Washington to look after the interests of the citizens who elected them, and who, indeed, would advocate and defend those local interests if not those very legislators? But they are also United States senators and United States representatives. The laws they make are binding on all Americans, not just on the voters who sent them to Washington. If the national interest could be defined as no more than the sum of all of the local interests represented by the 535 congressional members, then the adversary model would be the only one with which we need concern ourselves. It is certainly possible to imagine a system of government whose resources were so abundant that it could literally give every interest what it wanted and, indeed, there have been times in the American past when it seemed that we verged on such a system. But even if resources can be distributed equally to all claimants, values cannot.

The framers of the Constitution, for all of their belief in the beneficial interplay of interests, believed that the whole was larger than merely the sum of its parts. James Madison expressed his concern over what he called "the national character" and defended the inclusion of a Senate in the Constitution as a more reliable expression of that character than the House.

Madison wrote, in #63 of the *Federalist,* that national character "can never be sufficiently possessed by a numerous and changeable body. It can only be found in a number so small, that a sensible degree of the praise and blame of public measures may be the portion of each individual; or in an assembly so durably invested with public trust, that the pride and consequences of its members may be sensibly incorporated with the reputation and prosperity of the community."

Madison seemed to be making a case for the "unitary quality" of the Senate, saying, in effect, that its continuity made it a more national institution than the House. In a later passage in *Federalist* #63, Madison refers to the "cool and deliberate sense of community" in free governments that sometimes gives way to "irregular passions" and "temporary errors and delusions" on the part of the people. He stresses the need for a "temperate and respectable body of citizens" to intervene to quell the passions until "reason, justice, and truth can regain their authority over the public mind."

Representatives, with their proximity to the people by reason of their direct election and with their greater responsiveness by reason of their two-year term, were expected to resonate to popular passions. As Madison wrote in *Federalist*

#52, the House would have "an immediate dependence on, and intimate sympathy with, the people." This presupposed an adversary role; House members were to give voice to the concerns of their constituents in unmodulated volume. To do otherwise would be to impede the free interplay of interests that was at the heart of the constitutional design. The House was to be the arena of sentiments that were not only passionate but the products of numerically small and specialized segments of the population.

But can the considerable prerogatives of senators and a set of rules that promotes great individualism serve the public interest? At first glance it might seem unlikely that the values of unitary democracy could be promoted by a system of rules that provides so many opportunities for blockage and obstruction. But George Reedy notes, "The Senate does *not* prevent the majority from ruling; it merely prevents the majority from doing everything it wants to do when it wants to do it. The Senate does not grant the minority the right to rule. It merely grants the minority the right to block legislation until it has been demonstrated that there is a clearcut, consistent majority behind it and until it is apparent that the minority is willing to remain within the community when it is forced to give in to legislation that it considers abhorrent."[28]

Indeed, Jane Mansbridge has observed that protection and group unity are not always at odds, for the individual protection afforded by the veto can sometimes reinforce group unity.[29] This may be particularly applicable to small face-to-face groups like the Senate. While it is certainly true that political conflict based on the defense of parochial interests is a major force in the Senate, the simple compactness and the face-to-face quality of senatorial interaction may have the effect of muting and attenuating conflict. And, "while face-to-face contact is not logically related to the discovery of a common interest and can sometimes intensify conflict, it usually seems to encourage participants to find solutions they can all support."[30]

The framers of the Constitution created a Senate in which

all states would have equal voice so that the rights of the smallest and least populous states would be protected. The smallness of the Senate as a body and the rules that grew out of that compactness accentuate those protections of minority opinion, but they may also promote consensus by the simple fact that senators are likely to get to know one another and so take the measure of colleagues as individuals. "Face-to-face contact," Mansbridge writes, "works best for the unitary end of cementing friendship." She adds that "mutual knowledge and subtle communication make fuller empathy possible so that each member can more easily make the other's interest his or her own."[31]

But does the Senate qualify as a face-to-face body? One condition that has been laid down as a standard is that everyone in the body knows everyone else in it.[32]

The average senator, as I have already noted, does not know every last colleague, but there is evidence that senators know and interact with a higher percentage of colleagues than do House members. Michael Foley found that difference in committee size and the number of individual committee assignments between the House and the Senate resulted in the typical House member knowing about 11 percent of his or her colleagues and the average senator about one-third of the total membership of the Senate.[33]

The degree of personal intimacy in a circle of House friends is likely to be greater than that among senators with their more glancing contacts and the greater presence of staff as intermediaries. In the aggregate, however, the senator is able to take the personal measure of more of his or her colleagues. Such associations have a great impact on the institution at large. Networks of personal association in the Senate come closer to being institutionwide than in the House. Such networks, moreover, are less specialized by subject area or geography. Friendship of a kind peculiar to the Senate influences profoundly the way the Senate operates. Former senator Richard S. Schweiker, a Pennsylvania Republican, described the importance of personal relations in the Senate.

In the Senate reason prevails more, logic prevails more, and personal and close friendships are more important than they are in the House because there's no place to hide in the Senate. If you had a difference of opinion between House members of different parties, it very seldom got resolved or adjudicated in any way. It was just an accepted fact of life.

But if you clashed on the Senate floor, heatedly, with somebody, chances are that one or the other would make an effort by the end of the day to be congenial and converse and interact with that person, knowing that he differed. You sort of went out of your way after clashing with somebody to go over and say hello, shake his hand, wish him well.

At least part of the reason for the rancorous debate in the House comes out of the bitter partisan strife of the 1980s when beleaguered Republicans, out of power for almost forty years, resorted to a kind of procedural guerrilla warfare. Led by Representative Newt Gingrich, the Republicans were materially responsible for toppling Democratic Speaker Jim Wright. The Democrats used their majorities to beat down the Republicans, so when the GOP gained control of the House in the 1994 elections for the first time in forty years, it was payback time, and Democrats were on the receiving end of Republican high-handedness. With the vast majority of House seats being safe for one party or the other and with the core supporters of both Democrats and Republicans in these noncompetitive districts being among the most ideological voters, House members have every incentive to do battle on behalf of constituents who favor confrontation. Administering a tongue-lashing to a colleague and then withdrawing into the recesses of a large and segmented membership seems more typical of the House than of the Senate. Making amends for acrimonious comments made in debate seems more characteristic of the Senate than the House.

The Senate is a place where it is quite common for gestures of support to come from unexpected sources. At a time when Senator Edward M. Kennedy's personal conduct was the subject of some lurid articles in magazines and newspapers, his most staunch defender was Senator Orrin Hatch (R-Utah), his old political adversary on both the Human Resources and Judiciary Committees where the two had clashed on everything from abortion policy to the confirmation of Judge Clarence Thomas to the Supreme Court. And in 1990 when Senator Daniel Patrick Moynihan (D-N.Y.) faced a demonstration of angry students at Vassar College in Poughkeepsie, New York, who charged that his writings were racist, it was the Republican Minority Leader in the Senate, Bob Dole, who leaped to Moynihan's defense. "Pat Moynihan a racist? You've got to be kidding," Dole is reported to have said. "Pat has spent his life fighting for minorities, the down and out, and the left out. This strange story coming out of Poughkeepsie is absolutely preposterous."[34]

While such expressions across party and ideological lines are not unknown in the House, we shall see in the following chapter that there are some very dramatic differences between the House and Senate in regard to partisanship.

NOTES

1. U.S. Congress, House, *The Capitol,* 93rd Congress, 1st Session, 1973, p. 11.
2. *New York Times,* Monday, December 1, 1986.
3. Steven V. Roberts, "Pick a Seat, (but not) Any Seat," *New York Times,* Monday, December 1, 1986.
4. Ibid.
5. Roberts, op. cit.; Ross K. Baker, *Friend and Foe in the U.S. Senate* (New York: The Free Press, 1980), p. 95; and U.S. Congress, House, *The Capitol,* 96th Congress, 2d Session, 1981, p. 97.
6. Roberts, op. cit.
7. Baker, op. cit., p. 96.
8. *New York Times,* Wednesday, December 10, 1986.
9. Donald Riegle (with Trevor Armbrister), *O Congress* (Garden City, N.Y.: Doubleday, 1972), p. 147.
10. Richard F. Fenno, Jr., *Congressmen in Committee* (Boston: Little, Brown, 1973), p. 147.80

11. Steven S. Smith and Christopher J. Deering, *Committees in Congress* (Washington, D.C.: Congressional Quarterly Press, 1984), pp. 111–112. See also Richard F. Fenno, Jr., *Congressmen in Committee.*

12. Gilbert Y. Steiner, *The Congressional Conference Committee, Seventieth to Eightieth Congresses* (Urbana, Ill.: University of Illinois Press, 1951).

13. Richard F. Fenno, Jr., *The Power of the Purse* (Boston: Little Brown, 1966), and David Vogler, "Patterns of Dominance on Conference Committees," *Midwest Journal of Political Science,* 14 (1970), pp. 303–320.

14. John Manley, *The Politics of Finance* (Boston: Little, Brown, 1970).

15. John Ferejohn, "Who Wins in Conference Committee?" *Journal of Politics,* 27 (November 1975), pp. 1033–1046.

16. Gerald S. Strom and Barry S. Rundquist, "A Revised Theory of Winning in House-Senate Conferences," *American Political Science Review,* 71 (June 1977), pp. 448–453.

17. Richard F. Fenno, Jr., "Adjusting to the U.S. Senate," unpublished paper, photocopy, p. 16.81

18. Henry Cabot Lodge, "The Senate," *Scribner's Magazine,* 34 (1903), p. 542.

19. Lodge, op. cit., p. 545.

20. Woodrow Wilson, *Congressional Government* (Boston: Houghton Mifflin, 1885), pp. 216–217.

21. Senate Historical Office, *Oral History Interview with Floyd A. Riddick,* conducted by Donald A. Ritchie, Washington, D.C., June 26, 1978–February 15, 1979, pp. 16–17.

22. Malcolm E. Jewell and Samuel C. Patterson, *The Legislative Process in the United States,* 4th ed. (New York: Random House, 1986), pp. 102–103.

23. Walter J. Oleszek, *Congressional Procedures and the Policy Process,* 2d ed. (Washington, D.C.: CQ Press, 1984), p. 188.

24. Oleszek, *Congressional Procedures,* pp. 156–159.

25. Martin Tolchin, "Senate Deplores Disarray in New Chamber of Equals," *New York Times,* Sunday, November 24, 1984.

26. Quoted in Helen Dewar, "Senate Faces Institutional Identity Crisis," *Washington Post,* Monday, November 26, 1984.

27. See Jane J. Mansbridge, *Beyond Adversary Democracy* (Chicago: University of Chicago Press, 1983), and David J. Vogler and Sidney R. Waldman, *Congress and Democracy* (Washington, D.C.: Congressional Quarterly, 1985).

28. George E. Reedy, *The U.S. Senate* (New York: Crown, 1986), p. 197.

29. Mansbridge, op. cit., p. 263.

30. Ibid., p. 271.

31. Ibid., pp. 270–271.

32. Peter Laslett, "The Face to Face Society," in Peter Laslett, ed., *Philosophy, Politics, and Society* (Oxford: Blackwell, 1956), p. 157.

33. Michael Foley, *The New Senate* (New Haven: Yale University Press, 1980), p. 172.

34. James Feron, "Vassar Students End Sit-In; Moynihan Defends Lecture," *New York Times,* Friday, February 16, 1990.

3

Raw Numbers and Concurrent Majorities

Partisanship and Leadership in the Two Houses

REFLECTING ON HIS EXPERIENCE in the two chambers of Congress, a Democratic newcomer to the Senate, Jack Reed of Rhode Island, emphasized one distinction that he believed to be essential to understanding the differences between the House and the Senate:

I think that what happens in the Senate [is that] . . . people get to know each other better. I mean, you see more people. You work with them on different committees. You see them on the floor. You have to work with them. That's part of the Senate dynamic. You also know you'll see them the next day. The House is such a big place. You know the people on your committee or the regional members, or maybe somebody you have an interest in, but there are people who you might know by face and to nod to but you'd never had anything to do with. In that context, it's more anonymous. You just take a position and the heck with it.

The compactness of the Senate, its magnification of the role of the individual, and the opportunity for senators to take the personal measure of their colleagues yield, in the opinion of senators, a far less partisan body than the House. Yet, by one widely accepted standard of the intensity of partisanship in Congress—the percentage of times a majority of Democrats votes against a majority of Republicans on a broad range of issues—the House seems no more partisan than the Senate. Indeed, in several recent years, the percentage of recorded votes on which a majority of Democrats opposed a majority of Republicans was actually higher in the Senate than in the House, making it appear that polarization along party lines was actually higher in the Senate.[1]

The pattern of partisan differences between the two is neither consistent over recent years nor is it clear-cut. The data suffer from a problem found in all roll-call data—that such figures tell you how a member or a senator voted on final passage of a bill, not the many votes that preceded it or the intensity with which a member worked to pass or defeat the bill. The interviews with senators who previously served in the House suggest strongly that they perceive the Senate to be a less partisan place and that it is in the interpersonal negotiations that precede votes and in informal arrangements that the contrasts appear. One setting common to both houses in which differences in partisanship express themselves with particular force is in committee.

Bicameral Differences in Committee Partisanship

Committee service tends to be a major factor in determining with whom a legislator interacts, along with membership in one's state delegation in the chamber. Committees meet in relatively small rooms, share staff, caucus together, mark up bills together, and represent the chamber on conference committees. It would be logical, then, that the more committee settings in which legislators find themselves, the more colleagues they will have the opportunity to get to know. Because senators serve on more committees than House members, their circles of associations are larger and encompass more of the membership. While friendship and intimacy may be more intense among the House colleagues thrown together on a 30-member committee in a 435-member House, senators serving on 3 committees of 10 members each might have an opportunity to establish personal ties with fully a third of their colleagues in a 100-member Senate.[2]

The Iran-Contra hearings of 1987 provide an excellent opportunity to compare a House committee and a Senate committee working side by side on the same issue and determine how partisanship figured on each side.

The hearings were conducted not by a single committee consisting of House members and senators but by two separate committees meeting jointly to take testimony and file separate reports. Both were "select" committees; that is, they were temporary committees created for a specific purpose and would disband after issuing their reports.

Different views of partisanship came into play at the very beginning of the process of investigating illegal arms sales to Iran and diversion of the profits of those sales to the Contra guerrilla forces attempting to overthrow the anti-American government of Nicaragua. When House and Senate leaders selected members for the committee, their criteria as to the partisan spirit of those selected could hardly have been more different.

In the House, both Republican and Democratic leaders chose members for the intensity of their partisanship. Republican leader Bob Michel passed up two senior representatives from New York who occasionally voted with the Democrats in favor of three younger Republicans, Jim Courter of New Jersey, Michael DeWine of Ohio, and Bill McCollum of Florida, who could defend staunchly the Republican president. In the Senate, however, both Democratic leader Robert C. Byrd and Republican leader Bob Dole chose senators known for their mild partisanship. Byrd, the majority leader, made the first selections, based on moderate partisanship. Dole was reported to have looked over Byrd's list and made his choices on the same basis.[3]

Republican senator Paul Trible of Virginia ascribed the relatively mild partisanship of the Senate to its small size, saying, "You have to work with this person today even if you disagree with him because you may need him tomorrow." Citing the rules that govern the smaller chamber, William S. Cohen (R-Maine), another member of the Senate Iran-Contra Committee, said, "One or two people can tie this place in knots." He added, "In the House they can ignore [Republicans], but things that don't have bipartisan support don't get done here."[4]

Two plausible explanations for the milder partisanship of the Senate during most of the 1990s could be that, in any given election, either party was in striking distance of a majority and that party control had changed hands twice between 1981 and 1987. In the House, by contrast, the Democratic margin of control over the same period was never less than fifty seats and at one point was almost 100, the prospects of Republican control of the House seemed so unlikely that two respected scholars concluded in 1994 that "[House] Republicans are not entirely masters of their fate."[5]

Republicans became the House majority party in the elections of 1994, but their margin of control decreased in the two subsequent elections, so that by 2000, only a handful of votes separated the two parties in the House. If the possibility of turnover of control and closeness of numbers are factors that mute partisanship in a legislative body, it is difficult to prove it by the fierceness with which House Democrats and Republicans did battle in the years after the 1994 election. A more satisfactory explanation may be found elsewhere in the nature of the two chambers and their constiuent parts. The most important of those constituent parts are the committees of Congress.

Senate committees in general are joint enterprises run by the chair and the ranking minority member. The minority party members on a Senate committee are authentic and influential players. The influence enjoyed by minority party members is a combination of the courtesy and consideration toward the individual in the small Senate; the other component is a frank recognition that a single alienated senator can cause havoc. While the treatment accorded minority members on the House side varies from committee to committee, nowhere is it as deferential as in the Senate. In virtually every instance minority House members are, in the words of Senator Trible, "frankly irrelevant."[6]

The degree to which minority members on the House side are often marginalized—even those high in seniority who serve on prestige committees—was underscored for me in my interview with Senator Larry Craig, the Idaho Republican. I mentioned to Craig a newspaper photograph that had appeared that morning showing an imperious-looking Representative Dan Rostenkowski (D-Ill.), then chairman of the House Ways and Means Committee, speaking on the telephone. In the foreground of the photo and slightly out of focus was Representative Bill Archer (R-Tex.), then the ranking minority member of the committee. The story to which the photo was appended dealt with a party-line 24-14 vote in the committee approving a major part of President Clinton's budget plan. Craig laughed when I mentioned the photo and observed, "The reason the picture was out-of-focus was probably because they didn't want to show the tread marks on Bill's face. Bill Archer is a member of tremendous talent but he got rolled yesterday, run right over top of. That kind of thing would never happen in the Senate."

Some senators observed that the degree of partisanship on any committee, whether House or Senate, also depended on the nature of the subject matter and whether it tended to process legislation with strong ideological coloration or have within its jurisdiction policies that affected economic or professional interests. One senator recalled that the Senate Judiciary Committee, with its battles over abortion, was far more partisan than the now-abolished House Merchant Marine and Fisheries, where members of both parties from coastal districts worked harmoniously to foster fishing and shipping interests.

One notable exception to the rule that partisanship is more hard-edged on House committees than on Senate committees is House Appropriations. Senator Mark Andrews spoke of his own experience:

It's just awful for Republicans on some House committees. I didn't have to suffer through it, though, since I got on Appropriations in my second term. Once you were accepted on Appropriations, it didn't make any damn difference which side of the chairman you sat on.

When I got to the Senate, Mark Hatfield who had just become chairman of Senate Appropriations when we took control in 1981 said, "You're the only Republican member of the Senate who's had experience being sort of in the majority.' Now what he meant by that was, of course, that even in the Senate, the House Appropriations Committee had the reputation of being the most non-partisan committee in the House.

Leaders and Followers in the House and Senate

Once, when asked by a journalist about the powers wielded by the Majority Leader of the Senate, Senator George J. Mitchell (D-Me.) is said to have replied, "You have the power to kiss 99 asses."

Mitchell's response is a somewhat salty characterization of what Barbara D. Sinclair has termed "service leadership." Although she coined the term to apply to the House, it has even more applicability to the Senate.[7] Here again, size differences seem to account for House-Senate contrasts. Senator James Abourezk, a South Dakota Democrat, put the case bluntly:

There is a huge difference and it's only because there are so many House members. The leadership does not really have to pay attention to the individual members that the Senate leaders do.

Woodrow Wilson came very close to denying that formal leadership was even possible in the Senate. In 1885 he wrote:

The public now and again picks out here and there a Senator who seems to act and to speak with true instinct of statesmanship and who unmistakably merits the confidence of colleagues and of people. But such a man, however eminent, is never more than *a* Senator. No one is *the* Senator. No one may speak for his party as well as for himself; no one exercises the special trust of acknowledged leadership.[8]

While much has changed in the century since Wilson wrote, aside from a brief period in the late 1950s when Lyndon Johnson exercised a singular degree of control over the body, Wilson's observations are not wholly obsolete.

Differences have been noted as to the qualities most prevalent in House and Senate leaders. Neil MacNeil noted in the early 1960s that the Senate's greatest leaders have been its great orators, while the most eminent House leaders have been those who could persuade or force the House to act. Rarely, however, he noted, do these expressive and instrumental qualities exist in the same person. Significantly, he found them in Henry Clay, a man who began his legislative career in the Senate, switched to the House, where he was elected Speaker as a freshman in 1811, and finished his lawmaking career in the Senate.[9]

Senator Paul Sarbanes (D-Md.) dwelt on two differences between the House and Senate that affect leadership most profoundly: the House and Senate rules, and the ability of the House leadership to use the power of its majority. House leadership, according to Sarbanes, "has a superior ability to channel and focus things over what is available to Senate leadership." In regard to rules, Sarbanes emphasized the ability of individual senators to introduce amendments from the floor without needing to get the amendment approved by an arm of leadership. As for the power of 218 votes, the simple majority of the House, to be decisive, Sarbanes observed that both House and Senate leaders would prefer to cajole members into supporting them, because "it's probably a better way to lead." But if cajoling does not work, "the House leaders can just use the raw numbers to move the thing right along. In the Senate, one person, whether he's on the majority side or on the minority side, can keep leadership from moving the thing on through. You really have to say that in the Senate, leadership is in the hands of the membership."

The stark contrast between leadership in the House and Senate becomes even more vivid when one broadens the definition of leadership to include not only the top party and institutional leaders (Speaker of the House and floor leaders in the House and Senate) but committee chairs as well. Virtually every senator is either chairman of a committee or subcommittee or ranking minority member on one or the other. If leadership is so defined, every senator is a leader. This has been true for some time.

Robert Peabody noted that in the 93rd Congress (1973–1974) only one senator—Republican William V. Roth, Jr., of Delaware—did not hold at least one ranking minority position on either of his committees. That leadership resources were spread so evenly in the Senate led Peabody to conclude that "there is little reason to wonder at the lack of deference which even the lowliest freshman seems to accord his party leaders. Respect, trust, and accommodation are readily demonstrated, but very little awe or excessive veneration is apparent."[10] Fifty years earlier, George Rothwell Brown came to the same conclusion and stated it with unusual bluntness: "The facts are that there has never been any leadership in the Senate."[11]

Leadership positions are also now very widely dispersed in the House, with more than 200 people who chair or are ranking minority members on one standing committee or subcommittee or another. That is a remarkable dispersion of leadership resources, but it leaves more than half of the membership—typically the most junior—with no leadership position. Compare this to the Senate, where newly elected senators of the majority party present their certificates of election and are usually handed gavels. They may have spent their entire adult lives before coming to the Senate selling software or ranching, or playing basketball, but would literally have to shun leadership to prevent its being thrust on them.

Perhaps the greatest contrast in how the leadership in the House and Senate are regarded by members can be found in the testimony of those people who served only briefly in the House and never gained much seniority and were then elected to the Senate. One senator who had this experience was Montana Democrat Max S. Baucus, who in 1987 recalled, "I was a very junior member when I was in the House and the leadership was very remote to me. I've been here longer but there are also only one hundred of us and Bob Byrd, and Bob Dole, and Howard Baker are very approachable. I'm even friends with them. I never had that in the House."

While leadership in the House is vastly more member oriented and supportive of the rank-and-file than at any time in history, there is a discernible pyramid of hierarchy in the House that one does not find in the Senate. A Senate leader, indeed, can be likened to a lieutenant-general in an army composed only of major-generals or to the chair of an academic department in which all the faculty members are on lifetime tenure. So while House leaders rarely act in a high-handed and authoritarian manner with ordinary members, Senate leaders almost never do.

An analogy that might be used to describe the different relationships between leadership and members in the House and Senate is an ecclesiastical one: The House leader ministers to a flock; the Senate leader more nearly resembles the chaplain in a medieval court whose ministrations were highly personalized and phrased with the delicacy and diplomacy that acknowledges the power and vanity of his communicants.

An Epidemic of Staff: The Unelected
Leading the Overburdened

The size differences that give rise to Senate generalism and House specialization influence profoundly the role of staff members in both chambers. At the most basic level, it is important to note that senators' personal staffs are larger than the personal staffs of the House members. House members are entitled by House rules to hire eighteen full-time and four part-time employees. The average House member has an office staff of fifteen. The average Senate staff is thirty-one, but according to Senate rules senators are given staff allowances based on the population of their state. Accordingly, a senator from California or New York might have more than seventy assistants.[12]

In addition to personal staff, House chairmen and subcommittee chairmen and ranking minority members have professional staff to help them with the business of their committees, and since 1975, even the most junior senator has had committee staff assigned to him.

Spread so thinly across a range of committees whose subject matters may differ widely, the senator's relationship to staff is far different from that of the more focused House member. Because their ability to develop specialized knowledge is limited by the time that they can devote to any one committee responsibility, senators must rely on staff to fill in the gaps.

But senators can also tackle a wider range of national issues; they gain broader exposure through their multiple committee assignments and are generally less constrained than House members on the topics on which they can speak. Liberal rules of debate permit them to use the floor as a forum to raise new issues that need not even be related to pending legislation. Staff provides them with many of these issues.

Finally, the Senate has been called the "nursery of presidents." Sixteen senators have gone on to the presidency, and in every recent campaign a senator has been a major contender for one party or the other for the presidential nomination. The 2000 campaign produced as candidates Senators John McCain and Orrin Hatch and ex-senators Bill Bradley and Dan Quayle. The latter had also served as vice president. The last incumbent House member to be elected directly to the presidency was James A. Garfield in 1880, and U.S. representatives are more unusual figures on the presidential scene. Republican Jack Kemp and Democrat Richard Gephardt represented the House in the 1988 campaign but dropped out by the end of March of that year. Perhaps a more fitting title for the modern Senate should be "nursery of presidential hopefuls" inasmuch as only one incumbent senator has received a major party nomination since John F. Kennedy in 1960. That was George S. McGovern in 1972.

While there are restrictions against using congressional staff in presidential campaigns, it is a prohibition that is easily evaded. With their smaller staffs, House members lack the built-in advantage that senators have in mounting a national campaign. Few House members, moreover, have the national visibility enjoyed by senators and so they find it difficult to develop such an image given the limitation of staff resources.[13]

But even in the normal course of legislative business, the differences in the prominence of staff between the House and Senate are obvious. Viewers of the televised floor action in both houses rarely get a shot of a senator without a staffer close at hand. Normally forbidden to take staff onto the floor with them, House members engage in solitary combat, unsupported by staff retinues.

QUALITATIVE DIFFERENCES IN HOUSE AND SENATE STAFF

One surprising result from interviews with the senators who served in the House was that most of them simply considered Senate staff to be of better quality than House staff. The possibility that such a perception was held came up in one of the first interviews, with Senator Robert Taft, Jr. (R-Ohio). Taft felt that personal staff in the House tended to be "amateurs" while the "real pros" worked on the personal staff of senators. He felt that the "pros" on the House side were committee staff rather than those working in the personal office of the House member.

Senator William Hathaway echoed Taft's verdict but went further in explaining why there might be this qualitative difference.

The senators rely on them more heavily than the House members do, and I suppose you have a better chance of attracting good people with a six-year term than you have with a two-year term.

But it's also more responsibility. It's well known that senators give more responsibility to their staff than House members do.

Although the high rates of reelection of House members actually provide more job security for House staff, every one of the fourteen senators who had previously served in the House asserted that greater responsibilities were enjoyed by Senate staff. The broader responsibilities come from the fact that, in Senator John Culver's words, "senators are spread too thin and are too distracted. They have too many committee responsibilities. They can't handle these things by themselves and they end up relying excessively on staff." Culver added, "You have some key House staffers who are with powerful members or assigned to powerful committees who have influence comparable to or greater than Senate staff. Generally speaking, however, for the rank-and-file House members, there's just no comparison—either delegated or usurped—[with what] staff members are able to obtain or exercise on behalf of a senator."

Texas Republican Phil Gramm cited the larger size of Senate staffs as a factor contributing to their superiority over House staffs.

Senate staffs are bigger and this allows for more specialization. So if someone is going to talk to someone on my staff about a defense matter, I have a person who does nothing but defense work. The person went to Annapolis. They were in the navy. They were with the CIA for five years and they flat know their business. Anything that relates to national security and defense, we know about.

In the House there was no possibility that I could afford having a staff member just to deal with defense, even if I had been on the Armed Services Committee.

THE CAPTIVE SENATOR?

Because the senator is stretched thin and must delegate a great deal more to aides than is typically the case with House members, there is a danger of overdelegation. Every senator seemed to have his own horror story of a colleague who had become, in effect, a captive of his staff. Even after the passage of many years, Senator Richard Schweiker's indignation at such a captive senator had not cooled.

I won't use the guy's name, but I was working with a senator. We were co-sponsors on a bill. There were actually four of us, so we got together to work out some of our differences.

Well, we went to this senator's office who called the meeting and he didn't do any of the talking. His staff guy was trying to run four of us senators on this issue. I was just furious. I was really mad. This senator just sat back and let his staff run us, and we all went away resolving that we'd never work with that S.O.B. again. Imagine: He delegated to his staff the entire job of working this thing out and he sat there and had his staff be the prominent players with four of his colleagues. It was an insult.

I couldn't conceive of that happening in the House. A lot of times I've seen that happen in the Senate. I just couldn't see it happening in the House.

The suggestion that senators were more apt to become captives of their staff because of the need to delegate more broadly came through in interviews with a group of twenty lobbyists. While none of the lobbyists doubted that a House member might well allow himself to be dominated by staff, all said that the most extreme cases were more apt to be found in the Senate.

A partner in a small but prestigious Washington firm had his own horror story.

We had a case in this Congress in which we'd reached a point where we were having trouble with a particular senator. Our client's outside staff counsel had gone to school with this senator—college roommate types. So the client called me and asked if we minded having his outside counsel talk to the senator directly because things weren't where they should have been. I said, "Hell, no, I'll take all the help I can get in bringing this guy around."

So this senator says to his buddy of twenty-five years' standing, "I'm okay on this issue, but you've got a problem with my staff." A most revealing comment, right? He was saying, I agree with you but my staff doesn't, and therefore you have a problem.

Senator Warren B. Rudman was remarkably candid both in his acknowledgment of senators' lack of mastery of all the policy areas for which they are responsible and also the implications of this for the role of staff in the Senate:

I served on five subcommittees and there was no way I could keep up on the issues in all of them. The House members, that was all they did. That's their major assignment. They spend their lives immersed in one particular area. We tended to rely a heck of a lot more on staff except in those areas we chose to be our specialty. Defense was my specialty but in an Interior conference, it might well be that my staff were working something out while I was trying to get straightened out. That happened time and again with [Rep.] Sid Yates [D-Ill.], a good friend of mine. He was the expert. I couldn't compete with Sid on those issues. But I had staff that could.

Senators, lobbyists, and staff members alike seem to agree that Senate staffs have longer "leashes"—more latitude, more freedom to negotiate on behalf of their bosses—and, not surprisingly, are more likely to end up "downtown" as high-priced lobbyists or officials in the executive branch. Indeed, a study by Robert Salisbury and Kenneth Shepsle found that there was a higher staff turnover in the "fast track" of the Senate than there was among House staff members. House staff, particularly those working on standing committees, are more likely to be Capitol Hill lifers.[14]

If tomorrow all congressional staff disappeared, the House would be far better able to conduct its business than the Senate. With identical coverage of public policy, legislative responsibility, and oversight but with four and a half times the manpower and vastly greater specialized knowledge in the membership, the House would carry on. Barring some drastic limitations on the way senators currently spend their time and energy, the smaller body would simply be unable to cope with its burdens.

But while Senate staff is more influential, in general, than House staff, and even considering cases of staff dominance on the Senate side, the ultimate source of authority is the senator. The fact that most office-to-office contact on the Senate side is at the staff level should not obscure the fact that on important issues there is consultation between the principals. On nonroutine matters, the ground rules are established by the senators. In the words of an administrative assistant to a freshman senator, "It's *mano a mano*"—a hand-to-hand struggle between the principals.

Size and the Management of Conflict

Forging a consensus in the small and individualistic Senate under a system of rules whereby each senator has what amounts to a qualified veto has caused some observers to pronounce the Senate unmanageable. Without a question, the Senate is a highly inefficient body. But it must be recalled that if efficiency had been highly prized by the framers of the Constitution they probably would have created a one-house Congress. Indeed, the framers feared hasty action and the tendency of a majority to ride roughshod over the rights of minorities. The Senate is a shrine to the rights of the political minority and its rules confer considerable power on it to thwart the will of the majority.

Armed with such imposing power, each senator becomes an enforcer of the rights of the interests he or she represents. Like ambassadors from sovereign kingdoms, senators face one another as legal equals. Coercive tactics are inappropriate for such encounters, so consensus building through face-to-face contacts is the preferred method for managing conflict.

This produces two results—one institutional and one with implications for the larger political system.

The institutional result of face-to-face contact in a small Senate and the group-to-group contact in a large House of Representatives is that any given senator is much more likely to know any other senator than a House member is to know any other colleague. This firsthand knowledge of a colleague's background and constituency tends to deemphasize partisan or ideological traits. Close encounters of a personal kind can also lead to terrible vendettas, but the compactness of the Senate chamber leaves combatants few places to hide. There is a strong incentive toward damage control in the relationships among senators. House members, like air crews dropping bombs on an enemy they cannot see, take a more cold-blooded view of partisan warfare. You can drop your bombs and then retire to the vastness of a huge membership. Avoidance of hostile colleagues in the House is as easy as surrounding yourself with a group that is friendly. The rules of engagement in the Senate are largely personal; in the House they are distinctively partisan.

The implications for national politics is that the Senate is able to manage conflict somewhat more readily than the House. The consensus arrived at in the Senate on a given issue is virtually assured of having been at least influenced by the minority because of each member's equal powers within that body. The Senate, as an institution, stands more solidly behind its work product, which is perhaps one reason that less specialized senators fare so well in conference committees. A House member can claim to have been left out of a decision by reason of having been in a minority whose views were swept aside; that is a more difficult assertion for a senator to make. The legislation that comes out of the Senate, then, can be said to reflect a broader range of opinion.

House members who represent fewer interests than senators can articulate these issues more efficiently and often do so more forcefully and passionately. This contributes to the adversary style of the House. Spared the necessity to keep interpersonal relations in good repair to the extent that senators must, House members can express interests with passion and even ferocity. But the passion with which an interest is advocated has little to do with whether that interest is reflected in the legislation that comes out of the chamber.

The Senate is a more unitary body than the House not because political conflict is absent but because the minority side is more likely to have had an impact on its legislation than the minority side within the House. The Senate tends to be a place of concurrent majorities where all major segments of opinion need to concur but not necessarily be represented in the proportions in which they are found in the general public.

The House's role is to allow interests to be represented and articulated. It makes no representations that they will be influential or even heeded. It is a better reflection of the diversity of the country than is the Senate. The House is able to pick up, with almost seismographic sensitivity, what it is that is eating at Americans. Using a different metaphor, Senator Donald Riegle said, "If on any given day, you wanted to take the temperature of the country, all you'd need to do would be to take the temperature of the House of Representatives and you'd get a pretty good reading of what the country is thinking."

In a mass society in which citizens fear that government is slipping out of their grasp, the House remains accessible to citizens—it deals with their problems and opinions. It is, however, less good in its original role of being the place where citizens could register their objections to national policies through periodic elections. The Senate, we shall see, is not only the more unitary body of the two; it is also the more responsive.

NOTES

1. Norman J. Ornstein, Thomas E. Mann, and Michael J. Malbin, *Vital Statistics on Congress, 1997–1998* (Washington, D.C.: Congressional Quarterly Press, 1998), pp. 200–201 and 210.
2. See Gregory A. Caldeira and Samuel C. Patterson, "Political Friendship in the Legislature," a *Polimetrics* reprint (Columbus: Laboratory for Political and Social Research, n.d.), p. 963.
3. David E. Rosenbaum, "Do's and Don'ts of Party Cooperation," *New York Times,* Tuesday, October 27, 1987.
4. Ibid.
5. William F. Connelly, Jr., and John J. Pitney, Jr., *Congress' Permanent Minority?* (Lanham, Md.: Rowman and Littlefield, 1994), p. 171.
6. Rosenbaum, *op. cit.*
7. Barbara Sinclair, *Majority Leadership in the U.S. House* (Baltimore, Md.: Johns Hopkins Press, 1983).

8. Woodrow Wilson, *Congressional Government* (Boston: Houghton Mifflin, 1885), p. 213.
9. Neil MacNeil, *Forge of Democracy* (New York: David McKay, 1963), p. 376.
10. Robert L. Peabody, *Leadership in Congress* (Boston: Little, Brown, 1976), pp. 346–347.
11. George Rothwell Brown, *The Leadership in Congress* (Indianapolis, Ind.: Bobbs-Merrill, 1922), p. 254.
12. Roger H. Davidson and Walter J. Oleszek, *Congress and Its Members,* 2d ed. (Washington, D.C.: CQ Press, 1985), p. 245.
13. Malcolm E. Jewell and Samuel C. Patterson, *The Legislative Process in the United States,* 4th ed. (New York: Random House, 1986), p. 157.
14. Robert H. Salisbury and Kenneth A. Shepsle, "Congressional Staff Turnover and the Ties-That-Bind," *American Political Science Review,* 75 (June 1981), pp. 393–394, and Michael J. Malbin, *Unelected Representatives* (New York: Basic, 1980), pp. 86–87.

4

The Electoral Environments

THERE IS A RELATIONSHIP between House members and the roughly 700,000 people who make up their constituencies that the members speak of using words that we do not ordinarily associate with politics. They speak of "empathy" and "trust" in the relations with their constituents, and of "identifying" with them.[1] It is a language of intimacy and it flows naturally from the bond between a representative and a manageable political unit—the congressional district.

Some congressional districts are more complex than others. House members, moreover, do not experience the same degree of intimacy with their staunchest and most loyal supporters that they do with people who just happen to live in the district, but overall the relationships between House members and their districts and those between senators and their states are strikingly different. The most basic difference comes from the fact that House members can figuratively get their hands around a district. The senators interviewed spoke of an almost tactile sensation when describing techniques they used with their former House constituencies. Such feelings of intimacy are rare when a complete state is the constituency. Of the twenty-nine senators who formerly served in the House and were interviewed for this book, only the seven who came from states with only two House seats reported little or no decline in these feelings of intimacy after reaching the Senate. Senators James Abourezk and George McGovern of South Dakota, Max Baucus of Montana, William Hathaway of Maine, Mark Andrews of North Dakota, Larry Craig and Mike Crapo of Idaho, and Jack Reed of Rhode Island represented roughly half of the state and their transfer to the Senate was a change only in degree rather than an entirely novel experience.

The feeling of monumental change was, naturally enough, greatest in senators who had formerly represented districts in very populous states. Hugh Scott and Richard Schweiker of Pennsylvania and Phil Gramm of Texas, and Wyche Fowler of Georgia emphasized the dramatic quality of the transition. But the transition was also significant and noteworthy in senators from geographically small states with relatively large numbers of districts. One of these is Christopher Dodd—for him, the difference in intimacy between representing one of his state's six congressional districts and representing the entire state of Connecticut was summed up in how he spent his Saturday nights.

You're back in your district and on a Saturday night there might be, let's say, three events. And you'll go to two of them and you'll stay almost a couple of hours at each one. You'd be there for the cocktail hour, the dinner, the speeches, and even hanging around afterwards to say goodnight to the people.

In the Senate you might do three events on a Saturday night, but at one place you'll go to the cocktail hour and give a speech. And the next place you'll go to the dinner and you'll stand and wave from the podium because you've got to get to the next one. It's so detached. It's a terribly difficult transition to make if you've gotten very tactile and hands-on with your constituency. When you get to the Senate you've got to step back.

John Culver, who represented Iowa, spoke of the "intimacy and personal rapport" a House member establishes with his or her district, which is "extremely hard to duplicate on a state-wide basis." He said, "You really have genuine personal contacts of familiarity. These people are your neighbors. You really get to know them and they know you."

Senator Donald Riegle, who represented Michigan, said, "Having a constituency of roughly half a million people is a good size constituency in the sense that you could get your hands around a constituency that size and have a level of contact and intimacy that I value and miss."

The loss of intimacy expressed by so many of the House-members-turned-senators bears closer examination. Are they lamenting, literally, the diminished ability to relate to a larger, more amorphous, and more heterogeneous constituency as individuals? Without question, there is a reluctance on the part of large-state senators to exchange the handshaking of one-on-one campaigning characteristic of House elections for the "wholesale" politicking on statewide television. One gets a sense from a study based on observations and interviews of House members that personal contact and handshaking constituted for them a superior form of campaigning. Even one who recognized the need to use television in a statewide campaign expressed fear that he might be cast as a "celluloid candidate" by reason of his extensive use of the medium and insisted on at least some personal campaigning.[2]

Senators can, then, continue to make dawn visits to factory gates and shake hands personally with the voters even if only for the benefit of the cameras. Where conditions permit, most typically in races in small or low-population states, some senators attempt to duplicate in their campaigns the personal techniques they used as House members. In the most populous states you simply cannot shake enough hands to make much difference in an election.

In addition to the sense of intimacy experienced by House members toward their constituencies, the average congressional district is simply more knowable than the average state and these differences in complexity figure importantly in the electoral environments of House members and senators.

Differences in State and District Complexity: The Political Implications

The typical House district, even a complex one, is, of course, of more limited scope than an entire state. It is a smaller and less prominent stage on which to perform. And district lines are subject to adjustment every ten years to accommodate census changes, so there is an evanescent quality to the congressional district—something like a tent that can be folded up and moved. A state is permanent. It may gain or lose population, become prosperous or wither economically, but its borders are sacrosanct.

Each state is like a circus big top—lots of acts going on at the same time, a jumble of activity, cacophonous, and busy. A host of economic interests vie for the favor of government and legions of associations, ethnic groups, and political actors cavort on the sawdust.

Some congressional districts approximate this theatrical model, but most are places where interests run in a narrower track, where a single racial or ethnic group may be dominant, where a handful of large industries account for most of the payrolls. They are the sideshows, the specialty acts. They are off the midway and not likely to be recognized by the casual observer. The crossing of any state line is usually heralded by a sign welcoming you, but one would search in vain for a sign that says "Welcome to the 4th Congressional District."

NO PORTRAIT-IN-MINIATURE OF AMERICA: THE 11TH CONGRESSIONAL DISTRICT

In most instances the scope of the state in terms of its geographical size, diversity, size of population, and multiplicity of interests produces a picture of greater complexity than that which typically confronts a House member. The consequences of this greater complexity vary from state to state. As a general rule the greater complexity and breadth of scope presents senators with choices—sometimes of a politically treacherous nature—that House members do not have to confront. But at the same time, there are House districts with unusual configurations that produce a perilous terrain for the incumbent, and states whose composition gives a senator a virtual lifetime franchise from the voters. To be sure, the political skills of the individual senator and House member are powerful factors in reelection, but there are contextual peculiarities in a constituency from which even the most masterful politician cannot escape.

House districts can be astonishingly atypical of the nation at large. A good example of how far from the norm they can be is this nation's smallest congressional district, New York's 11th Congressional District represented since 1983 by Congressman Major Owens. In some ways Owens's district turns the nation's demography on its head. In the nation as a whole the white population is about 75 percent and the African-American population is about 12 percent. In New York's 11th Congressional District, it is 74 percent black and 16 percent white. In the United States at large about 11 percent of all households are headed by a female householder with no husband present. In New York's 11th such families constitute 28 percent of all households. The ten square miles of Representative Owens's district lie within the heart of the borough of Brooklyn. His constituents include not only a large number of American-born blacks but a sizeable number from the islands of the West Indies. Many of Owens's white constituents are ultra-religious Jews in the neighborhood of Crown Heights. In one sense, the 11th Congressional District is diverse, but in other ways it is not. There are no farms, military installations, recreational areas, or suburban communities in the 11th. There is one other group in conspicuously short supply in the New York 11th: Republicans. Owens first won his seat in 1982 with 91 percent of the vote against 6 percent for his Republican opponent. He won in 1984 and in his subsequent general elections by equivalent or even greater margins. Only in Democratic primaries do his opponents get as much as 20 percent. In this commanding electoral advantage that he enjoys, Representative Owens's performance is very much in line with the 75 percent of his colleagues who have only token opposition. In other words, only about 25 percent of all House seats are truly competitive.

Major Owens's district is in many ways like the new type of House district, the majority-minority district that is so called because its lines were drawn by a state legislature to insure the election of either an African-American or Latino member pursuant to the Voting Rights Act of 1965 and its 1982 amendments. The purpose of the law was to enable minority candidates to win seats in Congress in states where they had been, historically, the victims of discrimination. The first application of the law and its amendments came after the 1990 census. State legislatures rearranged congressional district lines not only to accommodate overall changes in their state's population but to maximize minority representation as well. The result was a surge in black members in the House from twenty-five in the 102nd Congress (1991–1993) to thirty-eight in the 103rd (1993–1995). Some breathtaking district boundaries were established because of the voting law including one celebrated district, North Carolina's 12th, that runs 190 miles—virtually the entire width of the state—from Durham in the North to Charlotte in the South. Even more remarkable was Louisiana's 4th Congressional District that was 600 miles long.[3]

The creation of majority-minority districts is by no means universally popular. While no one can deny that more black and Hispanic members have been elected and that they win by impressively large margins, the more extreme examples of drawing district lines so as to encompass as many minority voters as possible have come under court challenge. The practice has also been criticized by scholars who point out, for example, that few new African-American members will be produced by the practice of packing as many black voters as possible into a district. The limit of such districts has been reached. The point is also made that avenues of advancement to statewide office for black House members is impeded because those from majority-minority districts will have had little exposure to white voters whose votes they would need to win, for example, a seat in the U.S. Senate.[4]

Recent scholarship suggests that, on average, states are no more diverse demographically than congressional districts.

Paul Gronke has found that in terms of racial makeup, age distribution, and educational levels, the differences between states and congressional districts are slight. He acknowledges that the highly political process of drawing congressional district lines makes the House member's constituency far more one-sided in partisanship than the average state. He does not directly address the question of whether there is greater diversity of economic interest in states than there is in congressional districts.[5]

THE SENATORIAL TERRAIN:
AN ELEMENT OF RISK

In the minds of some senators, additional political risks come with greater diversity and complexity. There is even a kind of envy of the relatively uncomplicated political environment in which House members operate. Senator Paul Sarbanes, a Maryland Democrat who represented an urban district in Baltimore when he was in the House, seemed to reflect this view when he said of House members: "If your views are basically in line with those of your district you've got a lot of freedom. And even if they're not, you can usually make up for it through your constituency casework and developing a personal rapport with your district. That is much more difficult to do if you are a senator."

What Sarbanes is suggesting is that House members need only concern themselves with the limited range of issues that are of importance to their district. The many issues that a senator must confront in a considerably more complicated state make it virtually impossible to be "right" on all the issues.

The specifics of the greater complexity that awaits House members when they move to the Senate and confront statewide problems were supplied by Pennsylvania Republicans Hugh Scott and Richard Schweiker. Scott had represented an urban Philadelphia district and Schweiker a prosperous suburban Philadelphia constituency. For both, representing the more complex state meant a great adjustment. Scott, as a congressman, had pretty much restricted himself to "the social problems that come with an urban district: health, welfare, the environment, mass transit, and highways. With the state you still have those but you pick up agriculture, mining, and the impact of large, well-organized, powerful unions." Schweiker's district "did have a steel mill, but it was basically, even predominantly, a white-collar suburban district."

The complexity, by itself, required adaptation on the part of both former House members, but the new diversity carried with it an ominous and intimidating quality as well. In Scott's words, "I also picked up a much wider and more skillful collection of adversaries." The transition from the relatively simple congressional district to the generally more complex state involves, then, not only a greater and more bewildering array of interests but a broader range of potential antagonists and opponents. For these two Republicans from affluent districts in the Philadelphia area, organized labor had not been an important factor. Pennsylvania's blue-collar unions, which were a major political force statewide, traditionally supported Democrats and while neither Scott nor Schweiker was hostile to labor, the unions would have felt more comfortable with Democrats.

Stephen K. Bailey's classic study of the passage of the union-endorsed Employment Act of 1946 pointed to the differential impact of union influence in the two houses of Congress. He wrote, "As the political power of organized labor has grown . . . and as population movements into the cities have increased, it has become increasingly difficult for Senators . . . to ignore the interests and demands of the urban worker. A Representative from the 17th District in Illinois, for example, may find it possible to disregard the voice of the urban worker; a Senator representing the entire state, would do so only at considerable peril to his political future."[6]

All senators interviewed agreed that only a few issues arising out of the more complex senatorial constituency forced them to make choices they did not have to make in their House districts. Nonetheless, difficult political decisions that force senators to have to choose between the interests of one group

of constituents and those of another are part of the job for every
senator whose state is at all complex.

Senator George A. Smathers, a Democrat who represented
Florida in the Senate from 1951 until 1969 after serving two
years in the House, contrasted the simplicity and parochialism
of the interests of his south Florida district with the complexi-
ties of the entire state of Florida.

With congressmen it's all local. Everything is more local—the local
post office, the local industry, the local river, the local airport, the local Miami harbor. Why, if I could get the money to deepen the Miami harbor from fourteen to twenty-one feet, that alone would come
damn near to getting me reelected.

But at the state level, Miami not only wanted it, but Jacksonville
wanted it, Cape Canaveral wanted it, and Pensacola wanted it. And
you know that all of them can't get it. You've got bigger, broader
problems covering a wider spectrum of people.

Smathers cited two problems in particular that confronted
him as a senator that had not troubled him as a member of the
House and which arose from the size and diversity of his new
constituency. The first was that, in the 1950s, divisions among
many Floridians on civil rights were acute. Smathers recalled:

My Miami district was very liberal. It was a town with a lot of
foreign-born and minority groups. There was a large Jewish community and a lot of sophisticated people from New York had moved
down. Their attitude on civil rights would be classified as liberal.

But you go to Crestview, Florida, which is the county seat of
Okaloosa County, which is out in the panhandle, they're old cracker
folks. Or in Gadsden County that abuts Georgia—country Georgia.
The civil rights situation there was a different thing completely.

In the bitterly fought Florida Senate primary in 1950, not
only did Smathers modify his previous stand on civil rights, he
characterized incumbent Claude Pepper as being excessively
friendly to blacks. Once in the Senate, in Smathers's words,
"There was an adjustment in my record. I voted against the so-
called civil rights bills such as the one in 1957. Now looking

at it from heaven down, you'd know I was wrong. Looking at it as a practical political situation, I could not have gotten elected. I couldn't have gotten the votes in north and central Florida if I'd voted for those civil rights bills."

THE HOUSE PARADOX: THE BIPOLAR CONSTITUENCY

The House district can be about the safest environment for a congressional incumbent. Once he or she is entrenched, establishes name recognition, and raises enough campaign money to deter or defeat challenges, only conspicuous criminality or incredibly bad luck seems capable of dislodging the House incumbent. There are, however, exceptions: what might be called "bipolar districts" in which two major constituencies are antagonistic and the member finds himself in the position of satisfying one segment of his voters while alienating an equal number of others. The result can often be the defeat of the hapless member.

This has happened several times in recent years and usually as the result of a member having to take a stand on a piece of legislation in which both parts of his divided constituency have a large stake.

In 1990, Congressman Terry L. Bruce was in his third term representing Illinois's 19th Congressional District, in which was located both the University of Illinois at Champaign-Urbana and six large power plants that generated electricity from high-sulfur coal and the Amax coal mine in Keensburg, a producer of this highly polluting fuel.

Bruce had been elected in 1984 with the help of environmentalists from the Champaign-Urbana campus who were determined to see a drastic reduction in the amount of high-sulfur coal used in power plants. Coal miners, employees of the power company, and consumers, however, were just as anxious to use as much of the fuel as possible, not only to keep the mines running but to hold down utility costs which were likely to rise if the local power plant were forced to burn the more expensive low-sulfur coal. These clashing interests converged on Bruce and his political fortunes when Congress took up the job of reauthorizing the Clean Air Act in 1990. In the Bush administration's version of the reauthorization, 107 power plants nationally were targeted for stringent cutbacks in pollution—three of them were in Terry Bruce's 19th District.[7]

Another victim of the bipolar district was Representative Doug Bosco, representing a district in Northern California whose divisions became fatally apparent during the controversy over the Northern Spotted Owl, a bird whose habitat in the old-growth forests was said to be threatened by logging. Among Bosco's most powerful constituencies were ardent environmentalists including members of The Earth First!, a militant conservationist group referred to by their enemies as "tree-huggers." Another powerful interest in California's 1st Congressional District were the loggers whose jobs depended upon cutting down the very trees in which the owl nested and which the environmentalists in the district sought to protect. Bosco, caught between his polarized constituencies, lamented, "All of my constituents like trees. The problem is that 50 percent like them vertically and 50 percent like them horizontally." Bosco was defeated for reelection in 1990.[8]

These House districts in which major constituencies are so much at odds with one another are very much the exception to the rule, but they do illustrate an important point: Senators with their more diverse collection of interests may be better able than some House members to offset the negative effects of a single "killer vote." Senators are far more likely to have among their constituents potential winners whose influence can cancel out the influence of those who see themselves as having lost as the result of a vote cast by their senator. This diversity, however, may take its toll in other areas.

THE LOSS OF CONTROL: A SENATORIAL LAMENT

There is an unmistakable theme in the testimony of the senators who were interviewed that the House district was responsive to them and under their control to the extent that a state was not. It is as if by the laying on of hands House members can take the pulse of the district and apply the proper political therapy. They lose this when they exchange a district for a statewide constituency and many of them miss it.

A few of the senators, unprompted, went beyond their lamentations of the loss of intimacy to broach what may be the hidden issue: The state is less controllable an entity from a political standpoint. After decrying the loss of intimacy with constituents that attended his move to the Senate, one interviewee said, "What I'm getting at is that there is more uncertainty. The Senate seat is by definition more precarious politically than the average House seat." Senator Paul Sarbanes found that the greater attention lavished on senators by the media and the relative obscurity of the activities of House members was a situation that favored the political fortunes of the House member. He put it this way:

In the Senate, you're dependent on that intermediary to a much greater degree—the press, television are on you a lot. You need the TV coverage to reach statewide but it interferes with the message you put out to the voters.

South Dakota's James Abourezk put the district-state difference simply and directly. "House members have a good sense of what their district is. Senators have a harder time getting a handle on a state and it makes them more destructible than House members."

Presentation of self to the voters is generally much more under the control of the House member than of the senator. As Morris P. Fiorina observed in the late 1970s, "Congressmen are going home more, pressing the flesh, getting around. They are building a personal base of support, one dependent on personal contacts and favors."[9]

The very compactness and relative simplicity of most congressional districts, the relatively scant attention paid by the media to members in multidistrict states (and to their challengers as well), the unlikelihood that the member will be presented with serious political conflicts, and the ability to meet the voters directly present a political landscape of greater serenity to the House member. Challenges, if they come, occur in primaries. Recently, however, the decisions by voters in some states to apply term limits to members of their state legislatures has turned loose a horde of dispossessed state legislators who see a House seat as a tempting target. Large and complex states, however, foster more challengers, harbor more regional or interest group conflicts, and bathe senators in media attention that they may be able to control only imperfectly.

House-Senate Elections:
The Blessings of Obscurity

The observations of the former House members who won Senate seats that the district is a more controllable and manipulable political environment than the state receive confirmation on the different rates of success that members and senators enjoy in winning reelection. In only two elections since World War II has the percentage of senators gaining reelection been higher than that of House members seeking another term. It happened most recently in 1982, a recession year in which Democrats gained twenty-six House seats and many ousted members had been elected on Ronald Reagan's coattails in 1980. In other big-turnover years, such as 1964 and 1974, when more than fifty House seats changed hands, Senate reelection percentages exceeded those of the House, but it is normal for the reelection rate of House members to be much higher than for senators. In 1976, 1978, and 1980 House reelection percentages were more than thirty points better than Senate success rates. And for the forty years between 1946 and 1986, the average reelection percentage for Senate incumbents was a respectable 74.9 percent. For House members, however, the figure was close to 91 percent.[10] In 1998, the House re-election rate was more than 98 percent.

The most basic reason for the relatively greater degree of success for House incumbents over Senate incumbents is that senators are just larger, more visible, and more inviting targets. The size differential between the two chambers accounts for much of the quandary of the sitting senator becoming the sitting duck. For ideological groups to be able to claim that their contributions led to the defeat of 9 members of a body of 100 is a far more impressive boast than that they unseated 9 members in a body of 435. One is unlikely to see a hunter returning home with the trunk of his car festooned with squirrel carcasses, but he will proudly display a single moose or deer.

The apparent success in 1980 of an organization called the National Conservative Political Action Committee (NCPAC) illustrates the political payoff that comes from targeting incumbent senators. Beginning more than a year before the 1980 election, NCPAC ultimately put together a war chest of $1.2 million to defeat senators that the group characterizes as "the most distasteful."[11] This group included such familiar Democrats as Frank Church of Idaho, John Culver of Iowa, and Birch Bayh of Indiana as well as the 1972 Democratic presidential candidate George McGovern, who had continued his Senate career after suffering defeat at the hands of President Richard M. Nixon.

While the Republicans were stunningly successful in gaining thirty-three House seats in 1980—giving the House the largest number of Republicans since 1956—it was the ousting of the nine Democratic senators that NCPAC and other conservative groups regarded as their signal of triumph. Eighty percent of the money spent by the so-called independent-expenditure groups in 1980 went for negative campaigns directed against Senate Democrats. The House elections in 1980 showed the reverse pattern of expenditures by these groups, with most money being spent on behalf of incumbents, but in 1982 House Democrats were targeted by conservative groups in an effort that proved counterproductive in an election that saw Democrats gain twenty-six seats. The Democrats had been expected to win even more seats in that recession year, but adopted a defensive strategy designed to protect incumbents rather than support challengers—a clear reaction to the reverses suffered by House Democrats in 1980.[12]

Groups opposed to abortion—only one of the constellation of issues that animated NCPAC—developed a strategy for 1980 that would enable them to be depicted as "giant-killers" if they directed their efforts to the defeat of well-known liberal Democratic senators. These groups got "more bang for the buck" in their campaigns against incumbent senators than they would have against incumbent House members. Put another way, "It would take a brave group to announce its intention to defeat one-sixth of the *House* members up for reelection; during the past decade, at least 90 percent of all House incumbents who ran for reelection won their contests. Groups aiming at senators would have a clearer shot; only 60 percent of senators seeking reelection in 1978 were successful."[13]

While some people minimize the effect of NCPAC on the defeat of the liberal senators in 1980, few doubt that the strategy of John T. "Terry" Dolan, chairman of the NCPAC, was to focus on the Senate races because of the visibility of the targets. Peter Fenn, a Washington political consultant, worked in 1980 for Frank Church, the Idaho Democrat who was one of those "most distasteful" senators. Fenn asserts that lesser known House members as targets would have made NCPAC's job of raising money from conservative givers much more difficult.

Dolan's whole idea was that the Senate was the place you found those crazy, fuzzy-headed liberals and his pitch was that you have to get rid of these wackos. The people that Dolan appealed to knew and hated the Frank Churches, and Birch Bayhs, and George McGoverns. They wouldn't have known Les Au Coin [a liberal Democratic House member] from Adam. The only way Dolan could raise money was with those [senators] as targets. That's how Dolan got on the CBS Evening News and in *Newsweek* because he was dealing with the Senate and those guys who were well-enough known and his direct mail was going like gangbusters based on that strategy.

While there is unanimous agreement that the "incumbent advantage" redounds much more to the benefit of House members than to senators, there are a number of plausible explanation about why this difference is so marked. The incumbent advantage is far more formidable, as we have seen, in House elections since the deck can be stacked by a state legislature in the way it draws congressional district lines to favor incumbents. States are not subject to that kind of manipulation for political purposes. And while the distribution of a state's electorate cannot be manipulated against incumbent senators, neither can it be rigged in their favor.

Partisanship has also become an increasingly uncertain force in what lever the voter pulls in a voting booth during a congressional election. A CBS/New York Times poll of 1,062 registered adult voters just before the 1986 congressional elections explored their motivations and why they preferred one House candidate over another. More than 40 percent of those questioned said that the character and experience of the candidate counted most in their choice. Roughly a quarter said it was state or local issues, but only 9 percent pointed to a House candidate's party label as making the biggest difference in how they cast their vote.[14] Such surveys reinforce a point made by Thomas Mann and Raymond Wolfinger: "Party plays an important role for some voters in determining whether a candidate is attractive . . . but it is secondary to the images of the candidates themselves."[15]

Mann and Wolfinger make a further point that in elections in which voters emphasize character and experience, or at least the image of it, it is incumbents that benefit. Incumbents are seen as more visible and more attractive to voters than challengers. Indeed, 90 percent of all voters reported some contact with a House incumbent but only 44 percent reported contact with a House challenger.[16]

One reason for the positive image enjoyed by House incumbents that Mann and Wolfinger cite is the advantage of office. They enjoy, for example, the use of "franking privileges," the ability to send out printed materials free of postage. They are also in a position to intervene on behalf of constituents needing assistance in dealing with government. The newsletters, releases, ceremonial appearances, and occasions for symbolic but politically powerful gestures do weigh heavily in favor of the House incumbent.[17]

At least as compelling an ingredient for House incumbents' success according to Mann and Wolfinger is that House members rarely receive serious challenges. Senators, however, seem to be less able than House members to convert their incumbency into invulnerability. "Most Senate challengers," they say, "are big spenders and run competitive races, while the vast majority of House challengers have small budgets and even smaller chances of winning."[18]

Mann and Wolfinger offer two explanations for the inadequacy of challenges to House incumbents and the more competitive Senate challenges. The first is that there are so many districts with lopsided partisan majorities that upsets by minority party challengers in general elections are unlikely. They also point to the readiness and ability of well-funded Senate challengers to use the media—notably television—to make themselves known to voters. Many House districts—particularly those in large urban areas—do not lend themselves to the use of television.[19] Advertising rates in such metropolitan areas are very high and, since the districts themselves are small, a candidate would end up spending a great deal of money reaching voters who are unable to vote for him. Media coverage of House members and their challengers—as distinct from paid advertising—is also less extensive than that accorded to senators and their challengers. A New York television station would reach more than forty congressional districts in the New York/New Jersey/Connecticut metropolitan area. Adequate coverage of the activities of forty House members is impossible; adequate coverage of the activities of only six senators in those three states is relatively easy.

It is, perhaps, the "free media" difference between House and Senate challenges that contributes more to the differential rates of reelection success than paid campaign advertising. The differences in the attention paid to House members and senators in Washington by the national press is covered in a later chapter, but it is the choice by the local media of whom they prefer to cover and whose activities and what issues they tend to emphasize that affects outcomes.

It is not just the greater number of members of the House that makes coverage of their campaign less engrossing to the local media, but rather the nature of their activities. Over the past twenty-five years, members of the House have not only emphasized constituent problem solving and intervening on behalf of voters with the federal bureaucracy but have actually stimulated the demands of citizens for these services, which range from nominating district youngsters to service academies to helping the elderly iron out problems with their T-bills with the Treasury Department's Bureau of Public Debt. Morris Fiorina uses the term ombudsmanship* to describe this effort by House members to be champions of their constituents.[20]

This casework, by its very nature, is uncontroversial. There are no right or wrong sides to using your power to nominate a high school senior to Annapolis. There is no political or moral downside to introducing a special immigration bill to reunite a family or to seeing that an old soldier gets the medical care he needs from a Veterans Administration hospital. Does this mean that by emphasizing service to constituents House members are being irresponsible or untrue to their duties as legislators, who must, by definition, also involve themselves in a lawmaking process that can involve supporting or casting votes on bills that are indeed controversial? While such votes constitute a minority of all votes that a member casts and are not an everyday

*The term *ombudsman* is a Swedish word that means, literally, "representative" but has come to mean a citizen advocate who intervenes on behalf of individuals who experience problems with government bureaucracies.

occurrence, taking a controversial stand can alienate constituents; casework on behalf of constituents, however—unless it is bungled—involves no such risk.

While casework helps to establish a personal bond between members and voters, it is not an inherently interesting process. Except under special circumstances, journalists in the district would not cover the retrieval of a lost Social Security check or the mediation of a businessman's claim with the Small Business Administration. The very unspectacular nature of House members' activities enables them to reap a political dividend. "They are able to focus constituents' attention on activities and personal attributes that will enhance their popularity. In other words, they successfully "control' the information—limited, district-oriented and non-partisan in nature—that voters use to judge them."[21]

The administrative assistant to a New Jersey House member told me that the only time casework activity drew extensive press coverage was during the Vietnam War when the congressman arranged for a helicopter to fly a shipment of Passover matzoh to a group of Jewish sailors on a U.S. Navy warship in the South China Sea. Wanting the traditional holiday food, the sailors asked their families to enlist the help of the congressman. The congressman's efforts brought wide and favorable publicity.

Voters also learn directly about the House members from the services they receive from them, and the message they receive is about caring, responsive officials who are not merely willing but eager to do battle on behalf of their constituents. So while only 46 percent of the nation's eligible voters in a 1982 Gallup poll were able to identify their House member by name, by a margin of nearly 4 to 1 those surveyed said their representative was doing a good job. Indeed, in all demographic groups in the survey a majority of people approved of the job their House member was doing.[22]

The local press, radio, and television, by their very neglect of the public stands and legislative activities of House members, serve, in effect, the political needs of those House members. They allow the members to tell their own stories to the voters in understandably self-serving ways. In contrast, it is the very newsworthiness of the senators that causes attention and scrutiny to fall upon them. This, as we have seen, contributed to the mortality rate among Senate Democrats in 1980. The attention, then, is very much a mixed blessing because it is not subject to the senator's control. Too many media are interested in senatorial activities, and although senators try to shape and direct the press to what they consider their most desirable activities, much of what is said about them is beyond their manipulation. Senators may issue press releases, but only the most uncritical journalists will be content to write a story based on a press handout. Senator Paul Sarbanes likened the media to "the eyes and ears of the public." Television, in particular, he said,

is like a conveyor belt between you and the constituents. But it's a conveyor belt that interposes itself in terms of what it asks and how it reports and you don't have that much control over it.

Senator Phil Gramm pointed out that in his own state of Texas, with its thirty House seats, a member is unlikely to get coverage in media outside his own district, but "when you're representing the whole state every newspaper in the state is covering you as a local issue."

Senators appear, then, to be more associated in the public mind with major national issues than are House members. These matters are of more interest to the press, and word of senators' stands on issues filters back to the whole state. If senators take stands on divisive issues that are covered by the media back home, there can be a political price. As South Dakota Democrat James Abourezk put it:

Senate members, because their statements are picked up much more by the press than those of House members, are much more prone to controversy. In politics, the more controversy there is, the more enemies you make. The more enemies you make, the greater the chance of losing the election.

As already mentioned, the ways voters get to know senators and their challengers and House members and their opponents are quite distinct. Voter contact with House candidates is highly personal. Voters encounter the House candidates at coffees and small gatherings that promote eye contact and conversation. The encounters are reciprocal; communication flows in both directions. Senate candidates shake hands and attend town meetings but in large states they simply cannot do enough of this personal campaigning to have much impact. The communication by Senate candidates to voters is overwhelmingly through television. It is unilateral and impersonal, and it establishes no firm bond. Yet senators are compelled to use it, and one study indicated that television advertising was almost twice as important to Senate incumbents as a way to contact voters as it was to House incumbents. And if senators use television to tell their story to the voters, the voters form their opinions of their senators from what they see of them on television.[23]

But television for senators is the classic two-edged sword. It provides for those seeking to unseat an incumbent a formidable siege weapon. Ironically, the TV ads of the challengers in Senate elections seem to be the single most influential way to shape voters' evaluations. They appear to be more decisive than ads run by the incumbents.[24]

House challengers are less apt to have the money to run TV ads, but when they do the ads appear not to have the impact that is achieved by those of Senate challengers. In fact, very little that House challengers can do in the way of advertising seems to be able to generate positive feelings about them in the minds of voters. Indeed, if there is a disadvantaged class of politicians in America it is House challengers. Even when they use a technique employed to good advantage by House incumbents, it seems to do little for them—mailings to voters work effectively to get voters to think well of House incumbents, but they appear to have little payoff for challengers.[25]

Below even the level of evaluation is the primitive level of awareness of candidates and here again the very abundance of information on Senate campaigns—largely from the electronic media—throws both challenger and incumbent into high resolution and clarity in the public mind. Such a deluge of information devalues face-to-face contact between senatorial candidate and voter. This is particularly the case in large and populous states such as California where a political rally in the 1986 campaign between incumbent senator Alan Cranston and Republican challenger Ed Zschau was described as "three people around a television set." Gerald Warren, editor of the *San Diego Union,* observed that neither Cranston nor Zschau would be found "at a shopping center or at a plant gate pressing the flesh."[26]

In contrast to a Senate campaign in the state that is most populous and third in size was a House campaign in the third smallest House district in the country, New York's 14th which is known as the "Silk Stocking District" because of the enormous wealth of many of its residents. Historically, the district was much more uniform in affluence when it was largely the Upper East Side of Manhattan, but even now it is distinctive in what it demands of campaigners. In addition to the fact that a remarkable 51.4 percent of its inhabitants have college degrees, the district also has the nation's highest median household income, $74,780, and many of its inhabitants live in luxury condominiums, townhouses, and cooperative apartments.

"It's a district where you can't knock on doors because the doormen won't let you in," said one political consultant working for a candidate. He also observed that many of the district's wealthy residents prefer to have their phone numbers unlisted and even when called by campaigns they refuse to come to the phone. "I can't tell you how many maids we've called," lamented the consultant. While people abound on the streets of the district, candidates can never be sure they are residents. In an area as heavily visited as New York, "Everybody you meet is from Canada or somewhere," said a disgusted candidate.[27]

The Senate campaign, by contrast, is fought on an electronic battlefield with the paid political spot being the weapon of choice for incumbent and challenger alike. House campaigns—except under unusual circumstances—tend to be more like hand-to-hand combat in which the combatant in office fights with both hands free and the challenger is hog-tied. The Senate battle, moreover, is a more equal and uncertain one in which incumbents seem unable to come up with a tactical edge equivalent to that enjoyed by their House counterparts. The lack of media attention to House incumbents frees them to construct for themselves a positive political image among those voters who do know them. The same lack of media attention casts a shadow of obscurity on those who challenge members. Senate incumbents, to their political disadvantage, find that the very limelight in which they bask also illuminates those who seek to dislodge them.

ISSUES AND POLICY IN HOUSE AND SENATE ELECTIONS

We have seen that with some notable exceptions the greater complexity of the statewide political environment presents senators with much more uncertainty and considerably less control over events than House incumbents encounter with their simpler and more circumscribed congressional districts. At least part of this uncertainty for senators seems to be associated with the higher public profile they achieve, relative to House members. Recognizing that senators are more visible and that their visibility may, paradoxically, give stature to their challengers does not in itself provide a very complete picture of the differences in senator-representative vulnerability.

Does the visibility of the office of senator, or the senatorial election by itself, produce vulnerability or is there a difference in the very subject matter over which House and Senate elections are fought that influences the different rates of electoral success for incumbents?

The 1978 Michigan Election Study suggests that there may be profound differences between House and Senate elections in terms of the importance of policies—economic policies in particular.

James H. Kuklinski and Darrell M. West, using data from the Michigan study, concluded that neither those voters who saw their personal financial situations as having improved nor those who saw their income status as having deteriorated indicated that these economic changes had much to do with their choice of one Senate or House candidate over another. When the question, however, became what the future held for the economic well-being of voters, Kuklinski and West concluded that voters did indeed let their concerns for the future influence their choices in Senate elections. When asked about their expectations for the upcoming year and how this would affect their choice of a Democratic or Republican Senate candidate, the pessimists, midway in the administration of Democratic president Jimmy Carter, indicated that they would support the Republican senate candidates. Those who were more upbeat about their economic future showed stronger support for Democratic Senate candidates. Significantly, however, predictions about the immediate economic future seemed to have little influence on whether a voter would opt for a Democrat or Republican in a House contest.[28]

Kuklinski and West, noting that "House members have more successfully than their Senate counterparts isolated themselves from in-party economic performance, principally by establishing their roles as ombudsmen and providers of individualized services," conclude that a party-blind vote for a House member is probably a rational act from the voter's point of view inasmuch as "the individual voter . . . has benefitted from personalized [House member] services in the past—and expects to benefit in the future."[29] While they stop short of saying that senators alone are held to account for the policies of the president whose party affiliation they share, Kuklinski and West do seem to suggest that if senators chose to imitate House members in the provision of services and ombudsmenship, it would reduce their vulnerability to defeat. Many senators, of late, appear to be heeding this precept by assigning larger numbers of staff members to constituent problems and locating them in offices in the state. This would also, of course, reduce greatly the vulnerability of legislators on policy matters and make them answerable only for the effective delivery of government services.[30]

A more recent examination of how voters evaluate congressional candidates finds that although voters tend to have more information about Senate candidates than House candidates, they employ largely the same standards to judge both groups of candidates. According to this analysis, the traditionally dominant role of the Senate in foreign policy seems to exert little influence on voters, who hold House members almost as accountable for the state of the world as they do senators. In a related finding, the author of the study finds that voters demand of senators the same devotion to constituent services as they do members of the House.[31]

Responsiveness and the Democracies

In defending the creation of the Senate in *Federalist* #63, James Madison justified the length and staggered term of senators, their selection by the state legislatures, and the smallness of a chamber in which all states would have only two members by observing that "there are particular moments in public affairs, when the people, stimulated by some irregular passion, or some illicit advantage, or misled by the artful misrepresentations of interested men, may call for measures which they themselves will afterwards be the most ready to lament and condemn."

Buffered as they were by the state legislatures and long terms, senators would, presumably, be a bulwark against these "sudden and violent passions" that might overtake House members because of their greater vulnerability to being stampeded into unwise legislation by outraged citizens. What Madison and the other proponents of the Constitution wanted was, not an unresponsive Senate, but one that responded to popular demands only after careful deliberation.

Part of that protective bulwark was removed, of course, when the Seventeenth Amendment was ratified in 1913 and senators became elected directly by voters. Until 1900, moreover, rates of reelection for incumbent senators were always greater than those of House members, evidence that the Senate was a more stable body with less turnover; also the period of service for the average senator was longer than that of the average House member, even when the differences in the length of their terms was taken into account.

Since the beginning of the twentieth century, however, the incumbency advantage enjoyed by individual senators and the stability advantage enjoyed by the Senate as an institution has eroded somewhat. In fifteen of the forty-eight biennial congressional elections held between 1900 and 1996, the percentage of newly elected senators has exceeded the percentage of newly elected House members.

When most of the turnover results from defeat at the polls rather than voluntary retirement or death, a picture emerges of a Senate that is more susceptible to the winds of change than the founding fathers would either have imagined or approved of. The Senate, then, in electoral terms at least, has become the more responsive of the two chambers.

The shift has led two Senate experts to conclude that this reversal of electoral fortunes has also caused internal changes in the Senate, so that "the Senate can no longer be counted on for what the framers hoped it would provide"—a cooler, more deliberate body with a broader and more national view.[32]

Undeniably, lower reelection rates of senators seem to point to voters' holding them more accountable, but it is a considerable leap to conclude that a more electorally responsive Senate has produced a Senate that is a one-quarter-scale replica of the House. Even so, those who argue that the Senate can no longer be counted on to serve as the calm and deliberative counterpart to the impetuous House can usually find examples to buttress their argument.

In the first session of the 106th Congress (1999–2001), a

major campaign finance reform bill was passed in the House but succumbed to a filibuster in the Senate. Similarly, the Comprehensive Nuclear Test Ban Treaty failed to secure approval of the two-thirds of the Senate required for its ratification. Supporters of those two measures might contend that the House had acted responsibly in passing campaign finance reforms and that the Senate was beholden to big campaign contributors and its failure to ratify the treaty was evidence of a chamber in the grip of isolationists. But supporters of gun control and the overdue reform of the nation's banking system might have been more satisfied with the performance of the Senate. In the case of the banking bill, its ultimate success was the result of hard last-minute bargaining between the chairman of the Senate Banking Committee, Senator Phil Gramm (R-Tex.), and Treasury Secretary Lawrence Summers that succeeded despite the lingering animosity over of the Senate's trial of President Clinton on impeachment charges.

If willingness to bridge the gaps of divided government and solve a long-festering problem on a bipartisan basis is evidence of a more measured and deliberate approach to resolving conflicts, however, the Senate showed itself to good advantage on one of the most explosive issues in American politics. That issue was abortion and how it had become entangled with the payment of America's back dues to the United Nations. The failure of the United States to pay the dues over a period of years not only cast this nation in the role of the world's foremost deadbeat but also threatened its seat in the U.N.

A deal had been struck between the Clinton administration and the chairman of the Senate Foreign Relations Committee, Senator Jesse Helms (R-N.C.), to pay the dues conditional on some restructuring of the State Department. Helms, an ardent foe of abortion, had not insisted that antiabortion provisions be inserted in the legislation. The potential deal breaker was on the House side with Representative Christopher Smith (R-N.J.), chairman of the subcommittee of House Appropriations that funds overseas activities of the U.S. government.

Smith, also a foe of abortion, held up the dues money until the Clinton administration agreed to deny funding to any international organization that either provided abortions or counseled it to women in other countries. Eventually, the White House acceded to most of Smith's conditions. But what this episode suggests is that the Senate was more willing to spare the nation the embarrassment of losing its U.N. vote over an extraneous issue than was the House.

It is, at best, an open question as to whether the decline in the electoral fortunes of senators and the grater apparent responsiveness of the Senate has reversed the traditional roles of the two chambers. Perhaps the situation was best summed up by Janet Hook, the congressional correspondent for the *Los Angeles Times*, who said, "I can see the argument for saying that the Senate is becoming more like the House, but the House is not becoming any more deliberative."

The election of 1994 registered as a major deviation from the normal House elections of recent years by reason of the fifty-six seats that changed from Democratic to Republican and the shift of the majority to the GOP. But one fact bears repeating—that more than 90 percent of House members who sought reelection were, in fact, reelected. Republican gains occurred principally in open seats; twenty-two Republicans won in seats that been held by Democrats who had died, decided not to run again, or sought another office. Almost half the Democratic defeats were of freshmen, who are often the most vulnerable incumbents because they have had little time to establish name recognition. Incumbents of long-standing in that vast majority of House districts that had been drawn to give their party an overwhelming advantage had little trouble getting reelected. Referendums on national policy rarely take place in such districts.

House members can continue to align themselves quite comfortably with the simpler array of interests in their districts and take refuge behind House procedures that minimize embarrassing or controversial votes. If they concentrate their activities on serving their constituents through casework activities that have, in large measure, no policy content, they can generally immunize themselves from defeat. Not all House members choose this prudent, if timid, course, but it is available to them to an extent that it is not available to senators.

Senators, facing a daunting array of state interests, are often compelled to take stands that involve politically painful choices. They are prevented from adopting the strategy of merely conforming precisely to the interests of their constituencies because their constituencies are states, where it is unavoidable that there will be interests that will clash. They are also less able to take refuge behind friendly procedures in the Senate chamber. They can be forced to go on record with votes that are controversial and politically costly. In the House, procedures are so user friendly that members there can often appear to be on both sides of an issue.[33]

Some Senate elections contain implications for national policy that House elections have less frequently exhibited. The 1980 Senate election made the Republicans the majority party for the first time in twenty-five years. In that chamber the stage was set for the vast economic changes of the Reagan era. The 1986 Senate elections, which returned the Democrats to the majority, virtually closed the door on any major domestic policy accomplishments for President Reagan in the last two years of his term, lost him a Supreme Court nominee, Robert Bork, and seemed to preclude any further military aid to the Contra rebels in Nicaragua.

While it would be incorrect to argue that Senate elections are somehow more "national" than House elections because to do so would ignore such important factors as the quality of candidates and the importance of statewide issues, it has been possible over the years to read national trends and moods into them more unambiguously than into House elections. In the same vein, it would be equally inaccurate to say that House elections have no national policy implications, but the declining number of competitive House seats makes it difficult to achieve much of a swing in House elections. The 1994 results may be an exceptional case.

Senate elections are, in a sense, more national because the attention lavished on them by the national media makes them so. Moreover, the activities of contributors from beyond the borders of the state nationalize Senate elections. They have, accordingly, a kind of breadth of scope not associated with House elections. House members can gain reelection by the successful advocacy and articulation of a limited set of interests; senators are called upon to address a broad array of issues that embrace matters of concern to the nation as a whole.

But the difference in the electoral environments of House districts and whole states may have as much to do with the size of the legislative chamber to which the candidate belongs as to the number or variety of voters in the constituency. It is simply easier to find someone to hold accountable from the Senate than from the House when things go wrong. As political consultant Peter Fenn expressed it:

In the House there are 435 guys and, after all, one of them is my old friend Joe from down the street and I grew up with him and I'm not going to blame *him* that much for 20 percent interest rates, but you can bet your ass I'm going to blame that senator because he's only one of a hundred.

DO SENATORS TAKE THEIR ROLE SERIOUSLY?

In conversation with senators, the listener is left with the inescapable impression that they feel they deal with matters of greater weight and gravity than those who serve in the House and that speaking out on the great issues of the day comes with the territory of the United States Senate. South Dakota Democrat George McGovern expressed a view common among the older group of senators who began their congressional careers in the House.

Shortly after coming to the Senate, I made a series of speeches that were an examination of the contradictions in our kind of rigid fixation on Fidel Castro and I urged that we use Alliance for Progress [a program of economic aid to Latin America proposed by the Kennedy administration in 1961] not hostility toward Castro as the basis for our policy.

That was the kind of speech I felt comfortable with in the Senate. I guess I felt too much under the political gun to do it in the House. It wasn't that I was afraid to go on about things like that, but it was such a life-death struggle to save the farmers back home. The pressure of that one district problem was so intense that I was home every other weekend listening to it.

I was just so much more directly associated with the immediate concerns of my own district's problems than I was with the policies of the nation. Those things I found easier to examine in the Senate.

The level of issues the senator deals with is more apt to produce controversy than those locally oriented issues that seem to dominate House members' concerns. If senators see themselves—or are seen by the voters—as addressing the "big-ticket" issues, it is not surprising that they are held accountable for them. Some senators were adamant that senators should address these issues rather than take refuge in casework. As George McGovern put it, "If you don't talk about these things in the Senate, the system is not working the way it's supposed to."

The tendency of senators to identify with national and international issues is a result of both preference and an institutional bias in the Senate in favor of large, visible, and often controversial issues. Senator Thad Cochran (R-Miss.) described the breadth of the Senate's responsibilities:

The Senate is not just another legislative body. It has extra-legislative responsibilities such as treaty-ratification, confirmation of officials who are nominated by the executive, confirming all federal judges and officers of the armed forces. . . . The Senate decides who represents our country in international tribunals. The Senate decides which international agreements rise to the level of having the force of law. . . . So the Senate is the body that exercises these responsibilties and is kind of like the Supreme Court. The members take these responsibilities seriously, and more often than not, their decisions reflect that seriousness of purpose.

The very breadth of senators' committee responsibilities contrasted with the relative narrowness of House members' substantive focus means that senators typically are called on to speak out on a wider array of topics. In a sense, then, institutional imperatives force senators to be generalists whose views are solicited more frequently on a variety of topics, and these views are often newsworthy.

Constitutional distinctions such as those, for example, in treaty ratification confront senators with an area of controversy from which House members are exempted. Politically touchy treaties, such as the 1999 Comprehensive Test-Ban Treaty that would have halted U.S. nuclear testing presented senators with a gauntlet that House members do not have to run.

The proportion of legislators assigned to the committees dealing with national security and foreign policy issues—perennially topics of great controversy—varies between the House and Senate. In the 99th Congress (1985–1986), for example, almost 60 percent of the members of the Senate were assigned to the following committees: the Appropriations Committee's Subcommittee on Defense and Foreign Operations, the Armed Services Committee, and the Foreign Relations Committee. There are four parallel committees in the House, yet less than 25 percent of the membership of the House was assigned to those committees dealing with international relations and national security. The stake of the Senate in these areas of public policy is more than twice as large as that of the House. In a sense, then, institutional imperatives combine with a sense of being "senatorial" to direct senators into issues that are more salient to the public and media and at the same time more controversial.

The Senate's role as the institution that produces presidential possibilities also works to promote issue stands on the part of senators. The toughness with which Senator Joseph R. Biden, Jr., took on President Reagan's judicial nominees in 1987 and 1988 was intensified by his presidential ambitions. But presidential quests that impel senators to take novel or radical positions in order to cater to national party constituencies can backfire on those who fail to get the nomination. They often end up having to explain to the voters of their state why they took such uncharacteristic positions. Going national and taking stands that appealed to a national Democratic constituency vastly more liberal than the electorates in their states was a factor in the 1980 defeat of three prominent senators. George McGovern of South Dakota became associated with opposition to American foreign policy; Frank Church of Idaho exposed excesses on the part of the CIA; and Birch Bayh of Indiana was seen as an advocate of liberalized abortion policy.

Howard Paster, who served as Bayh's chief legislative assistant, acknowledged that Bayh's 1976 bid for the Democratic presidential nomination caused him to take positions that put him at odds with Indiana voters, but argued that even those senators without presidential ambitions take up risky issues and causes.

Senators are more apt to play a role in cosmic issues that don't have a direct payback for their constituency. That sometimes can cause them either to neglect home or to be perceived to be detached from home and it can catch up with them in a political way.

The 2000 campaign of Senator John McCain (R-Ariz.) led him into the dangerous realm of religion when he denounced Reverend Pat Robertson and Reverend Jerry Falwell, who supported his rival, Governor George W. Bush. Had he not sought the nomination, it is unlikely that McCain would have become involved in such an explosive issue as the political role of the "religious right."

But there is evidence that the public expects senators to tackle big and important issues. A CBS/New York Times poll of a random sample of 1,254 adults, which coincided with the celebration of the 200th anniversary of the Constitution, found that 51 percent (as opposed to 35 percent) felt that the Senate was "likely to take a long-range view of issues" more than the House and, by a 54 to 29 percent margin, that the House "better represents the views of the people that elected them" than do members of the Senate.[34]

Do citizens still expect senators to be "senatorial"—more measured and less impulsive in judgment, less mechanistically tied to the specific views of their constituents? We have already noted that the expectations voters have of House and Senate candidates seem not to be very different and that the electorate expects senators as well as House members to attend to their problems. There is, however, evidence that Americans continue to have considerably more information about Senate candidates than about House candidates and their expectations of the House and Senate as institutions are also different. Americans appear not to want senators to act like House members. They are, however, not necessarily willing to reward that detachment and independence of mind with a long lease on the office.

DOES COMPETITION INFLUENCE THE INSTITUTIONAL PERSONALITIES OF THE HOUSE AND SENATE?

Having established the greater competitiveness of Senate elections and the greater vulnerability of Senate incumbents, we can now address the question of whether the differences in the uncertainties that surround House and Senate elections have any impact on the manner in which the two houses conduct their business.

The Senate has seen greater partisan amplitudes than the House. In the decade of the 1980s, party control in the Senate changed twice—after the 1980 election when the Republicans became the majority party and in 1986 when the Democrats reestablished their majority. During that same period, the House Democrats retained the majority they had enjoyed since 1955. Only in the election of 1994 did majority control in the House change hands. This Democratic lock on House partisanship was interpreted as being a source of the greater partisanship in the House.

Quite apart from the partisanship difference, additional effects have been observed. Two long-term students of Senate

elections, Alan Abramowitz and Jeffrey Segal made the case
that the greater competitiveness of Senate elections and the
closer division of seats between Democrats and Republicans in
the Senate in the 1980s produced "a stronger sense of collective responsibility for policy outcomes in the Senate than in
the House, because Senators realized that there was a real
chance of a change in party control based on these outcomes.
There was, in addition, a greater incentive for cooperation between the majority and minority parties in the Senate because
each side realized that its position could change after the next
election."[35]

The closeness of the number of seats occupied by Democrats and Republicans after the 1996 and 1998 elections produced quite the opposite effect in the House. Here, the
connection between broader trends in the electorate and the internal dynamics of the House can be seen clearly. Southern
House districts, once overwhelmingly Democratic, are now
preponderantly Republican. The increase in African-American
voters and the subsequent creation of majority-minority districts in which black voters (most of whom are Democrats) constitute a majority have produced an upsurge in black House
membership. "Since black members of Congress tended to reflect the liberal orientation of their constituents, they reinforced
the liberal wing of the Democratic caucus [in the House], while
new Republican representatives from the South tended to be
more conservative than their Democratic predecessors [and] as
the party identification of Southern whites changed, so did the
number of House seats from the South held by Republicans."[36]

These trends caused both the House Democrats and House
Republicans to become more homogeneous, with Democrats
being more consistently liberal, reflecting the ideology of their
districts, and Republicans more uniformly conservative, reflecting the philosophy of their constitutents. This split produced much greater partisanship in the House, and as the gap
between Republicans and Democrats narrowed to less than a
dozen seats in 2000, the animosities, if anything, grew more in-

tense. It is here that the more politically diverse composition of the electorate in entire states produced a membership in the Senate that was less polarized. Segal and Abramowitz suggested that greater collective accountability seemed also to be associated with greater personal responsibility for legislative decisions on the part of individual senators than is the case among House members.

The idea that senators have a larger stake in the institution and feel more personal responsibility for the work of the Senate was readily accepted by both Democratic and Republican senators who were interviewed for this book. All ascribed this to the smaller size of the Senate. Senator Christopher Dodd (D-Conn.) made his case with characteristic bluntness: "Yeah, it's a smaller group you're dealing with—100 people rather than 435. That in itself, just the math, has an impact. And the profiles of the individuals here are just higher. In the House, out of 435 people, you might have just 50 people—maybe—who are high profile. The remaining 380 are just part of the ground troops." While conceding that some senators could be as constituency-oriented as any House member, they stated, "Senators do appear to be more willing than House members to look beyond the immediate reaction of the voters in their own state and to weigh the consequences of their actions for the well-being of the nation."[37]

The greater disposition of senators to have a more national outlook than House members seemed, in the eyes of these two observers, to emerge from two sets of perceptions: one among House members and the other among senators. House members assumed that the Democrats would be in the majority for the foreseeable future. Accordingly, there was little that any single House member could do to affect the partisan balance. Therefore, "members of both parties in the House have little motivation to consider the national consequences of their actions."[38] The view from the Senate, according to their analysis, was that the greater likelihood that party control will shift "means that senators must be concerned about the national reputations of their parties," and the competitiveness of their elections "may force senators to consider the consequences of their actions for the nation as well as for their own constituents."[39]

One may challenge the assertion that senators' perspectives are more national than those of House members on matters of policy, but there is one area in which the national orientation of senators is beyond question: campaign fund-raising.

PACs and Deep Pockets:
The Financing of House and Senate Campaigns

The money to conduct congressional campaigns comes from three sources: contributions by individuals; contributions from state or national party organizations (such as the Democratic Congressional Campaign Committee for Democratic House candidates or the Republican Senatorial Campaign Committee for GOP Senate candidates); and contributions from organizations known as political action committees (PACs). Among PACs, the examples of most interest are multicandidate PACs. These are like political mutual funds in which a donor who may not want to put all of his or her money in the campaign of a single candidate will donate instead to a PAC whose directors will decide where the contribution of that person and of thousands of others would be best directed. Some PACs solicit funds to help liberal members, others to help members and senators whose votes have helped the labor unions; still other PACs are set up by a single company to give money to the campaigns of friendly members; the most powerful, the trade association PACs, are organized by entire industries as part of their lobbying activities. One example of lobbying activities by an industry is the National Cable Television Association, which is based in Washington and to which all local cable television companies belong. These companies' membership dues in the trade association are based on the number of cable subscribers they have, and the dues enable NCTA to operate a PAC that targets money for the campaigns of those who have been, or might be, friendly or influential on matters relating to the industry.

While PACs have become more important since 1974 when changes in the Federal Election Campaign Act made it easier for PACs to raise and disburse money to candidates in federal elections, it is still the individual contribution that is the most important source of campaign funds for congressional elections in both House and Senate races. There are, however, differences in the sources of funds between House and Senate elections.

Senate candidates rely less on PAC money than do those running for House seats. In contrast, Senate campaigns receive a larger percentage of their total receipts from individuals than do House candidates. In 1996, for example, PAC donations constituted about 25 percent of House campaign receipts but only 16 percent of contributions going to Senate candidates. At the same time, the contributions of individual givers to House campaigns accounted for about 52 percent of receipts, while individuals' donations accounted for almost 60 percent of Senate campaign receipts.[40]

Senate campaigns tend to draw more heavily than House campaigns on individual contributors for two reasons. First, Senate candidates—both incumbents and challengers—receive more publicity than their House counterparts and have a larger constituency geographically. According to Larry Sabato, this visibility of Senate candidates enables them to solicit money from individual contributors, especially through the use of direct mail advertising.[41]

The second reason is that fund-raising by direct mail is not practical in a House campaign. It is very expensive and the primary target of the mailing would be only a few hundred thousand households in the average congressional district. Given the relative anonymity of House members even within their own districts, it is unlikely that the representative's solicitation would elicit much of a response from a household halfway across the country. Yet this is one important way that money is raised by senators. Senators can use direct mail solicitation not only because they are so much better known—a Senator Ted Kennedy is as well known in Illinois as in his own home state of Massachusetts—but because their very visibility allows them to raise the money to invest in expensive mailings. Expenses such as mail solicitation are built into the large overhead costs of a Senate campaign.

It is not only in the area of direct mail solicitation that the senator's financial scope is national. Washington lobbyist Howard Paster described the broader fund-raising environment of senators:

Unless the House member is the chairman of a big committee or some other bigshot, he can't fly out to Chicago or Miami or Los Angeles or St. Louis and raise money from individuals.

The fund-raising event in which individuals contribute to a congressional campaign by buying a ticket costing several hundred dollars or more is used differently by senators and House members. Unless the House member is a party leader or committee chair, the fund-raising event will be held either in Washington, D.C., or in the district itself. If the event is held in Washington it will be attended by lobbyists who have purchased the tickets. These lobbyists will normally represent interests that fall within the jurisdiction of the member's committee. Sometimes groups of members will hold joint fundraisers. Groups of members will also drop in on events being held by their colleagues. The presence of several members adds to the drawing power of the event since ticket buyers will have more than one congressional hand to shake.

The senator's fund-raising universe is broader and more glittering. The visibility of senators gives them a celebrity value that enables them to tap the most affluent and politically aware individuals anywhere in the country. As one lobbyist observed, "Most House guys can't go to [socialite and philanthropist] Mary Lasker's place on the Upper East Side for a fund-raiser. Almost any Democratic senator who really asks can get a fundraiser at Mary Lasker's."

For the House member, the political action committee represents a very efficient way to raise money. Jay Berman, the Washington lobbyist for the recording industry, comments, "It's just very convenient when a new House member comes to Washington for him to identify some PACs, and their contributions will be the core of that guy's fund-raising."

From the PAC director's point of view, House members can offer a bigger return than can senators. For one thing, we have already observed the impressive ability of House incumbents to win reelection. PAC directors, not surprisingly, will direct contributions to the campaigns of those who will likely be voting in the next Congress on matters that concern the PAC. There is, accordingly, a heavy bias among PACs, in general, to incumbents of both parties. Although most PACs indicate that they show no preference as to whether their contributions go to House or Senate campaigns, those who do indicate a preference tend to favor the House and, within the House, the incumbent.[42]

While helping those most likely to be making policy contributes to the pro-incumbent, pro-House bias of PACs, there is also the fact that PACs can get "more bang for the buck" by giving contributions to a House campaign that may cost $500,000 to wage than by giving it to a $10 million Senate campaign in which the money is, in effect, "lost" among many other individual and PAC donations. Their money is more likely to be visible and appreciated by the House member waging the lower cost campaign, and it also helps those most likely to win. But influential senior House members with token opposition have taken to raising huge sums of money from contributors in order to scare away potential opponents. A $5,000 contribution by a PAC to one of these members would not stand out very distinctly.

PACs by their nature will always favor the most likely winners and support those in whose coffers the PAC coin will have the greatest luster: typically, incumbent House members. PACs with corporate or trade association connections will key their contributions to the member whose committee jurisdiction covers policies important to those industries. Senators or senatorial challengers do appear to be favored by one type of PAC—the one that represents a single large corporation. These company-connected PACs may have facilities in many states and the percentage of Senate elections to which they contribute will be high. They may also perceive a broader and more national perspective on the part of senators and find the very breadth of senators' committee assignments appealing.

Representation, Responsiveness, and the Two Forms of Democracy

Looking back on this chapter, we have seen that the electoral environments in which senators and House members operate are quite different. The intimacy and sense of being in control that characterize House members' relationships with their districts have few parallels in senators' relationships with their statewide constituencies, except in the smallest states.

House members may be sent to Washington by constituents with whom they can feel intimate, but their legislative decision making occurs in a setting of little intimacy. As we saw in the previous chapter, it is the Senate that enables members to better interact on the one-to-one basis that promotes unitary democracy in Congress. "It is the means by which legislators come to perceive overlapping interests, to emphathize with colleagues and to recognize common principles—the means, in other words, by which they come to make decisions on the basis of common interests."[43]

There is a paradox to be found in the fact that House members are sent by constituents with whom they feel great closeness to represent them in a vast, anonymous, and often anomic House. Senators, by contrast, are delegated by sprawling, complex, and unknowable constituencies to interact in a highly personal way in a compact and intimate chamber.

The relationship between members of the House and their

constituents influences profoundly the approach to legislation that they bring to Washington. In close, direct, and almost continuous contact with voters, House members hear the interests of those they represent expressed with great intensity. But even if House members did not stick so closely to their constituents, the greater simplicity of the average congressional district would still enable them to divine constituent interests far more readily than a senator can. But it is in the expression of those interests in their respective chambers that the differences in home state interactions and Capitol Hill interactions between senators and representatives become critical in whether adversary or unitary democracy emerges.

While it is not clear that voters send House members and senators to Washington with the expectation that they will sail close to the prevailing winds of district interests or that with senators there is an expectation that from time to time they will have the freedom to go off on a tack, the view among the senators I interviewed was that they saw themselves dealing with a broader array of issues and problems, and there was also a feeling among most of the senators that constituents, in the words of Senator Chris Dodd, "see senators as being involved in national issues. There's an expectation in people's minds. They may not understand the constitutional distinctions between a congressman and a senator when it comes to foreign policy but they sense that senators are supposed to be involved in that job." Though the rules of the Senate promote a kind of aggressive individualism associated with adversary democracy that puts senators in a better position to foster their constituents' interests, "senators, of course, can use their greater freedom . . . to raise broader issues."[44]

If, indeed, senators cast their debate and frame their concerns more in national terms, the Senate would appear to be the chamber where the values of unitary democracy are furthered. There was, however, a feeling among the senators interviewed that uncertainty about reelection was pushing senators into exaggerated defensive strategies of fund-raising that made them beholden to the very interests they were expected to stand above. Paradoxically, House members, for whom no broader vision is demanded, are reelected with inexorable regularity.

But even here, the higher electoral mortality of senators represents a greater responsiveness to national political trends. While House members can insulate and innoculate themselves from these trends by stressing service and dedication to the limited interests of the district, senators cannot usually do enough of these favors to make a difference. Sensing, albeit imperfectly, that Senate elections are the means to register sentiments about the trends of national policy and the course of the broader political system, voters unilaterally impose unitary standards of accountability on the upper chamber.

One strategy adopted by fearful Senate incumbents is to emulate the localism of House members by becoming what former New York senator Alfonse D'Amato called "a pothole senator." While senators have long been free to choose from any number of representational styles, it may be more difficult for senators to restrict themselves only to noncontroversial activities. There is pressure both from colleagues and from voters that may impel even the most parochially minded senator toward a broader focus. These senators may still prefer to deal with potholes but, at the very least, they will be potholes on Interstate 95.

NOTES

1. Richard F. Fenno, Jr., *Homestyle* (Boston: Little Brown, 1978), p. 55.
2. Richard F. Fenno, Jr., *The United States Senate: A Bicameral Perspective* (Washington, D.C.: American Enterprise Institute, 1982), pp. 24–25.
3. Ronald Smothers, "Fairness or Gerrymander? Justices Study "Serpentine' District," *New York Times,* Friday, April 16, 1993, and "Segregated and Unequal," *Wall Street Journal,* Monday, January 10, 1994.
4. See Carol M. Swain, *Black Faces, Black Interests: The Representation of African Americans in Congress* (Cambridge, Mass.: Harvard University Press, 1993).
5. Paul Gronke, *Settings, Institutions, Campaigns, and the Vote* (Ann Arbor: University of Michigan Press, forthcoming).
6. Stephen Kemp Bailey, *Congress Makes a Law* (New York: Columbia University

Press, 1950), pp. 126–127. The 17th District of Illinois currently embraces such industrial towns as Rock Island and Peoria and is not nearly so rural as it was in 1950 when Bailey used it as an example of a district without much blue-collar influence.

7. Michael Weisskopf, "Between a Rock and a Bunch of Lobbies," *Washington Post National Weekly Edition,* February 12–18, 1990.

8. Susan F. Rasky, "California, the Congressional Giant, Has the Numbers, But Not the Solidarity," *New York Times,* Monday, November 26, 1990.

9. Morris P. Fiorina, *Congress: Keystone of the Washington Establishment* (New Haven, Conn.: Yale University Press, 1977), p. 61.

10. Jacqueline Calmes, "House Incumbents Achieve Record Success Rate in 1986," *Congressional Quarterly Weekly Report,* November 15, 1986, p. 2891.

11. *Washington Post,* Friday, August 17, 1979.

12. Gary C. Jacobson, "Money in the 1980 and 1982 Congressional Elections," in Michael J. Malbin, ed., *Money and Politics in the United States* (Chatham, N.J.: Chatham House, 1984), pp. 52–54, and Gary C. Jacobson and Samuel Kernell, *Strategy and Choice in Congressional Elections,* 2d ed. (New Haven, Conn.: Yale University Press, 1983), p. 102.

13. Marjorie Randon Hershey, *Running for Office* (Chatham: N.J.: Chatham House, 1984), p. 166.

14. CBS/New York Times Poll, *Politics, 1986,* September–October 1986.

15. Thomas E. Mann and Raymond E. Wolfinger, "Candidates and Parties in Congressional Elections," *American Political Science Review,* 74 (September 1980), p. 626.

16. Ibid.

17. The two most influential works on the effective use of their incumbency by House members are Fiorina, op. cit., who makes the simple point that the expansion of the scope of government—often at public demand—causes more citizens to get trapped in the toils of the federal bureaucracy and to turn to members of Congress to protect them from a government whose expansion they favored. Another picture is painted by David Mayhew in *Congress: The Electoral Connection* (New Haven, Conn.: Yale University Press, 1974), which points out that internal resources in the House itself enable members to advertise their accomplishments to voters, claim credit for benefits they have brought to their districts, and take positions (often in the form of posturing) on issues that align them with the majority of the electorate. See also Bruce E. Cain, John A. Ferejohn, and Morris P. Fiorina, *The Personal Vote* (Cambridge: Harvard University Press, 1987).

18. Mann and Wolfinger, op. cit., p. 627.

19. See Paul Gronke, op. cit., who points out, "House members face inefficient media markets, yet benefit from districts with uneven numbers of partisans. The situation in states is reversed: efficient media market but balanced numbers of partisans."

20. Fiorina, op. cit., pp. 58–60.

21. James H. Kuklinski and Darrell M. West, "Economic Expectations and Voting Behavior in United States House and Senate Elections," *American Political Science Review,* 75 (June 1981), p. 438.

22. "Only 46% Can Name Congressional Representative," *Washington Post,* Sunday, August 1, 1982.

23. Alan I. Abramowitz, "A Comparison of Voting for U.S. Senator and Representative in 1978," *American Political Science Review,* 74 (September 1980), pp. 635–637.

24. Ibid.
25. Gary G. Jacobson and Samuel Kernell, *Strategy and Choice in Congressional Elections,* pp. 19–34.
26. R. W. Apple, Jr., "California Senate Race Reflects Electronic Era," *New York Times,* Sunday, October 19, 1986. See also Glenn R. Parker, "Interpreting Candidate Awareness in U.S. Congressional Elections," *Legislative Studies Quarterly,* 6 (May 1981), pp. 219–233.
27. James Bennet, "East Side Race, Both Phones and Parties Are Unlisted," *New York Times,* Sunday, February 21, 1993.
28. Kuklinski and West, op. cit., pp. 436–447.
29. Ibid., p. 446.
30. The percentage of congressional staff assigned to work in state and district offices rather than in Washington has risen sharply for the Senate. In 1972, only 12.5 percent of Senate staff was in the states. A decade later it was almost 28 percent. House members, however, still assign a higher percentage of their staffs to district offices. For 1983, it was 36.6 percent. See Norman J. Ornstein et al., *Vital Statistics on Congress,* 1984–1985 ed. (Washington, D.C.: American Enterprise Institute, 1984), p. 123.
31. Gronke, op. cit.
32. Figures compiled by John R. Alford and John R. Hibbing, in "The Electorally Distinct Senate," paper prepared for presentation at the Norman Thomas Conference on Senate Exceptionalism, Vanderbilt University, Nashville, Tenn., October 21–23, 1999.
33. Mayhew, *Congress: The Electoral Connection.*
34. CBS/New York Times Poll, May 25, 1987.
35. Alan I. Abramowitz and Jeffrey A. Segal, *Senate Elections* (Ann Arbor, Mich.: University of Michigan Press, 1992), p. 288.
36. James P. Pfiffner, "President Clinton, Newt Gingrich, and the 104th Congress," in Nelson W. Polsby and Raymond E. Wolfinger (eds.), *On Parties* (Berkeley, Calif.: Institute of Governmental Studies Press, 1999), p. 139.
37. Abramowitz and Segal, p. 24.
38. Ibid.
39. Abramowitz and Segal, loc. cit.
40. "PACs Bearing Gifts," *Congressional Quarterly Weekly Report,* June 16, 1990, p. 1470, and Richard L. Berke, "Clinton Eases Plan in Campaign Funds," *New York Times,* Friday, March 26, 1993, and Norman J. Ornstein, Thomas E. Mann, and Michael J. Malbin, *Vital Statistics on Congress* (Washington, D.C.: Congressional Quarterly Press, 1998), pp. 103–104.
41. Larry J. Sabato, *PAC Power* (New York: W.W. Norton, 1985), pp. 74 and 77.
42. Ibid.
43. David J. Vogler and Sidney R. Waldman, *Congress and Democracy* (Washington, D.C.: Congressional Quarterly Press, 1985), p. 116.
44. Ibid., p. 87.

5

The Attentive Elites
Lobbyists and Journalists on House-Senate Differences

APART FROM THE congressional establishment itself, which consists of the members and senators and their staffs, the two groups with whom legislators have the most direct and personal contact are journalists and lobbyists. They are the most important elements in the supporting cast of Congress. Their attentiveness to the institutions and the members as individuals is of such consequence that it is impossible to imagine the modern Congress without them. In the course of representing their clients' interests to Congress, lobbyists often become valuable personal friends of members and senators. Their presence in the legislative process—far from being intrusive—is probably indispensable. As purveyors of information, witnesses at hearings, suppliers of political resources, they are integral to the legislative process.

Journalists have a similarly symbiotic relationship with legislators. Without the comments and tape footage of members and senators, newspaper columns and TV news would be impossible. At the same time, it is the journalists—above all others—who tell the story of Congress and its members to the world.

In this chapter we examine the relationships between these important supporting actors and the main cast of players, the legislators themselves. And we look at those relationships in terms of the ways they appear in both the House and Senate.

The treatment accorded the House and Senate is not identical. Reporters and lobbyists see them in different ways, present themselves in different ways to members of each house, and emphasize different features of the two legislative bodies. Some lobbyists and journalists prefer to work the House; others indicate a preference for the Senate. Why this is the case is part of the subject of this chapter, but the relationship between the various news media and the two houses of Congress receives first attention. What emerges is a very distinctive set of perceptions of the two legislative bodies on the part of reporters and lobbyists.

The Camera on Bicameralism:
Journalists and Congress

The lead story on NBC-TV's *Today* show the morning after the 1986 congressional elections was an unexpectedly strong showing by Democrats that enabled them to reclaim control of the U.S. Senate after six years as the minority party.

The first set of live interviews conducted by co-host Bryant Gumbel was with two senators and one member of the House: soon-to-be Senate minority leader Bob Dole; Senator Joseph Biden, a Delaware Democrat; and Representative Jack Kemp, a New York Republican. Kemp's involvement in the interview was not to solicit his views on the outcome of House elections—a result barely noted in the hubbub over the Senate—but to question him in his capacity as a Republican presidential hopeful for 1988. Indeed, the House races figured in only the most minor way in either the news coverage or the interview.

And why, indeed, should the House elections have merited more than tangential comment? An estimate by the *Congressional Quarterly* undertaken a week before the election showed that 340 of the 435 seats in the House were "safe" seats in which the incumbent or candidate of the party locally dominant was unbeatable. In the mere one-quarter of all House seats in

which actual political competition was taking place, the strug-
gles were being waged by incumbents who could be identified
by only a minority of voters[1] and challengers whose visibility
was so low that only 44 percent of voters typically reported
even having had any contact with them.[2]

The next set of *Today* show interviews took place shortly
after the 7:30 A.M. break to local stations. Two of the newly
elected Democratic senators and the lone Republican who captured a previously held Democratic seat were interviewed. Still,
no comment from a House member other than from aspiring
presidential candidate Kemp. Just before the end of the first
hour, however, mention was made of a specific House race
when co-anchor Gumbel mentioned that of the two children of
the late Senator Robert F. Kennedy who were seeking House
seats, only Joseph P. Kennedy II, who was running for the
Massachusetts seat once held by his uncle, John F. Kennedy,
had prevailed. Apart from the bare reporting of the overall
House results—a gain of six seats for the Democrats, the appearance of a presidential hopeful who just happened to hold a
House seat, and a snippet of America's most intriguing political family—the fate of one of the two houses of the national
legislature was barely mentioned.

At the beginning of the next hour, however, it appeared as
if the House would finally be featured. Congressional correspondent Bob Kur, on the south side of the Capitol building,
reported the overall results. He chose four individual House
contests to expand upon. One was a contest in Iowa's 6th Congressional District in which Fred Grandy, the character known
as "Gopher" on the TV series *The Loveboat*, was elected. The
second was in Georgia's 4th Congressional District where
Democrat Ben Jones, who played the character "Cooter" in the
TV car-chase series *The Dukes of Hazzard*, was defeated by Republican Pat Swindall. Jones beat Swindall in a rematch in
1988 after Swindall was indicted for lying to a federal grand
jury. The combination of celebrity and scandal made the 1988
race in the 4th District newsworthy again. Two other contests

merited specific mention: Kentucky's 4th, where former Detroit and Philadelphia ace pitcher Jim Bunning had won as a Republican, and Maryland's 4th, where former Atlanta Hawks and Washington Capitols basketball star Tom McMillen was winning as a Democrat.

But the first half of the second hour of *Today* was not to be without its interview with a newly elected member of the House. The choice to represent the House was not Speaker-presumptive Jim Wright or even an up-and-coming backbencher who had served a few terms. It was, rather, Joseph Kennedy II, who symbolized the coming of age of another political generation of Kennedys rather than anything notable about the House of Representatives itself. In the aftermath of the 1988 congressional elections, the young Kennedy again provided one of the few stories in the popular media about a House member. Representative Kennedy, reportedly "bored" with his work on the Banking Committee, had enlisted the aid of his uncle, Senator Edward M. Kennedy, to secure a seat on the House Appropriations Committee. This senatorial interference was promptly rebuffed and the appropriations seat went to Representative Chester Atkins (D-Mass.).[3]

So it is with the House and Senate. Senators who may possess little more than a certificate of election receive the attention that House members can earn only if they have an almost freakish quality. To be noticed in the Senate does not, to be sure, come about simply because you happen to be a senator, but to rise above the huddled and undifferentiated masses of the House may require traits that are less political than theatrical.

Richard F. Fenno has spoken of an "all-encompassing pro-senator bias on the part of the media."[4] While this verdict was meant to apply to the greater interest on the part of the local media in Senate campaigns over House campaigns, the same conclusion could be reached about coverage in Washington, although perhaps less categorically.

The percentage of legislators mentioned on the major networks' nightly news programs shows a pattern that consistently and heavily favors the Senate over the House. Data on the percentage of House and Senate members mentioned on these programs at least once in the course of a year were computed over a fourteen-year period beginning in 1969. In the average year over that period 89 percent of the total membership of the Senate would be mentioned at least on the nightly network news but only 37 percent of the House membership. The best year for the House was 1981 when 55 percent of its membership received at least one mention. That same year, 99 percent of all senators made an appearance on the news shows—the only uncovered senator being Hawaii Democrat Spark Matsunaga.[5]

One reason for a greater attentiveness to the work of the Senate on the part of the Capitol Hill press corps is already familiar to us: The size difference between the House and Senate favors the Senate. "It is easier and faster," Stephen Hess writes, "to build a coherent story with a smaller cast of characters. The House of Representatives is too much like *War and Peace;* the Senate is more on the scale of *Crime and Punishment.* "[6] The single notable exception to the media's preference for Senate stories came in the 1994 election, when both House and Senate were captured by the Republicans. Because the Senate had twice switched hands in the 1980s, the turnover there was less of a story than the Republicans' majority in the House, which had been Democratic since the election of 1954.

Factors that derive from the size of the legislative body seem to explain much of what journalists find fascinating in the Senate. One obvious appeal of the senator over a House member is that it requires fewer of them to stand out above the crowd. For one thing, the crowd is smaller, which means that journalists find it easier to get a sense of the identities of and relationships among 100 members rather than 435.

In practical terms, however, journalists are not even really dealing with a cast of 435 and a cast of 100. A compilation of the number of times senators were mentioned on network television evening news programs in 1981–1982 showed that roughly a half dozen senators were mentioned 100 or more times during the course of the year and another half dozen were mentioned three times or less. Indeed, the number of senators mentioned fifty or more times was only eighteen. That means that 72 percent of the membership was mentioned less than once a week.[7]

Christopher Matthews, press secretary to former Speaker Thomas P. O'Neill and now host of the MSNBC and CNBC program *Hardball*, made much the same observation about the House. "The House is like your senior year in high school," Matthews said. "You look in the yearbook and it's always the same people who are getting letters for track, starring in the school play, and getting elected to the National Honor Society. The rest of them are a bunch of nobodies."

Journalists also feel that the compactness of the Senate and the smaller cast of characters make it easier to sort out the players. Ann Compton, who covered the House for ABC television news, made this point:

It's easier to go after some identifiable name [to interview] and the Senate is just a smaller kettle of fish. It's easier to cover the jockeyings of a hundred members, but really you end up covering only thirty or forty. And that thirty or forty you really pay attention to on a regular basis consists primarily of chairmen and ranking minority members.

While stating a general preference for the manageability of the Senate for reporters, Compton raised an important qualification to the size advantage enjoyed by the Senate in the eyes of journalists: the number of definitive sources in the House may not be much larger than that in the Senate.

Linda Wertheimer, a congressional correspondent for National Public Radio, asserted flatly, "As a practical matter it's not any more difficult to cover the House than the Senate. In the House you need to know about fifty people well and sort of have an idea of who's who on an issue."

Journalists looking for a congressional spokesperson on an issue do appear to be drawn to those who can be identified as experts. "The national media need specialists; when they choose which senator to interview, it is often exactly because the senator can be counted on to be recognized as an expert."[8]

Stephen Hess established in his study of which senators receive the greatest media attention that journalists take the very logical step of going to those in the Senate whose leadership role or committee assignment gives them a plausible claim on expertise. But, as we have seen, the media appear to show a more generalized preference for senators over House members that seems not to be directly associated with expertise. Stated more bluntly, it is more likely that just any old senator will appear on the evening news than that any random House member will be interviewed. What does this generalized preference reflect? One possibility is that senators are deemed to be more knowledgeable and authoritative than House members.

This interpretation was rejected by every journalist I interviewed. Typical was the response of Associated Press correspondent Karen Ball who asserted, "In the House, these guys are specialists on things they really want to be specialists on. Therefore, they get very deeply involved in something. But in the Senate, those guys have to have an opinion on everything and sort of act like they know everything."

It does not take much skill reading between the lines to find that Ball may even prefer to cover the House. Indeed, there is a generalized pattern of preference among both print and TV and radio reporters that, from a working journalist's viewpoint, the House assignment is more fulfilling and simply more fun. As Karen Tumulty of *Time* magazine explained: "I vastly prefer covering the House. The specialization makes it in a lot of ways easier to cover because you have a very clear idea of who you go to on what. The House members are far more accessible and on any given day you can get immediately a far broader range of opinion."

But there seems to be no strong connection between the satisfaction that journalists experience in covering the House and any sense that House members have a clear expertise advantage. Moreover, despite this preference for the House on the part of the working press, the amount of coverage on newspaper front pages and evening news programs continues to show a pro-Senate bias.

IF JOURNALISTS LIKE THE HOUSE SO MUCH, WHY DO WE
SEE SO MUCH OF SENATORS?

Considering first the conditions inside Congress that give rise to the media preference for senators, there is the manner in which the committee assignments systems of the House and Senate operate. As we've seen, the average House member is assigned to a single major committee while senators serve on three or more major committees. Any given senator, then, is better situated to speak out on a range of issues than is the typical House member because of the breadth and diversity of committee assignments in the Senate. If it is true that journalists seek out spokespersons who have at least the appearance of expertise, then one result would be that senators would be called upon by reporters more readily simply because the diversity of their committee assignments gives them some claim on familiarity in more areas.

A good example of a senator being placed where a reporter might want to reach was Daniel Patrick Moynihan of New York, who served as chairman of the Finance Committee and also on the Foreign Relations Committee and the Environment and Public Works Committee. Theoretically, then, in a single day he could be called upon to air his views on health care reform, the situation in Bosnia, and the toxic waste cleanup program. In contrast, three of Moynihan's House colleagues from New York served only on Ways and Means, the House committee that is the counterpart to Moynihan's Finance Committee. So while they might have been sought out for their expertise on health care matters, it would have been unlikely that a reporter would have sought them out for interviews on foreign policy or the environment. Here again, the Senate's small size and the correspondingly broad range of committee responsibilities that senators are given works in its favor on media coverage.

There is also the possibility, of course, that Senator Moynihan was being interviewed because he was Senator Moynihan and that his visibility as a former UN ambassador, sociologist, and social critic had more news value than his detailed knowledge on a particular topic.

That possibility points to another characteristic of the Senate that causes its members to be more mediaworthy: those who come to the Senate with reputations already established in other fields.

People with established star quality in other professions have tended to run first for the Senate rather than the House. A glance at the 106th Congress reveals a considerable number of people whose renown antedates their Senate service and whose celebrity was helpful in winning one of the 100 seats in the smaller chamber.

Beginning at the "B"s with Kentucky Republican Jim Bunning, we see a former Philadelphia Phillies and Detroit Tigers pitcher who came to the Senate from the House in 1998. Further into the alphabet is Senator Edward M. Kennedy, sole surviving brother of President John F. Kennedy and Senator Robert Kennedy. He is followed closely by presidential candidate John McCain, war hero who was elected as an Arizona Republican in 1986. Virginia boasts two senators associated with famous women: John Warner, a Republican, who was once married to actress Elizabeth Taylor, and Charles S. Robb, married to the daughter of the late president Lyndon B. Johnson. Tennessee Republican Fred Thompson had served as counsel on the well-televised Watergate hearings in 1973–74, but is perhaps best known for his roles in movies such as *Cape Fear*, in which he played opposite Robert DeNiro, and *The Hunt for Red October*.

Although he enjoyed a regional reputation as a talk-show host, North Carolina Republican Jesse Helms became the most prominent spokesman for ultra-conservative causes through his Senate service. Hess lists him as the fifth most-mentioned senator in the 1981–1982 period and puts Helms, Moynihan, and Kennedy in a category he designates as "originals"—"from the reporters' perspective they are the most fun to write about."[9]

Does the House have originals? It does, but not in such relative profusion. There is the irrepressible Representative James A. Traficant, Jr., of Ohio who announced publicly that the president could "shove his veto pen up his deficit." There is the low-keyed Speaker, Dennis Hastert, and the smooth, articulate Democratic leader, Dick Gephardt of Missouri. As with the Senate, journalists of both the pencil and the camera turn to leaders and experts for their news stories.[10] The House, however, has so many formal leaders and experts that they outnumber the entire membership of the Senate.

There are roughly 150 committees and subcommittees in the House. While chairmen of full committees often chair one of its subcommittees, that still leaves more than 100 people who can call themselves "Mr. Chairman" or "Madame Chairwoman." Those 100 people do not even include the party leaders on both sides of the partisan aisle. Spokesmanship, then, is relatively devalued in the House in terms of both its profusion and its narrowness of focus compared to a Senate in which far fewer people with much broader responsibilities are available for interviews.

Among national reporters, particularly those associated with newspapers, the size difference comes down to a difference in access to the individual: House members are generally accessible to both print and electronic media. Senators will usually be readily available only to correspondents from the major networks, and for one to grant an immediate interview to a reporter from even the most prestigious newspaper is not an automatic occurrence. Steven V. Roberts, who covered both the House and the Senate for the *New York Times,* contrasted the two chambers. Reflecting first on the prominence of staff—a factor we have already noted—Roberts observed:

Senators have their Praetorian guard around them, squads of press secretaries. Sometimes, it takes two or three days to get an appointment with a senator. It takes about an hour to get an appointment with a House member if he doesn't actually pick up the phone immediately when you call.

In fact, part of the problem with the House is beating people off. You get calls from House members' press secretaries saying, "Don't you want to talk to my boss?" You get enough of them and you say, "All right, all right, I'll talk to your boss."

THE PRO-SENATE BIAS OF EDITORS AND PRODUCERS

It would be an unwarranted conclusion, however, to assert that reporters simply prefer senators over House members as spokespersons and subjects for interviews. Indeed, the preference that some reporters show for the House hints at a more complicated explanation for the greater prominence of senators in the media, most notably in television news. The complication is that the TV reporters in front of the camera or behind the pencil are not the final word as to which story is broadcast or printed. Newspaper editors and television producers are normally the ultimate authority. Reporters from all media insisted that the preference for Senate stories over House stories among the reporters was not clear-cut, but that among editors and producers, who decide which story the public will see, the senatorial story usually wins hands down. Radio reporter Linda Wertheimer reflected the opinion of the overwhelming majority of journalists interviewed when she asserted:

The Senate is more attractive to editors and producers, certainly. . . . In the House you don't have a lot of big-picture guys. Members of the House don't wake up the morning after the election and understand that they are in the direct line of succession to the presidency, as senators do.

Knowing that a story featuring a senator or with a Senate dateline is more likely to appear on the evening news or on the front page might well incline reporters to offer a senatorial story to an editor or producer. This pressure is probably somewhat greater on television reporters than on newspaper journalists. A newspaperman argued that television reporters are aware of the pro-Senate bias on the part of their producers and act accordingly.

The whole goal of TV network reporters is to get on TV yourself. Phil Jones [formerly congressional correspondent for CBS Evening News] wants to be seen and say, "Hi, I'm Phil Jones," and at the end say, "This is Phil Jones at the Senate." That's their bread and butter and determines their salary. If a producer likes Senate tape better than House tape and you need to please the producer, you'll be inclined to do the story with senators.

Although Helen Dewar, who covers Capitol Hill for the *Washington Post* prefers covering the Senate because, as she puts it, "The Senate is good theater if you have an appreciation for odd things," she concedes that the House is "more alive, more vibrant, more right out in the open and in your face." She agrees with those journalists who say that their editors and producers prefer stories with Senate datelines, but she says of the Senate, "It drives editors nuts. They call me up in the press gallery and they say, 'When are they going to vote?' And I'll say, 'Do you want the long version or the short version?' "

Among editorial decision makers in journalism, then, there is also a tendency to favor the Senate. While reporters may not share in this preference, they appear to defer to it. In those news organizations that assign one individual to cover the House and another to cover the Senate, the Senate assignment is usually clearly the more highly prized. Richard Benedetto of *USA Today* stated flatly, "For a journalist to be transferred from covering the House to covering the Senate would be regarded as a promotion in any news organization with which I'm familiar."

DO PRINT REPORTERS LOVE THE HOUSE
WHILE CAMERA JOURNALISTS FAVOR THE SENATE?

Some journalists argue that print reporters favor the House and television reporters prefer the Senate. This argument tends to be made by print journalists, one of whom is Thomas Edsall of the *Washington Post.*

House members are much more accessible to the print media. There's a House lobby right behind the chamber and you can hang out there. I used to find that you could get more of a feel for what was going on just hanging out there. As the members came in to vote, you'd grab the guy. They're much more casual than in the Senate. There is no place in the Senate where only the press and members were allowed. You'd have to go into the Mansfield Room adjacent to the chamber with all the lobbyists and get a doorkeeper to go in there and get the senator you want to talk to. And, of course, he's got to agree to come out. It's a real pain.

Access to leaders is even more important than access to rank-and-file members of the House and Senate from the journalists' point of view, and there had been a distinct preference among print journalists for the House style of leadership press conference over that of the Senate, especially after the voluble Newt Gingrich became Speaker in 1995. Changes in the House Republican leadership after the 1998 election cast some less compelling figures into the top positions in the party. As Helen Dewar of the *Washington Post* recalled: "It was fun covering Gingrich if you could figure out what he was saying all the time. [Dennis] Hastert is kind of soft-spoken and indirect. He doesn't hold many press conferences." Dewar believes that reporters' preferences for covering congressional leaders depends on the personalities of the top people and their accessibility rather than on an arbitrary standard that gives one house precedence over the other. Indeed, in 1999, she observed that "[Senate Majority leader Trent] Lott tends to make more news than they do at House press conferences. . . . You can get him a lot. It's fairly easy access. You just go downstairs and wait outside his office."

Charles Green of the Knight-Ridder papers points out that one reason print reporters tended to favor the House is that television cameras are not normally allowed in the Speaker's lobby. This gives the press an advantage over television and provides a kind of crossroads for journalists and members for which no parallel exists in the Senate.

If print reporters like to cover the House, House members prefer to talk to newspaper people than to television correspondents, according to a survey of press secretaries who work for House members. One reason is that it is simply more difficult to get on television than to have a story written—especially in a local paper. The same may also be true of Senate secretaries for the same reason—a staff member such as a press secretary might speak on behalf of a senator to a print reporter and be quoted in a newspaper or news magazine as an authoritative source in the senator's office. Television reporters, however, want the actual senator and will rarely if ever use footage of a staff member.[11] But the fact that their press secretaries prefer to interact with print reporters is not the same as saying that senators themselves choose print over television. They make themselves available to television reporters in the Senate TV gallery when a news story is breaking that might require senatorial comment. Seated in front of what one television reporter called "the most famous row of books in America" in the Senate's radio and TV gallery, those senators who have the knack for the quick, pithy comment that comes across well on a "sound bite" luxuriate in the national visibility they achieve.[12]

While print reporters praise the access and openness of the House and its leaders, there appears to be no systematic difference as to which house is preferred by print and television reporters that might enable us to say, for example, that print journalists favor the House and television reporters the Senate. The reason for this is an apparent distinction in the minds of journalists between the "play" a story receives and the professional satisfaction the journalist receives. Reporters, as we have heard, want to file stories that are printed or broadcast and producers seem to favor Senate stories over House stories, all things being equal. This does not mean, however, that reporters necessarily favor the Senate. They are making a pragmatic judgment as to what is likely to get them on page one or a story on the evening news. Charles Green of Knight-Ridder reflected this set of calculations when he indicated a preference for covering the Senate in terms of getting stories published, "but in terms of having a more interesting assignment," said Green, "it would certainly be the House."

TELEVISION IN CONGRESS:
IS THE HOUSE'S MEDIA RIDE OVER?

The media advantage that the Senate had enjoyed in modern times seemed to be jeopardized in 1979 when the House authorized live coverage of its floor proceedings. While the number of people who became faithful viewers of the C-SPAN coverage of the House was not large, videotapes of speeches and debates began to be used extensively by the network news programs. Since there were no television cameras permitted on the floor of the Senate—the only television allowed being the occasional coverage of hearings—the House proceedings became the only game in town until 1986, when Senate television coverage began.

The immediate advantage enjoyed by the House in permitting coverage of floor proceedings can best be explained by this fact: For more than 190 years the public could learn of the normal activities of Congress only after they had occurred. Here was a window on Congress showing the House conducting its business for all to see. From the perspective of the television networks, moreover, the House was making it incredibly easy for them to get footage of Congress in action. By taping House proceedings from C-SPAN, stations had an ample supply of fresh, vivid material available without having to dispatch correspondents or camera crews.

There is no question that the House gained an immediate advantage over the Senate in the amount of broadcast-worthy material it was generating. The euphoria within the House was notable, perhaps even excessive. Former Speaker of the House Thomas P. "Tip" O'Neill boasted in his memoirs:

Thanks to television, the House of Representatives is now recognized as the dominant branch of Congress. In 1986, the Senate brought in TV cameras as well. But senators ramble on for hours, whereas our members can speak for only five minutes. . . . Now that the Senate is on television, the prestige of the House should continue to increase.[13]

The optimism of the former Speaker was understandable but probably unwarranted. Reporters are not attracted solely by the brevity or closely reasoned quality of a speech; they are also interested in who says it and how it is said. If editors and producers are convinced that something is said better by a senator because of the star qualities they associate with the Senate, then the Senate will continue to receive the bulk of attention from the media, particularly television.

There is a political factor that also needs to be considered in assessing the advantage the House has been said to have gained from the first use of television: The onset of the TV age in the House coincided closely with the political upheaval of 1980, which saw the White House fall to the Republicans and the Senate captured by that party for the first time in a quarter century. The House Democrats were, quite simply, the only Democratic game in town.

Where would a journalist turn for a Democratic opinion? Some turned to spokespersons from the Democratic National Committee, but most regarded the House as the locus of the loyal opposition in the years 1981 through 1986. By being Democratic in a federal system dominated by the Republicans, the House received an institutional boost from journalists eager to ascertain Democratic positions.

The principal threat to the media hegemony of the Senate is the increase in the number of news-gathering organizations covering Congress. The development of satellite technology has enabled local TV stations that were formerly at the mercy of the networks to transmit their own coverage directly from Capitol Hill. More stations with the capacity to cover Congress means an escalation in the demand for spokespersons. With only 100 spokespersons, the Senate may not be able to provide TV producers with the high-profile senators they want for their sound bites and those producers may settle for the less luminous stars of the House.

That development will please the reporters to whom I spoke who were such strong partisans of the House of Representatives. One such journalist is Cokie Roberts. When I pointed out to her that her preference for covering the House might be explained by her family history—her father, the late Hale Boggs of Louisiana, had served as Majority Leader and her mother, Lindy Boggs, had been a Democratic member from Louisiana—she acknowledged the bias. "I was always amazed as I was growing up that there were people who were prejudiced against other people. In our home, we were raised with only two prejudices: against Republicans and senators."

The Legislative Stages: A View from the Lobby

While there is no accurate count of the number of people engaged in lobbying in Washington, more than 10,000 organizations have a presence in the nation's capital. Some of them occupy whole buildings or floors of buildings. Some operate out of small, crowded offices with volunteer staffs, and others may be represented by a single attorney in a large, prestigious law firm. The people who represent these groups may have representatives working on Capitol Hill almost continuously while Congress is in session; others may have all their lobbying accomplished in a single visit.

Organizations that lobby Congress fall into two large categories: membership organizations and nonmembership organizations. The first group contains "peak business associations" such as the National Association of Manufacturers and the U.S. Chamber of Commerce that are federations of thousands of member businesses and industries and advance the cause of business in the most general sense. Then there are trade associations that lobby for individual industries, from manufacturers of formaldehyde foam to the canners of tuna fish. There are labor unions, farm groups, and professional associations (such as the American Medical Association), as well as advocacy groups like the National Organization for Women. Nonmembership organizations consist primarily of individual corporations such as the Ford Motor Company, which maintains a large Washington office. But the nonmembership category would also include Stanford University and CBS.[14] There are also individuals such as the winemakers Ernest and Julio Gallo who hired a lobbyist to press for a provision in the 1986 tax reform law enabling them to keep the company in the family.

Some groups and individuals are represented by people known cynically as "hired guns," lawyers and public relations specialists who may be their sole Washington representatives or augment their permanent office staffs.

It can be taken as a general principle that the interests lobbyists represent will determine, in large measure, who they deal with in Congress. Congress is specialized and so are lobbyists. Almost no one lobbies "Congress" on a routine basis. Most lobbyists, especially if they represent a single corporation or industry, will ultimately become familiar with one group of senators and members and their staff and know little about others.

A lobbyist who represents a big pharmaceutical firm may deal principally with the House Commerce Committee and the Senate Health, Education, Labor and Pensions, and Environment and Public Works Committees, and never have anything to do with the Armed Services Committees of either house or the two panels that deal with foreign relations. In contrast, the lobbyist for a pro-Israel group may be aware of the players on the House Judiciary Committee but will certainly know a great deal more about the House Foreign Affairs Committee and the Senate Foreign Relations Committee.

The differences between lobbying in the House and in the Senate are less obvious. On the basis of interviews with a dozen lobbyists, these differences come down to two factors that, as already noted, are closely associated: the distinctive constitutional responsibilities of each house, and the size difference that produces a very different set of internal rules and procedures for each chamber and affects the prominence of individual members, the degree of specialization in either chamber, and the role of staff members. It is not always easy to disentangle these two factors. The founding fathers, while they did not stipulate that the Senate be less than a quarter the size of the House, did envision a more compact chamber, and the Senate went on to adopt rules appropriate to that chamber's compactness.

But size alone does not define the difference. For example, the Constitution accords to the Senate exclusive authority to confirm presidential nominations of high governmental officials, including ambassadors, and vests in the Senate the sole power to advise and consent in the ratification of treaties. The framers wanted the Senate, as the body in which all states had equal representation, to be the repository of the pre-constitutional sovereignty of the states, albeit in a circumscribed form.[15] The Senate, accordingly, has normally been the principal antagonist to the president on foreign policy and the focus of attention in clashes over the conduct of U.S. diplomacy.

The difference between the House and Senate from the perspective of the dozen lobbyists interviewed could be summed up in two terms: size and scope. The size of the Senate is smaller and the scope of its members, by reason of their chamber's size and its constitutional role, is broader. The House is larger and the scope of its members, by reason of this larger size, is narrower but also better defined. From these differences in size and scope emerge five subsidiary distinctions that lobbyists make: (1) the big picture versus the small picture; (2) direct contact versus staff contact; (3) designer lobbying versus mass-market lobbying; (4) House champions versus Senate champions; and (5) predictability versus unpredictability.

When asking lobbyists about bicameral differences one must always bear in mind that many of them worked either as congressional staff or even as members and senators before they took up the lobbying trade. They have residual loyalties to their old chamber and this tends to influence their views. Nonetheless, there appeared to be a general feeling among the lobbyists that the level at which issues were discussed was loftier when they were dealing with senators. Some lobbyists attributed it to the people attracted to the Senate. As a lobbyist with a Senate background now working in the foreign policy field said, "The policy-oriented people come to the Senate."

What this means in practice for the lobbyist is that he or she must make a presentation to a senator in terms that underscore the broader implications of the issue they are pressing. A civil rights lobbyist said, "When you want to persuade a senator to do what you want him to do, most likely you are going to have to argue in loftier terms than you would with a House member . . . what's in the national interest or what the profound consequences of this legislation may be. In the House you get into the nitty-gritty with more detail."

Supporting the argument that the big picture must be drawn for senators but that technicalities are the stuff of House members is the notion shared by several lobbyists that senators disdain those of their colleagues who relish detail work.

Some lobbyists confessed that they ask House members to do things for them that they would be hesitant to request of a senator. A member of a prominent Washington lobbying firm enlisted the help of a House member to block an amendment that would have been financially damaging to one of his clients. "I don't think I would have asked a senator to do this. It was a little bit esoteric."

Then, reflecting on what he would have done had this timely intervention of his friendly House member not killed the amendment, he mused: "I probably would have found a senator and argued to him the broader public policy reasons as to why the amendment was bad."

It would probably be too strong to say that lobbyists see certain activities as "senators-only" work and other categories as proper for House members; however, distinctions are made not only as to the kind of issue a senator might be better activated on and the issue better pushed by a member but as to the manner in which the same issue should be "pitched" to a senator or a member. One gets the feeling in talking to lobbyists that certain technical or narrowly drawn issues are seen as "beneath" senators unless they can be ornamented with high-level implications.

I mentioned this senatorial association with high-level policy questions in the previous chapter on the House and Senate electoral environments and why senators seem more vulnerable politically. It appears that at least two sets of political actors associate senators more than members with the highest-level policy questions: lobbyists and senators themselves. As George McGovern recalled: "You see it on the floor debates and in the committees. There are more appeals to history and less to the immediate claims and current passions."

Lobbyists interested in more parochial concerns or pressing issues not susceptible to appeals to the national interest tend to have less of a sense of this distinction. A lobbyist for a pharmaceutical firm told me:

OSHA [Occupational Safety and Health Administration] is a national issue. It applies to everybody. I let the [pharmaceutical trade association] or the U.S. Chamber of Commerce lobbyists deal with that. I'll tell a senator how many of our employees are in his state and localize the issue. So I don't deal in grand issues. I let other people do that.

What are the reasons most lobbyists who are in a position to do so aim their pitches to senators on a loftier trajectory? One reason supplied by lobbyists and senators alike is that senators have a perception of themselves as being more concerned with high-level policy questions and that lobbyists have learned to appeal to them on a level different from that used with House members. Representing states, senators are, *a fortiori,* more broad-gauged in their concerns than members, but the difference seems to be more one of kind than simply of degree.

Most lobbyists felt that senators were more immune from petty political pressures and consequently independent-minded. The diversity of interests they represent renders them less vulnerable to the types of pressures that might intimidate a House member, according to this view. A lobbyist for a trade association observed, "It's a lot easier for a senator to say no to his real estate lobby. A senator is more likely to have people on both sides of an issue. They don't run so often and can balance off interests over a broader period of time."

This view is not shared by all lobbyists. A lobbyist with one of Washington's most influential firms felt that senators were much more subject to cross-pressures: "They've got to weigh the competing interests. You always want to tell the people you're lobbying what the downsides are, but if you're dealing with a senator from a major state, the chances of his having downsides are much greater." This was distinctly a minority position among lobbyists. Most would agree with Donald Matthews that while some lobbies in a senator's state can inflict mortal damage for a wrong vote, "Senate terms are long and constituencies large and heterogeneous [and] senators are seldom without discretion."[16]

Those lobbyists who saw senators as more insulated from pressure by reason of the diversity of interests in their states and the length of their term were the ones most likely to place their appeals to senators on a loftier plane. We have already seen evidence in Chapter 4 that the tendency of some senators to identify themselves with large and important issues may subject them to greater political peril than House members who emphasize service to constituents. Senators are also mindful that the larger statewide constituency encompasses a greater variety of interests and political challenges. But some, at least, appear to see the larger environment as a test of their political creativity and the Senate as a place to deal with issues of a more transcendent nature.

The overwhelming majority of lobbyists felt that senators had more political "wiggle room" than House members. Typical of the comments on the differences in the scope of interests was one from the head of a trade association, who said, "House guys operate under a very narrow window politically." Another, the head lobbyist of a major industrial conglomerate, commented: "Senators act as brokers for a fairly diverse set of interests, but an awful lot of these House guys come from constituencies where they have to articulate a pretty narrow set of demands."

Aside from the two lobbyists who felt that senators were often more constrained politically because of the greater likelihood of conflict between different interests in their states, the consensus was that senators can be less parochial, more nationally minded, and, most significant from a lobbyist's perspective, bolder.

But there is another persuasive, if less noble, explanation for the more general and macropolitical appeals that lobbyists often feel they must employ with senators: Senators know less than House members.

More often than not they don't know what the hell you're talking about. Yeah, you need to talk in concepts—what's good for America—but I don't think that's because they have any deeper feelings for America than the guys in the House. I think it's just because they don't know the details as well. You can't talk to them any other way.

This assertion by a lobbyist for a major trade association is a variant of statements made by almost all the lobbyists interviewed.

Some lobbyists have horror stories about the lack of specific knowledge senators have of amendments that they themselves have introduced. One Washington representative of a trade association in the health field told of a meeting with a off174 HOUSE AND SENATE

Republican senator from an eastern state. The senator's state was home to a large number of health product firms. The senator had introduced an amendment aimed at helping the elderly to secure low-cost medicines but the measure also contained a provision that the lobbyist saw as damaging to the industries he represented. The senator assured the lobbyist, "Look, I want to do what I can for the elderly on this amendment, but I certainly wouldn't want to do anything that's going to hurt your industry and I know there's nothing in my proposal that would do that." At that point, according to the lobbyist, the senator paused and looked imploringly at his staff and asked, "There's nothing like that in my amendment, is there?" Somewhat abashedly his administrative assistant said that there was indeed such a formula in the amendment that would impose restrictions on the industry.

Lobbyists were unanimous in asserting, however, that even when a senator was personally uninformed about the details of legislation—even his or her own—this did not imply that the senator could not quickly get the information from those who had it at their fingertips: the senator's staff. Senate staff enables senators to operate at a more cosmic policy level but also, by its very quality and abundance, forces them to be even more generalized and superficial in their grasp of policy.

DIRECT CONTACT VERSUS STAFF CONTACT

One area of House-Senate differences that every lobbyist cited was that personal contact with members was typical in dealing with the House. In the Senate, one-on-one meetings with senators were unusual. Lobbyist-staff encounters were the norm in the Senate and while most lobbyists' meetings on the House side were also with staff, there was a more routine and regular quality to lobbyists' contacts with House members.

One lobbyist reflected, "I had been a Senate denizen all my years of working on the Hill, but the ease of access to House members is one of those things that has come as a revelation to me. The general rule on the Senate side is that you usually have to be satisfied with seeing staff."

But lobbyists in general feel more confident dealing with Senate staff than with House staff. A lobbyist for a civil rights group said, "Senate staff really is in a way junior senators." Another lobbyist, this one from a major pharmaceutical firm, said, "Senate staff know pretty much what their bosses want. They speak with a degree of authority. It's much more a mixed bag on the House side."

The lobbyists perceive Senate staff as having considerable authority. A lobbyist for a major trade association said bluntly, "If your arguments convince the Senate staffer, you've convinced the senator. You don't have to see him." Indeed, in terms of a lobbyist's negotiations with a congressional office, it is typically the case that agreements can, in effect, be clinched with Senate staff. The senator may be brought in at the penultimate stage for what is almost a formalistic or ceremonial meeting with the lobbyist if indeed a meeting is required at all. House members become personally involved at a much earlier stage and usually vest their staff with more restricted negotiating authority.

Lobbyists who represent corporations or trade associations identify a kind of protocol involving senators that is not widespread on the House side. It is a ritual akin to those we associate with international summit conferences, whereby extensive lower level staff work on both sides precedes a ceremonial signing of documents by presidents and prime ministers.

Senatorial summitry operates in the following fashion: Lobbyists make contacts with Senate offices to persuade the senator to sponsor or kill an amendment or bill, make a statement on the floor, help a lobbyist's client with the bureaucracy, or any one of a number of actions senators are called upon to perform. Negotiations proceed which, depending on the size and complexity of the lobbying group, may involve those people who work the Hill for an interest group. These lobbyists may not be the executives who head trade associations, or the senior partners in a law firm that lobbies, but often they too get involved personally.

When most of the detail work is disposed of by the Senate staff and their counterparts in the lobbying group, or if a problem develops with the senator, a new set of individuals enters the arena: the principals.

A lobbyist for a large industrial firm told me about his negotiations with the office of Edward M. Kennedy for the Massachusetts Democrat to introduce a bill of interest to the corporation. "The staff and I negotiated the bill," the lobbyist said. "Now that all the details are nailed down, we'll bring in Kennedy and [the CEO of the company] to shake hands."

Corporate and trade association lobbyists also agree with the blunt assessment made by a lobbyist for a trade association—you need a CEO to see a senator. What he meant was that if he needed to see a senator he would need someone of the stature of a chief executive officer of a corporation to underscore the importance of his concern. This does not mean that lobbyists, on their own, could not get access to the senator personally. Rather, it is that the deployment of a client who is deemed to be of equal rank to the senator is called for. This, however, should not be interpreted to mean that CEOs can see senators whenever they choose. More than one CEO has come to Washington with the expectation of a private meeting with a senator only to find himself one member of a larger audience or to have the meeting blown off completely by the senator.

DESIGNER AND MASS-MARKET LOBBYING

Lobbyists will often work House members (other than key chairmen of committees) as part of a group; this is almost never done with senators—the latter receive individual attention. The "wholesale," "mass-market" lobbying of groups of House members and the "retail" or "designer" lobbying of senators as individuals are products of the smaller size of the Senate and the vastly greater amount of personal influence enjoyed by the individual.

There are occasions, however, such as the vote on the North American Free Trade Agreement (NAFTA) in November, 1993, in which House members received highly individualized attention, even very junior members whose influence is quite limited.

The average member of the House can become influential in a variety of ways: by encouraging the consensus of those who serve with the member on a committee; by being an acknowledged power in a geographical bloc; by being an expert on House rules; or even by being a vote counter. All of these, however, involve getting large numbers of colleagues to line up behind you. Senators generally are seen as forces in their own right. Given the intense individualism in the Senate, it is unusual for senators to view themselves as part of a bloc. They do, however, look to colleagues to provide expertise, or political cover or innoculation on controversial issues. Sam Nunn of Georgia, for example, was the Senate's acknowledged expert on national defense, and there were few others like him in that body. In that capacity he not only gave informed judgments on military issues but could provide cover for a colleague who could point to the respected Georgia Democrat on a controversial issue and tell his constituents, "But Sam Nunn also voted for it." His vote against the use of military force against Iran in 1990 made it easier for other Democrats who opposed the war. Nunn's expertise was strengthened by his role as chairman of the Armed Services Committee. In the House, though, there are many more of these individuals whose influence extends beyond their own single vote.

As we have seen, moreover, House members are more apt to be part of social networks, sports groups, or informal socio-legislative groups than are senators. Lobbyists know that their jobs can be made somewhat easier by lobbying groups of members. Thomas A. Dine, who formerly served as director of the American-Israel Public Affairs Committee (AIPAC), the pro-Israel lobby in Washington, drew a distinction between the approach he takes with senators and the one he takes with House members.

The closest thing to a group of friends I know of in the Senate that's kind of intimate is [Jim] Sasser, [David] Pryor, [Dale] Bumpers, and [Don] Riegle. They sit together and they kid around a lot.

But in the House! This past week I was discussing strategy on the Foreign Aid Authorization Bill and some other matters at Larry Smith's house [Larry Smith, a House Democrat from Florida] and Larry had invited [Robert] Torricelli, Mel Levine, Gary Ackerman, Howard Berman, and myself and we all sat around and talked. That kind of discussion would never take place with senators.

I call on Howard Metzenbaum. I call on Bob Dole. One more thing—four members came to Larry Smith's house. No aides. If that meeting had taken place at a senator's home, if such a thing can be imagined, each one of them would have brought a staff person.

Lobbying in the House, then, would appear at first blush to be more cost effective. House members seem not to resent being dealt with in groups and the social dynamics of the House are conducive to group formation. But the picture is not so clear because of the size difference and the related differential in influence between senators and House members. As one lobbyist described the process of developing support for a measure, to achieve equivalence with a single senator "you've got to get a group of congressmen. You need lots of bodies in the House, but with five senators you've got a genuine national movement going." A single senator straying off the reservation can cause a lobbyist a bigger headache than the defection of a horde of House members. AIPAC's former director Thomas Dine recalled one such incident:

In 1984 there was an [anti-Israel] amendment by Nick Joe Rahall of West Virginia. He had thirty votes.

Since that vote I have not worried about that thirty. I know who they are. I've dealt with all thirty of them. They would all probably vote the same way again. But when we can get 390 votes, 410 votes, that thirty doesn't cause me to lose sleep.

But take the vote in October 1985 to delay the Jordan arms sale. The vote was 97–1, I think. Chris Dodd [Democratic senator from Connecticut] was that one vote and strictly on a procedural matter. I've been all over him ever since.

But Dine's issues were quite different from the vast majority of those dealt with by most lobbyists. His were highly visible, well-reported "big-ticket" items in a policy on which the Senate is regarded as preeminent. In like manner, every one of the lobbyists I interviewed who represented a corporation or a trade association spent at least some time lobbying the House Ways and Means Committee because of its dominant role in tax policy. These issues are usually highly technical.

Key House members such as chairs of standing committees can no more be lobbied *en masse* than senators, and the wholesale approach can only be used with relatively junior House members. Internet lobbyist Harris Miller made the following point: "If I were dealing with any issue near John Dingell's purview [John D. Dingell, D-Mich., ranking Democrat on the House Commerce Committee], which I do with some of the insurance issues, I'd ignore him at risk to my clients and myself. On immigration, I have to pay as much attention to [Kentucky Democratic representative Romano L.] Mazzoli and [Texas Democratic representative Kika] DeLa Garza as I do to senators like [Vermont Democrat Patrick] Leahy, Kennedy, and Biden."

There are interesting exceptions to the use of the designer approach with senators and the mass-marketing approach with House members. Kenneth Duberstein, the former White House lobbyist, recalled the 1982 tax bill, known by its acronym TEFRA (Tax Equity and Fiscal Responsibility Act), when House Republicans had deserted the White House and were not supporting the measure. Duberstein said, "It was going down the tubes and we lobbied that [in the House] as if it were a Senate vote. We went one-to-one. Most of the meetings the president had on TEFRA were bringing in the congressmen one-on-one to meet with the president. House Republicans— one-on-one—we used a Senate strategy to work in the House." The reason for this approach was the unusual closeness of the vote in the House.

On the critical trade issues of the 1990s such as NAFTA and the normalization of trade relations with China in 2000,

Senate passage was taken for granted, but White House lobbyists had to fight for every last House vote.

So while the general approach used by lobbyists is to go after groups—generally small groups—in the House and to approach senators as individuals, there are circumstances under
which a reversal of tactics is called for. Duberstein provided examples of the White House using group lobbying with senators
when time was an element and the administration feared it
would be barred from selling AWACs (airborne surveillance
planes) to Saudi Arabia in 1981. "We took the Senate and lobbied it like the House," recalled Duberstein. "We went to
groups—small groups of senators—and put them together."

While these exceptions are interesting and important, the
norm described by all lobbyists is that of using the mass-
marketing approach in the House and the designer style in the
Senate, except in the case of House committee chairmen, who
are given the same personal and undivided attention as senators. The nature of the issue being lobbied also dictates which
approach is likely to be most effective. Tax issues find lobbyists going one-on-one with House members as meticulously as
senators would be lobbied on major presidential nominations
requiring Senate approval or on issues in the foreign policy
area.

HOUSE CHAMPIONS VERSUS SENATE CHAMPIONS: WHO CARRIES YOUR WATER?

Lobbyists call upon House members and senators not only
to introduce, support, and kill bills and amendments but also to
champion their issues and even to rescue them. Is there any
general rule among lobbyists as to whether House members or
senators are more effective in "carrying water"?

Lobbyists found it somewhat easier to interest House members in taking on an issue because of the considerably greater
ease of access to these members. House members are also
likely to ask more probing questions of the lobbyist because,
as we have seen, their grasp of the intricacies of issues is gen-

erally better. For lobbyists, clearly, this can be a mixed blessing. And the advantage in getting a well-informed hearing from a House member is contrasted, by some lobbyists, with the greater amount of influence enjoyed by individual senators. A civil rights lobbyist noted, "If you can get a champion in the Senate you have a much greater possibility of success than if you did likewise in the House."

Most lobbyists felt uncomfortable making such a stark distinction on the question of whether to enlist a senator or House member, and all asserted that their decisions would be dictated by the nature of the issue involved. Nonetheless, a small majority of the lobbyists conceded that, all things being equal, they would prefer to be championed by a senator.

The question of whether or not the House member is more constrained than the senator in taking on an issue by virtue of the member's smaller number of committee assignments is one that divides the lobbyists fairly evenly. Lobbyist Jay Berman made the case that senators have more room to operate. "The senator can operate more effectively," said Berman, "because senators who want to be players and who have some jurisdictional responsibilities are going to have a greater opportunity to be players than House members who have comparable jurisdictional responsibilities."

Harris Miller took a different view. "In the House," Miller said, "with its greater dispersion of influence, almost anybody can get involved. You'll find a lot of different places to do things in the House, but in the Senate, because of deference and simply because of time constraints, it makes more sense to leave it to the chairman. It's difficult to get someone in the Senate to take on an issue when it's not at all within their area of expertise."

It seems debatable, from the lobbyist's point of view, whether the greater influence of individual senators and their larger number of committee assignments would make them better issue champions than House members with their greater ability to take on and comprehend new issues. The individual

senator certainly looms larger in the Senate than the average
House member does in the House, but the senator is also
strapped for time to concentrate on an issue, much less to expend the resources to take a lead on it.

Some recent research indicates that the breadth of Senate
committee assignments and the lack of constraint that comes
with membership on those panels enable senators to use their
committees as bases to champion issues more than is the case
with House members and their committees. But at the same
time, senators are picking and choosing more and more among
issues on which they are willing to take a leadership role. In
many instances they are passing on their discarded issues to
House members from their state.[17]

While tactical subtleties abound, it does seem that there is
a fairly clear set of advantages and disadvantages to using either a senator or a House member to take a leadership role on
an issue or even to embrace it in a less conspicuous way. The
calculation might run something like this for the lobbyist: A
senator is less likely than a House member to take up my cause
but in the more remote event that the senator does agree to
champion my issue, the vastly greater amount of personal influence and public visibility that senators can draw on can, in
competent hands, produce desired results.

A civil rights lobbyist interviewed in 1986 before the
Democrats recaptured the Senate from the Republicans mused
on who would be best to take up the issues he cared about.

The Senate clearly gets more attention from the media and the spotlight is more usually focused on individual senators and the Senate
as a body; therefore, you might want the Senate as a platform, but for
the last six years you have the Democrats and most of your champions controlling the House and they control the committees and subcommittees and the hearings.

But the civil rights lobbyist conceded that for the kinds of
issues that he pressed, the Senate was the place to go. He

shared this preference with the other "cause" lobbyists. These lobbyists for nonprofit organizations that are concerned with issues ranging from the Middle East to the environment to civil rights said that issues with national implications, as opposed to more detailed and technical legislation, were best pursued in the Senate. They seemed to feel that senators warm to these issues and that the media warm to senators. If you can infuse one of the senators with passion for your cause and convince him or her that great policy consequences can be read in it, the senator can be an estimable catalyst and attract national attention.

There is one additional calculation a lobbyist might want to make in framing a legislative strategy that involved a senator: Does the senator come from a state with a large population or a state with few people? Recent research suggests strongly that senators from big-population states tend to be more interested in policy questions and senators from sparsely populated states incline more to constituency politics and the securing of benefits for their states. Lobbyists can gain access to senators from less-populous states much more easily than they can get to senators from places like New York or California. With fewer and less complex state interests, the senators from small-population states simply have more flexibility.[18] Lobbyists also ease their access to members of Congress with campaign contributions. A single donation is likely to show up far more prominently on the contributors' list of a senator from a low-population state than it would be for a senator from a state that has many people seeking access.

WHICH HOUSE IS MORE PREDICTABLE?— THE VERDICT OF THE LOBBYISTS

Most lobbyists deal with a fairly constant set of players— both members and staff—on Capitol Hill. Much lobbying, moreover, takes place within the context of policy "subgovernments"—relatively small groups of lobbyists, members, staff, and bureaucrats who combine to routinely make policy in specialized and noncontroversial areas of which the press and public are generally oblivious.[19] The relationships between lobbyists for a particular industry or large corporation and members and senators whose states and districts are home to those interests are remarkably stable. A lobbyist for a firm in the entertainment business in Hollywood said, "If somebody is trying to stick it to us on the Appropriations Committee, we have a California guy on that committee. We have a California guy on Commerce and a California guy on Ways and Means." Lobbyists who represent a broad and changing group of clients find that their cast of characters is more varied, but even they work through members they already know to get access to members they know less well.

Even in this relatively stable environment, unpleasant surprises come up. Like the old adage of navy pilots that flying off a carrier is hours of boredom punctuated by moments of terror, even the orderly life of a lobbyist can be rocked by the unexpected. Where is the unexpected most likely to take place? The lobbyists interviewed came down squarely on the side of the Senate as the body with the most surprises.

And we have already observed the power of the individual senator to "break all the toys in the sandbox," to use John Culver's expression, meaning that leadership is less able to guide the Senate according to the kind of timetable that House leaders have come to rely on. A man who lobbies insurance interests reflected, "At the end of every year, there is a series of articles in the newspapers about how [former Senate Majority Leader Robert C.] Byrd really had things under control and moving right along, brought his Defense Authorization Bill up in May or late April and then the world crashed in around his ears. Yes, I'd say the Senate is more unpredictable."

Someone who lobbies on a much different issue—civil rights—had much the same assessment: "One person in the Senate can foul things up whether it's in the committee or on the floor. That's much harder to do on the House side. It's difficult to prepare adequately for a Senate lobbying campaign, to plan a strict timetable. You can come up with a relatively strict timetable that you'll meet most of the time in the House, but you have to give the Senate a lot of leeway." The chamber's unpredictability is so important a problem for senators that a pledge to impose discipline on the schedule was a major factor in the victory of Senator George Mitchell of Maine in the race for majority leader in 1988.

Issues, Interests, and Complexity in the Two Houses

Journalists and lobbyists, as we have seen, approach the House and Senate with somewhat different expectations of the two chambers and its members. From journalists—most notably newspaper editors and TV news producers—there is an expectation that senators are able to address themselves to a broader array of issues and somehow see the larger picture. Most lobbyists see senators as enjoying a latitude in their actions and being able to balance off interests in such a way as to allow more flexibility than that permitted House members. Lobbyists certainly appear to frame their appeals differently to those in the Senate and those in the House. At least some of this more general scope with its direct or indirect message of national implications may be a product of the need to adjust to senators' imperfect knowledge of details. However, some lobbyists do find that invoking the general good on the Senate side is at least a useful way to get the attention of a senator.

A tantalizing question is whether the pursuit of an interest is best pressed in the House or the Senate. While a great deal of that calculation, from a lobbyist's point of view, would have to do with such things as the nature of the issue, the quality of personal ties to a member or senator, or any number of other factors having to do with committee jurisdiction, it may be that some *kinds* of issues fare better in the Senate and other kinds fare better in the House for reasons stemming from the very nature of the two bodies.

Without question, the great flexibility of the decision-making process in the Senate puts senators "in a better position to further constituents' interests than representatives are. This too strengthens adversary democracy in the Senate relative to the House."[20] Senate rules enable a senator to take up an issue at almost any point in the legislative process and force consideration of it by the entire membership. The senator, moreover, need have no association with the committee that has jurisdiction over the issue. The House, with its Rules Committee acting as an arm of leadership and more of a determination role taken by committees, offers fewer opportunities for just any representative to champion just any issue.

But would a senator be the person to turn to if a lobbyist wanted a champion for a relatively minor issue or one with strictly local implications or one that affected few people? Given the size and complexity of their constituencies, the diffuseness of their committee responsibilities, and the image that they and others have of their proper role, a senator would probably not be the one to enlist to champion a highly localized issue affecting few people. This would apply less to senators from small-population states. The openness of the legislative process in the Senate certainly makes it easier for any given issue to be considered, but, as we have seen, senators do not promote any given issue. Indeed, "senators are most likely to use their influence on behalf of those with the resources to communicate their interests most strongly."[21]

While all senators are equal, all issues clearly are not equal. The Senate, accordingly, is probably a poor place to press issues that senators would regard as too narrow or too limited. But don't such issues deserve to be heard and considered? Is it not important that there be a place in the federal system that is receptive to issues that may affect few people or are essentially local in nature? One of the most thoughtful observers of Congress, former representative Richard Bolling of Missouri, declared, "The House is the only place that the little interests get heard." One might go even further and say that in the House all issues are created equal.

What seems to emerge is a picture of a Senate whose procedures promote the consideration of some kinds of interests. So while the Senate may be said to be adversary in its procedures in that it is a relatively open field for the championing of interests and issues at almost any point in the legislative process, the scope and substance of the interest seem to have an influence on whether or not senators will take it up. The tendency of the Senate to deal in larger aggregates than the House suggests that the Senate, while adversary in process, is unitary in outcome. The House, with its greater control over the legislative process by party leaders, is procedurally unitary. Its receptivity to small issues and its tendency to frame legislation that takes account of a myriad of small interests make it adversary in outcome. Every member of the House is assumed to have one or more interests sacred to his or her district and these interests are respected by all, because all House members have them. The legislative work products of the House bear the marks of this fragmentation.

NOTES

1. George Gallup, "Only 46% Can Name Congressional Representatives," *Washington Post,* Sunday, August 1, 1982.
2. Alan I. Abramowitz, "A Comparison of Voting for U.S. Senator and Representative in 1978," *American Political Science Review,* 74 (September 1980), pp. 633–640.
3. *New York Times,* Wednesday, December 7, 1988.
4. Fenno, *The United States Senate,* p. 11.
5. Timothy E. Cook, "Newsmakers, Lawmakers and Leaders: Who Gets on the Network News from Congress," paper presented at the annual meeting of the American Political Science Association, Washington, D.C., August 30–September 2, 1984, pp. 9–11.
6. Stephen Hess, *The Ultimate Insiders* (Washington, D.C.: The Brookings Institution, 1986), p. 91.
7. Ibid., p. 136.
8. Ibid., p. 37.

9. Stephen Hess, "Being Newsworthy," *Society,* 24 (Jan./Feb., 1987), p. 39.
10. Cook, op. cit., pp. 13–17.
11. Stephen Hess, "A Note on Senate Press Secretaries and Media Strategies," Brookings Discussion Papers in Governmental Studies (Washington, D.C.: The Brookings Institution, April 1987), pp. 18–19.
12. Larry Warren, "The Other Side of the Camera: A TV Reporter's Stint as a Congressional Aide," *PS,* 19 (Winter 1986), pp. 43–48.
13. Thomas P. O'Neill, with William Novak, *Man of the House* (New York: Random House, 1987), p. 290.
14. These categories are provided in Kay Lehman Schlozman and John T. Tierney, *Organized Interests and American Democracy* (New York: Harper and Row, 1986), pp. 38–51.
15. *The Federalist,* #62.
16. Donald R. Matthews, *U.S. Senators and Their World* (New York: Random House, 1960), p. 188.
17. Steven S. Smith, "Informal Leadership in the Senate: Opportunities, Resources, and Motivations," paper prepared for the Project on Congressional Leadership of the Everett McKinley Dirksen Congressional Center and the Congressional Research Service, September 30, 1987, pp. 4–10.
18. See Frances E. Lee and Bruce I. Oppenheimer, *Sizing Up the Senate* (Chicago: University of Chicago Press, 1999).
19. See Randall B. Ripley and Grace A. Franklin, *Congress, the Bureaucracy, and Public Policy,* 4th ed. (Chicago: Dorsey Press, 1987), pp. 6–10.
20. David J. Vogler and Sidney R. Waldman, *Congress and Democracy* (Washington, D.C.: Congressional Quarterly Press, 1985), p. 87.
21. Ibid.

6

Convergence, Divergence, and Persistence

Are the House and Senate Becoming More Alike?

"IN EVERY RESPECT 'Their High Mightiness, the Senate,' attracted less attention than the younger, popularly elected members of the House. . . . Although the ladies were permitted to sit on the Senate floor, and were restricted in the House to the galleries, they found their favorite orators in the lower chamber. Over in the House members have a great propensity to speak to the galleries and for the newspaper."[1] These observations on House-Senate differences made in the early years of the nineteenth century strike us as inconsistent with what we have learned about the characteristics of the two chambers from Chapters 2 through 5. We hear of a House esteemed for its oratory and its members making remarks in the hopes of being quoted by journalists while the "national graybeards" of the Senate "hold all wit and humor in abomination" and conduct "somniferous debates" before resolving "not to expend a few dollars."[2]

Despite the distinctive roles granted to the House and Senate by the Constitution, the characteristics of the two and their relationships to each other are not static, as we saw in Chapter 1. The House, which was less than three times the size of the Senate in 1789, is now more than four times its size, the ceiling of 435 having been imposed by statute in 1911. Three years later the Seventeenth Amendment was ratified giving the people the right to elect U.S. senators directly and stripping the state legislatures of the function. During World War I, the first limitation on debate in the Senate since the earliest days of the institution was imposed, Rule 22. It was modified in 1975 to ease somewhat the ability to muster a vote of cloture to limit the filibuster. The House authorized the televising of its floor debates in 1979 and seven years later the Senate duplicated the action. This recitation of just a few of the changes over the course of 200 years is meant only to suggest that relationships we think of as fixed and established are subject to alterations either by formal action or by custom and usage. The very committees that seem today such a natural component of a legislative body have no documentary basis in the Constitution any more than do political action committees or the practice of having the House initiate appropriations bills.

Changes in the institutional personalities of the two bodies can also take place over a much shorter time period than two centuries. Accordingly, it could be said in 1970, "The essence of the Senate is that it is a great forum, an echo chamber, a publicity machine. Thus 'passing bills,' which is central to the life of the House, is peripheral to the Senate."[3] Only sixteen years later, the appraisal was different: "There is unprecedented opportunity for individual [House] members to present themselves as analysts, commentators, polemicists, and specialists in quick reaction to events around the world."[4]

As for the House being an efficient legislative machine, even in an era of budget surpluses, there has been little in the way of raw materials to process. A cap on expenditures instituted in 1997 and the declared unwillingness by both parties to touch the Social Security surplus that for so many years had served as a kind of emergency fund, has limited large-scale initiatives by either the president or Congress. The most noteworthy accomplishment of Congress at the end of 1999 had been the repeal of a seventy-year-old banking law, if one does not count the impeachment of President Clinton. The appropriations bills eventually become law, but it is a system that involves very few members and frees the rest to pursue symbolic activities and constituent-oriented duties that solidify their ties to the voters and the interests they work to cultivate.[5]

Thus the behavior of members adapts to alterations in the way the legislative system operates, but the legislative system also responds to changes in members and their objectives. The House was changed profoundly by a reform movement that began in the late 1960s and reached its zenith after the election of the House class of 1974—a group of younger Democrats elected in reaction to the Watergate scandal. It was a movement whose magnitude had no parallel in the Senate. By the time this reform surge had spent its force, the institution had been changed profoundly. Power that had been held by two groups of senior members—party leaders such as the Speaker and roughly twenty chairmen of standing committees—was more broadly dispersed. Subcommittees, which had existed only at the sufferance of the chairmen of standing committees, were institutionalized. By the simple reform of the committee system, more House members were able to refer to themselves as "Mr. Chairman" or "Madame Chairwoman" and to participate actively in the legislative process. Those reforms and others made the House a different place, but they did not necessarily make it more like the Senate.

There has been a tendency to seize upon some changes whose long-term effects are by no means certain and suggest that they represent, or at least presage, vast and permanent changes in the essential character of the House and Senate with the cumulative effect of making them more alike.

After the Republicans became the majority party in the House in 1994, the new speaker, Newt Gingrich, assumed extraordinary powers that gave him unprecedented influence on the legislative process. The procedure for assigning Republican members to committees was placed under the Speaker's direct control, enabling him to bypass a number of veteran Republicans whose seniority would normally have placed them in

line to be chairmen. The new committee chairs were literally
handpicked by Gingrich. Committee chairs were also limited to
three consecutive terms and even the Speaker would have to re-
linquish his post after eight years. Gingrich also eliminated
twenty-five subcommittees, thus reducing the number of members who could wield a gavel and speak authoritatively. But the
effect of these dramatic changes was, if anything, to make the
House even more different from the Senate, where leadership
continued to be more problematical and committee seniority
absolutely sacrosanct.

The purpose of this chapter is to examine the proposition
that changes in both chambers and their political environments
in recent years have caused them to converge. Almost no one
says that they have become more distinct, one from the other.
But there is an important third position—while some House
members have come to act like senators in some areas and
some senators have begun to assume characteristics of House
members in some areas, important differences persist. These
differences are of such a fundamental nature as to make the apparent points of convergence—or at least the scope of duration
of that convergence—open to question.

The Case for Convergence

Scholars and journalists who see the House and Senate becoming more alike cite a number of examples to substantiate
their claim. Viewed broadly, the points of convergence relate to
the following: procedures; interpersonal and institutional loyalties; campaigning behavior; policy expertise; and the value of
leadership positions.

Those who make the case for convergence find evidence for
the following:

1. The House has suffered a decline in the efficiency of its
legislative process and has become a more unpredictable body
—in the manner of the Senate.

2. A heavier Senate workload and an increase in the num-

bers and the attendant rise of influence of staff have caused a deterioration in the interpersonal comity and accommodation that has long defined the Senate. This shift is associated with a decline of institutional loyalty, disillusionment, and a more rapid turnover of members and seems to point to more chances for stardom in the House.

3. Senators are beginning to experience greater electoral insecurity and to act more like House members by campaigning almost constantly for six years, as the House members do for the two years of their incumbency.

4. Senators are actually becoming more engrossed in the minutiae of legislation and House members are acting like generalists—an apparently dramatic role reversal.

5. The value of leadership positions in the House—both party and committee—has diminished, and the hierarchy of the House has become more flattened to resemble that of the Senate where power is more evenly distributed.[6]

Let us look first at the question of changes in the legislative process in both chambers. The case was made by Norman Ornstein in 1981 that the control over the legislative process exerted by the formal leaders of the House had been eroded by the dispersion of power to the many new centers of power in the subcommittee, producing "an ad hoc institution without firm control over its own schedule or priorities—much like the Senate."[7]

THE HOUSE: UP FROM ANARCHY

One expression of the enfeebled grasp of the Speaker and his lieutenants was that "the House floor is often a free-for-all, rarely a ratification point for decisions pre-structured by one or two specialists."[8] While Ornstein's observation more accurately describes the time at which it was made, what he may actually have observed was a House in a state of flux due to temporary forces.

The early 1980s were indeed a period of uncertain leadership in the House. The Democrats were demoralized by the decline in the fortunes of the Carter administration and its ultimate defeat by Ronald Reagan. In the 1981–1983 period, Speaker Thomas "Tip" O'Neill had lost effective control of the House even though the Democrats enjoyed a numerical majority. The most consistent policymaking force in the House was a combination of House Republicans, who were remarkably cohesive in their support for Reagan administration policies, and a group of Sunbelt Democrats, the so-called "Boll Weevils," who voted with the GOP members on such crucial issues as budget-cutting and tax-cutting legislation.

The situation changed abruptly after the election of 1982 with a twenty-six-seat gain by Democrats in the House that eliminated much of the influence of the Boll Weevil Democrats. Few of these new Democrats became affiliated with the Boll Weevils. Even the humiliating loss by Walter Mondale to President Reagan in 1984 did not materially affect Democratic strength in the House.

Far from being a free-for-all, the end of the O'Neill years saw House leadership with its hand firmly on the wheel. So effective did this control appear to be that Alan Ehrenhalt could write in 1986, "The O'Neill years have seen the floor evolve into a much more efficient legislative machine, with most major bills brought there under procedures barring more than a handful of amendments. . . . House leaders and the Rules Committee have kept the terms of debate and amendment under tight control."[9]

From 1994 until 1996, Newt Gingrich was absolute master of the House. He enjoyed powers that Democratic speakers of the previous four decades could only have dreamed of. But in July 1997, a revolt was hatched against Gingrich. It failed, but it demonstrated that there were Republicans who were unhappy with his leadership style. When Gingrich resigned his speakership after the 1998 election losses by the GOP, his ultimate replacement was the soft-spoken J. Dennis Hastert, whose low-keyed approach was fitting in light of the narrowness of the Republicans' majority. Despite this momentary period of unassertive leadership, the House is, by its very nature, an institution that needs a strong guiding hand, and no one appreciates this fact more than the members themselves. Senator Richard Schweiker said it simply in 1986: "The House is still autocratic and the Senate is in chaos. I don't think that's really changing."

The laissez-faire atmosphere in the House that was discerned in the early 1980s as evidence of the House becoming more like the Senate has also been a victim of limited legislative output. The slender margin of majority control and political polarization of the House means, among other things, that only "must-pass" bills are going to be enacted along with the very few bills that are unusually popular, such as lifting the earnings limit on those who receive Social Security. The main centers of activity in the House are the Budget Committee, with its responsibility for the budget resolution and reconciliation bills; the Appropriations Committee, with its jurisdiction over the thirteen appropriations bills (or the continuing resolution that is passed in the absence of them) and supplemental appropriations bills to augment money already appropriated to any agency or program; and Ways and Means, because of its jurisdiction over tax matters.

If the processing and passage of bills is the measure by which we judge a well-functioning House, relatively few players are involved in the key legislation, and what measures are enacted bear the strong imprint of committee and party leaders. Far from being a free-for-all, the contemporary House is like a vast bridge tournament with a few players and scores of kibitzers.

Indeed, it is the activity of kibitzing to which many of the excluded members turn in a Congress with so little legislative action. Committees that process only one piece of legislation in a year, such as the House International Relations Committee, have little to offer their members other than a platform for media appearances.

The Senate, in contrast, seemed in danger of turning into a well-regimented clone of the House in the early 1980s. "The Senate," Ornstein wrote, "has become *more* formal and impersonal, *more* tightly organized through its 'reformed' committee system, and developed *more* rigid floor rules and procedures."[10] By the first session of the 99th Congress in 1985, Senator Thomas Eagleton, a Democrat of Missouri, was rising on the floor to proclaim the Senate to be "in a state of incipient anarchy." Eagleton's Missouri colleague, Senator John Danforth, a Republican, had only one quarrel with Eagleton's characterization of the Senate. He suggested deletion of the modifier "incipient" and substituting for it the phrase "fully developed." What anarchy means, Danforth reminded his colleague, is "everyone is a law unto himself."[11]

It is important to look back again to the early 1980s and remark that although the observations about a more docile and tractable Senate were probably accurate at the time they were made, the Senate is by nature such an individualistic body that such periods do not last long.

The use of the filibuster, which seemed to be coming under tighter control in the late 1970s, is now used or threatened as a device to block consideration of legislation with considerable abandon. While the termination of the filibuster has become somewhat easier, it is still an effective enough tactic that even the mere threat by a senator that he or she will filibuster a bill will often cause the leaders to shelve the measure. No longer used exclusively to block action on civil rights bills by willful segregationists or even as a device to protect the interests of small states, the filibuster is now used, according to Senator Charles Grassley, for "piddly little issues." Arizona Democrat Dennis DeConcini saw its capricious use as a "disservice to the institution and to the orderly consideration of issues here."[12]

The image of a more docile Senate and a more unruly

House seems to have been a transitory phenomenon. Contemporary observers see the House as an orderly and mostly predictable place and the Senate as a thicket of unexpected snares and pitfalls.

The evolution of the Senate into a place of anonymous members who offer little to one another in the way of comity or friendship and the emergence of House members who stand out by reason of their individual qualities also bear examination as an indicator of convergence.

A decline in the quality and quantity of interpersonal relationships in the Senate, if it could be documented, would constitute a profound change in the institution. Recalling Chapters 2 and 3 and the discussion of the powerful effect of chamber size on the way business is conducted in the two houses, the elaborateness of House rules and the simplicity and brevity of Senate rules mean much is left to personal negotiation in the Senate between members of that body. The rise in importance of staff as intermediaries between overworked and overcommitted senators has already been noted. It is almost unheard of to be able to talk to a senator for more than a few minutes without hearing complaints about the workload or about the increased importance of staff. Neither of these changes can be denied. But whether the interpersonal contacts so important to the conduct of Senate business have been seriously damaged is another matter.

Friendship among U.S. senators is a habitually misunderstood feature of the upper chamber. Few senators are buddies, although there was more social interaction outside the walls of the Senate in the past than there is now. What senators call friendship, and what is vitally important to the smooth operation of the Senate, is a kind of stable business relationship based on trust and reciprocity that grows up between people who may have never exchanged a confidence, or traded volleys on a tennis court, or drunk bourbon together. Hostility among senators also tends to run in fairly narrow channels. Almost all senators profess distaste for highly dogmatic and inflexible colleagues, and there are always a few senators in every era pointed to by their fellow members as troublesome and obstructionist, but widespread and enduring uncivility is not characteristic of the Senate. Even a chaotic Senate is not necessarily a vicious and unfriendly place.[13]

Among the senators and former senators with House service who were interviewed, there was unanimous agreement that senators were overburdened, and that staff members handled much more office-to-office negotiation. All, however, felt that interpersonal comity was still a defining feature of the Senate and none felt that the House and Senate were at all alike in terms of the quality of member-on-member dealings.

Senators as different in temperament and philosophy as Montana Democrat Max Baucus and Texas Republican Phil Gramm emphasized the greater importance of the personal touch in the Senate than in the House and the greater disposition to tolerate deviant, even egregiously bad, behavior. They also observed that, unlike the House, you might conceivably have to deal with all ninety-nine of your colleagues. Baucus recalled: "I found that in the House I dealt with a good number of members personally but rarely with any others. Over here it is different. The variety and spectrum of who you deal with is proportionately much greater than in the House." Gramm observed, "I could give you three or four names right off the bat of people who are just genuinely disliked—who are notorious for being obnoxious and abusive—but people don't call their hand. The rules are such that it's better to tolerate it than get all stirred up."

Senators who served before 1980 make much the same observation. John Culver, who felt, on the whole, that the House and Senate were becoming more alike, qualified his endorsement of convergence by observing, "There's a lot more logrolling in the Senate. Also there's the feeling that if I get it through the Senate and write my press release, I'll drop it in conference because I've done my thing politically. So everybody in the Senate is just a lot more accommodating in terms of the political interests of the members than the House can afford to be." Culver's observation about the prevalence of Senate log-rolling, or swapping political favors and voting for colleagues' bills on the expectation that the gesture will be returned, was shared by all those interviewed.

A number of the senators interviewed did, however, mention that they had detected a breakdown in Senate comity and a rise in interpersonal friction at the time the Republicans became the majority in the chamber in 1981. One senator who went out of his way to comment on this period was Michigan Democrat Donald Riegle.

When the Republicans won control of the Senate on the strength of Reagan's victory in 1980, they achieved in the Senate a remarkable degree of political and partisan solidarity and that introduced into the Senate a somewhat higher level of partisanship. I think, generally speaking, it was less than in the House but I think it was higher than it had been before 1981.

If Riegle's judgment is correct, an observer looking at the Senate in the early 1980s might well have come to the conclusion that comity had declined. Republicans in both chambers were remarkably cohesive in support of the Reagan administration's programs, but this hardening of partisan lines was a strange and unfamiliar sensation for many senators.

It was during this period that Kansas Republican Bob Dole took over the chairmanship of the Finance Committee from longtime chairman Russell Long (D-La.). Dole began to hold closed-door meetings for the Republican members of the committee. On one occasion Long attempted to gain entry to such a meeting and was turned away at the door by a staff member who informed the astonished former chairman that it was a Republicans-only meeting.

Long, who believed that revenge is always more tasty when eaten cold, bided his time. In short order, the Reagan administration proposed to withhold any taxes that might be due the federal government on interest or dividend payments at the time the payments were made to customers by banks or businesses rather than have the recipients pay when they filed their taxes. It was basically a scheme to get money to the Treasury more quickly. The plan came under attack by Wisconsin Republican Bob Kasten, who characterized it as an attack on people living on fixed incomes. Kasten, however, was a junior member who had arrayed against him both the White House and Finance Committee chairman Dole.

Then, with no apparent motive, Russell Long threw his considerable prestige into the battle on Kasten's side. Dole asked why he was opposing a plan that seemed to be such a good policy. Long is reported to have reminded Dole about the partisan meeting and the door that had been slammed in his face. With Long's assistance, Kasten's effort to block the administration plan succeeded and Dole had occasion in defeat to reflect upon the price that is paid in the Senate for excessive partisanship and disrespect to a senior colleague of whatever party.

The importance of good collegial relationships seems to be well understood even by the newest members of the Senate. If there has been a long-term decline in the importance of collegiality, it was not to be found in the views of Senator Timothy Wirth (D-Colo.), who was elected in 1986 and retired in 1993.

One of the things that's so impressive about this place is the personal relationships that exist over here. Because of the filibuster and the fact that so much gets done by unanimous consent and the comity that's needed to support that kind of system, what grows up is a great deal of personal rapport among members of the Senate that is real.

People talk about this place being a club. It has to be a club in order to get unanimous consent. But underneath that grow up very strong, very real relationships. It takes a while to develop those relationships so that people know your style and approach enough to trust you and take you seriously.

Again, it appears that a snapshot in time taken in the early 1980s showed a Senate that was uncharacteristically partisan due, in large measure, to the unfamiliarity of Republicans with the sensation of being the majority party in the chamber.

High turnover in the personnel of the Senate in some recent elections gave credence to the image of a more transitory and anomic membership. The elections of 1978 and 1980 were notable for the large number of new senators produced. The Senate that was sworn in on January 15, 1979, had twenty new members and there were eighteen freshmen on hand for induction on January 3, 1981. Reading these figures, one could easily conclude that turnover was destroying continuity in the Senate and making it a more anonymous and less collegial body. But the elections of 1982 and 1984 produced only twelve freshmen between them. The abnormally large number of thirteen casualties inflicted on the members in the 1986 elections did not, however, signal a return to high rates of turnover. It was probably a reflection of the weakness of those Republican senators elected on Ronald Reagan's coattails in 1980 who did not enjoy that advantage six years later. By 1988, with the election of ten new senators the turnover rate came close to the post-1960 average of eleven Senate freshmen for each new Congress.

Another average year for Senate turnovers was 1992, with eleven, but by the early spring of 1994, nine senators had already announced their retirements. This meant that the average post-1960 turnover rate of eleven was already being approached without a single ballot having been cast and without a single defeat. When likely defeats were added to these numbers, 1994 seemed to be a reprise of the high-turnover years of 1978 and 1980 and could well lead an observer to the conclusion that turnover was changing the nature of the Senate.

But in 1994 the most dramatic turnover came in the House as the result of an unprecedented number of retirements and a Republican gain of fifty-two seats. While there was an eight-seat pickup by the Republicans in the Senate, the changes there were not so great as in the House. Looking back on the decade of the 1990s, the turnover rate in the House, as defined by percentage of new members after each congressional election, was indeed consistently higher than that of the Senate. But even if a senator serves a single term, he or she still has a greater opportunity to get to know a larger percentage of the Senate's 100 members than a House member with a single term would have to become acquainted with the other 434 voting members of the House. This reality was expressed by Senator Wayne Allard, a Colorado Republican who came to the Senate in 1996 after spending six years in the House.

You get to know each other more personally on the Senate side than on the House side. You've got 435 members over there and they just don't have a chance to get to know each other. Over here, I know all the members of the opposite party by their first names, but over in the House I couldn't say that. I usually know my own party pretty well and I worked hard to get to know the House members, but after each election, you'd get a whole bunch of new ones and you'd have to re-learn again. And you fall behind on names over there because after each election you've got a whole bunch of new faces that have come in.

Is it also the case that "recent House members rank with Senate celebrities in public recognition and/or acclaim?"[14] The rise and fall in the bicameral stardom quotient is perhaps the most slippery indicator of convergence or nonconvergence. Between the years 1994 and 1998, the most visible but also the least-liked member of Congress, if the public opinion polls could be believed, was House Speaker Newt Gingrich. His successor, J. Dennis Hastert, could probably walk down the main street of most American towns and not be recognized. While the Senate has lost such distinctive and visible members as Bill Bradley and Daniel Patrick Moynihan, it retains Ted Kennedy, whose appearance on the floor never fails to elicit gasps from the visitors' gallery, ex-actor Fred Thompson, and 2000 presidential hopeful John McCain. The House lost one of its most intriguing members when Representative Sonny Bono, formerly of the Sonny and Cher singing duo, was killed in a skiing accident in January 1998. Representatives Fred "Gopher" Grandy and Ben "Cooter" Jones are no longer in Congress. So while citizens might remember the portly, silver-haired Henry

Hyde from the impeachment proceedings, or former professional football players J. C. Watts and Steve Largent from their playing days, it would be surprising if even the most politically aware citizens could identify 5 percent of the House membership unless they were addicted to watching C-SPAN.

Another expression of convergence would be a decline in the loyalty of its members to the Senate. And one measure of that institutional loyalty is whether senators want to remain there. The 1994 retirement announcements—many of them from relatively young senators—suggest that the level of disenchantment either with politics in general or the Senate in particular has rarely been greater. Three Senate departures—by Florida's Lawton Chiles, California's Pete Wilson, and Idaho's Dirk Kempthorne—led these former Senators to governorships. But in Chiles's case, the transition was not direct and in Wilson's case, there was very likely a calculation that presidential ambitions were better advanced from Sacramento than from Washington. If a senator on a presidential trajectory chooses to leave the upper chamber for the more promising turf of a state capitol, this tells us more about the senator's attachment to the presidency than about loyalty to the Senate.

Only two incumbent senators—John McCain and Orrin Hatch—chose to seek presidential nominations in 2000, and neither did so at the sacrifice of their Senate seats. So while there is undoubtedly a high level of disaffection with political careers, it is unclear whether the Senate is being singled out. The fact that 15 percent of House incumbents in 1992 and another 10 percent in 1994 chose not to seek reelection suggests that the Senate is not unique. The large number of 1994 departures seemed less a sign of disenchantment with the Senate than with a more generalized loathing of campaigning in an era of highly negative politics and the high-pressure fund-raising activities that are associated with it.

If we look to the words of senators themselves, there is often criticism of the Senate for its archaic and often anarchic ways, but little real Senate bashing. Indeed, the sense of satisfaction at being a senator or having been one is uniform across the fourteen people interviewed who served in both bodies.

I asked all the senators I interviewed whether they had ever had any second thoughts about leaving the House for the Senate. The responses varied only in the vehemence of their assertion of the superiority of the Senate.

From liberal Democrat Don Riegle came the statement: "I like the chance to make things happen in a direct way. I think that opportunity is available only in the Senate." Conservative Republican Phil Gramm simply said, "I'm glad to be out of the House." From former senator Hugh Scott, who came to the House in 1941 and the Senate in 1959, there was this recollection: "I was totally elated to be in the Senate; completely exuberant about it. If I missed anything about the House, it was the luncheons of the Pennsylvania delegation, but as for the proceedings of the House, it was a large disorganized team hitting pop flies into the infield." From Max Baucus, who entered the House in 1974 and the Senate in 1978, came this appraisal of his decision to run for the Senate: "It's clear to me personally that I made the right decision. One has greater opportunity to develop issues that interest one and, historically, senators have been able to marshal constituencies outside their own state."

These were not uncritical judgments. Timothy Wirth faulted the Senate's technological backwardness. Max Baucus and Wyche Fowler lamented the loss of the circle of friends they had in the House. Don Riegle, Chris Dodd, and Paul Sarbanes deplored the loss of intimacy that comes when you trade a congressional district for a state. Virtually everyone complained about obstructionism and delay in the legislative process but none expressed anything but the most qualified and attenuated nostalgia for the House and none proclaimed the Senate to be nothing more than a downsized House or wanted it to move in that direction.

One factor that appeared to be both a symptom and a cause of the decline in interpersonal comity detected in the early 1980s was the role of staff. In Chapter 3 I discussed the greater prominence of staff in the Senate than in the House but made only passing note of its effect on senators' relations with colleagues. In David Kozak's study of sixteen senators, the prominence of staff was a commonly cited difference between House and Senate. One of Kozak's respondents complained, in the context of a discussion of staff, "You don't see the other senators that much. We are more isolated from our colleagues."[15] Unquestionably, the modern Senate office does resemble a small corporation in both numbers and complexity. Much office-to-office contact is carried on by staff members. But it would be a mistake to conclude that the important bilateral and multilateral agreements among senators are cooked up by the staffs and merely rubber-stamped by the senators. Interoffice consultations among staff typically take place only after the principals involved—the senators themselves—have authorized negotiations. Senate staff, for all its importance, rarely does anything more than implement decisions made by senators who have agreed on the broad outlines of a deal. As the staff member of the freshman Democrat quipped, it is, in the final analysis, "*mano a mano*."

Senator Timothy Wirth asserted, "More business gets done among members here than in the House. In the House you assign your staff people to work it out because there are so many members in the House. Over here, you don't get anything done unless you talk personally to the other guy."

What Wirth said does not detract from the relatively greater importance of the staff on the Senate side than on the House side, but it does tell us that, for all of the buffering and cosseting, senators have not become complete creatures of their staffs and that deals must still be struck among principals, not their agents. Senators are almost certainly more poorly informed on details than their House colleagues and more apt to use staff expertise to fill gaps, but they are in no way inferior to House members in discerning the politics of a situation or even in simply being well informed enough about the substance of policy to make sound decisions with their colleagues.

There is considerable support for at least part of the third element of convergence theory and that is that the difference between the two-year term of House members and the six-year term of senators has narrowed because of a high attrition rate at the polls for incumbent senators. Apprehensive about defeat, many senators have expanded the active phase of their campaigning to the point that they resemble House members.

Traditionally, the difference between the abbreviated House term and the elongated Senate term was so great that the Senate was looked upon as a kind of semi-retirement. House Speaker Thomas Brackett Reed (1889–1891 and 1895–1899) thought so little of the activity level of the upper chamber that he described the Senate as a place where good representatives go when they die. During the time when election to the Senate was by vote of the state legislature, the combination of insulation from popular control and length of term made the Senate a very safe and relaxed place to be. James A. Garfield, who served in the House for seventeen years, believed that the necessity to stand for election every two years was injurious to health and that, at the very least, "a seat in the Senate will delay the catastrophe."[16]

Representative Oscar W. Underwood, an Alabama Democrat, who was serving as majority leader of the House in the aftermath of the great Democratic triumph in 1912, found life in a House leadership position so taxing that "his wife felt he might find sanctuary in the Senate."[17] At the same time, however, "Senator John Bankhead, the senior senator, and other friends counseled him against surrendering his tenacious hold on the Ninth District Congressional seat for the uncertainties of a Senate campaign."[18]

These "uncertainties" were part of a new set of considerations that attended the ratification of the Seventeenth Amendment in 1913. With the disappearance of the margin of safety provided by the state legislatures, the principal buffer left to senators was the six-year term. The political calculation for would-be senators became more complicated. Those who occupied safe House seats, like Underwood, would have to strike a balance between the more perilous new electoral environment of the U.S. senator and the potential for more influence. George W. Norris, a Nebraska Republican and prominent progressive, had his eyes on the future when he pondered a run for the Senate in 1912, the last congressional election before the ratification of the direct-election amendment, and "decided to risk the chances of promotion to the Senate. There, crowded chambers and stifling procedure could not silence an outspoken man."[19]

With the removal of the political insulation of state legislative elections that often produced senators who were under the thumb of political bosses but whose safety was assured, the six-year term loomed more impressively as a safety margin. Sometimes, the allure of the six-year term in the Senate, with its promise of vastly greater influence, had a practical appeal as well. Consider the calculations made by Democratic House member Estes Kefauver of Tennessee when he considered a run in 1948 against incumbent senator Arthur T. "Tom" Stewart.

Against his loss of House seniority and his assurance of effective support in his home district, the Senate would offer a stronger power base from which to work toward realization of his legislative objectives. . . . There were strong personal considerations, too: he did not want his children to be reared in an apartment, but he was reluctant to buy a house when he had to face the risk of being retired from Congress every two years.[20]

Even though "Kefauver was established solidly as a representative and could be elected as long as he wished to stay in the House," he defended to his father his decision to run for the Senate with the argument that " 'I've served long enough in the House . . . I can't keep on living in an apartment and running for reelection every two years. My family deserves a normal life, in a home of their own.' "[21] Kefauver defeated

Stewart in 1948 and went on to spend the next fifteen years in the Senate.

What is so remarkable about the apparent safety of House seats is that the obligation to run every two years—even if it amounts to no more than a formality—generates apprehension in many House members. "House members see electoral uncertainty where outsiders would fail to unearth a single objective indicator of it."[22] House members fear general elections, and if general elections are no problem because of the partisan cast of the district, they obsess about primaries. If they fear that they will be overtaken by complacency, they fret about redistricting. The impressive margins by which so many House members win reelection and the consistent success of their reelection bids, even in such anti-incumbent years as 1992 when 88 percent of incumbents were elected, seem to be little compensation for the fact that every two-year interval could turn out to be a hinge of history, a climactic event.

House members are aware that the attachments of voters are not to the political party with which the candidates identify but to more flimsy and transient factors of a more personal nature. Members who find favor with the voters in one election can find themselves out of favor two years later. Without strong party attachments among voters to draw on, House members must rise or fall on their own merits or shortcomings.[23]

House members, when transported to the Senate, tend to see the electoral vulnerabilities differently. In the discussion of congressional districts and states in Chapter 4, there was a feeling expressed by most senators interviewed that a kind of intimacy prevailed in the relationship between a House member and his district that had few parallels in the bonds between senators and their states. Only among those senators from states with only two congressional districts and the one who had served at large was this sense of lost intimacy not pronounced. But what might look very comfortable from the Senate does not, evidently, put many minds to rest in the House. In the Senate, with its vastly more complicated and politically perilous terrain, the House district does seem almost pastoral in its simplicity and coziness, but for those still in the House, fate is never tempted with complacency.

The usual ambitions for advancement to the Senate that are harbored by many House members were disrupted by the big stakes involved in the election of 2000. If fewer than half a dozen House seats were to change hands, majority control would pass from Republicans to Democrats. Leaders of both parties in the House found themselves pleading with members who held safe seats not to seek a Senate seat. While it was seen to be less likely that control of the Senate might change hands, both Majority Leader Trent Lott and Minority Leader Tom Daschle tried their best to lure well-entrenched House members to make the run for the Senate. This put House and Senate leaders of the same party in an unusual competition. Typically, the lure to keep House members from seeking the Senate was the promise of a better committee assignment. Representative Mark Foley of Florida had just been rewarded with a coveted seat on the House Ways and Means Committee. He scrapped his plan to run for the Senate seat being vacated by Senator Connie Mack when Representative Thomas M. Davis, III, of Virginia, chairman of the National Republican Campaign Committee, took him aside and told him pointedly, "Mark, we just put you on Ways and Means—it's a huge investment."[24]

Despite House members' own apprehensions about reelection, senators who once served in the House regard the obligation of their former colleagues to go before the voters every two years as something of a formality. Senator Paul Sarbanes, a Maryland Democrat said, "Look. People talk about congressmen having to run every two years. Well, if they have a marginal district, that's a real problem. But most of them don't have marginal districts. Most of them have safe districts and they are not, in any real sense, running every two years."

Senator James Abourezk stressed the protection afforded by the six-year term but added an important qualification:

After a while in the Senate you say, "Jesus, God, they're running all the time over there in the House and I don't have to run. It's my second year and I'm still in office and they're opening doors for me and cheering my speeches and laughing at my jokes. My God, I might just forget to go home." Well, House members never forget to go back home. They're forced to and Senate members that don't are the ones that lose.

Evidence of the diminution of the importance of the term differential between House and Senate is found in the fund-raising behavior of senators. The trend toward earlier and almost-continual fund-raising activity was detected in the early 1980s.[25] Unlike senators of the past, who waited until their re-election year to raise funds in earnest, modern senators are spending their fifth or even fourth years in intensive fund-raising activities, and their first in paying off the previous campaign.

The reason for this preemptive fund-raising among senators is that their opponents are more likely than House challengers to attract media attention. Only a media-based strategy by an incumbent can ward them off. Incumbents can get a great deal of free media, but they are also forced to buy it at rates that have climbed into the stratosphere.

A six-year term in the United States Senate lasts 2,189 days. The cost of the average Senate campaign is now about $3 million. Setting aside a few days for vacation, this means that the average senator must raise $1,600 a day for every day in office. This breaks down to $100 for every waking hour.[26] It has also become something of an axiom in political campaigning that "early" money is better than "late" money. A sizable war chest of an incumbent can have the effect of deterring a challenger. Raising money, accordingly, becomes not only a resource for waging a campaign against a challenger but a strong disincentive for a potential rival to even think of becoming a declared challenger.

For most of the twenty-nine senators interviewed, the principal expression of convergence is in this trend toward almost continual campaigning. The most pointed expression of this trend is in the expansion of fund-raising activities to encompass practically the entire six-year term. One senator, Idaho's Larry Craig, claimed that fund-raising was actually easier for him in the Senate than in the House because out-of-state contributors "recognize the difference between a senator and a House member."

Many lobbyists seem distressed by the aggressiveness of Senate fund-raising appeals. David Rubinstein, a former high official in the Carter White House, said, "Senators always have had their hand out. They're raising money for elections that have limitless costs. California, New York—you can never raise enough money and because of that feeling of never having enough money, you're always raising it."

The tone of dismay was captured by former senator John Culver of Iowa: "Nowadays senators come in with debts and the financial stresses of the campaign. They owe people money and the only way to get it is to go to the special interests right away rather than have that grace period of four or five years that was intended for them to be able to take a second look at the House judgment on the public policy question and give it a sober, reflective look."

Without question, the Senate as an institution now resonates to changes in the mood of the electorate in a manner dramatically at variance with the plan of the framers of the Constitution while the House seems immune to them. The high turnover in the Senate and, until recently, the remarkable stability of the House seemed to be producing a "devolution of the lower house into a relatively inflexible repository of stable, local interests and the associated birth of a popular upper house, functioning as a sensitive barometer of national mood."[27] What is less clear is whether this has caused changes in the behavior of senators away from the "sober and reflective" role described by Culver.

If it is true that the traditional respite from campaign activities on the part of U.S. senators has given way to a term-long period of fund-raising, have senators generally trimmed their sails to the prevailing political winds? Has the period of senatorial statesmanship, in which a measure of political boldness might be practiced, given way to greater caution and a tendency to behave according to the perceived wishes of the constituency?

One very obvious indication that senators are becoming more like House members in their relations with their constituencies is the growing frequency of trips from Washington back to the state. The percentage of House members who go home about once a week was as recently as 1980 far greater than the percentage of senators who do. The percentage of senators who visited their state less frequently than every two weeks was much higher than that of House members.[28]

As a group, senators traditionally were not as diligent in fence-mending as were House members, but after the debacles of 1980 and 1986, at least some senators are emulating the attentiveness of congressmen. Senator Alfonse D'Amato (R-N.Y.) proudly called himself a "pothole senator" as a badge of honor for his attentiveness to his constituency. When D'Amato's colleague from New York, Democratic senator Daniel Patrick Moynihan (characterized by one journalist as a "scholar-senator"), visited the upstate city of Elmira, the local paper noted that "it took Moynihan six years to return." Elsewhere in the paper, it was reported that D'Amato had visited the town ten times.[29] In spite of D'Amato's diligence in visiting out-of-the-way places, he suffered defeat in 1998.

Senators are now using communications techniques such as "postal-patron" mailings that blanket the state and organizing town meetings to meet voters face-to-face. While these House-tested techniques for political success are finding much more favor among senators, and while some might even relish the designation "pothole senator," others, for a variety of reasons, will not emulate the conduct of House members.

Different styles have always prevailed in the Senate, ranging from those who think of themselves as instructed delegates who, as one senator put it, "are as nervous as a Christmas goose" on every vote for fear that it will be out of line with the wishes of the state to those who are almost defiantly independent. As Donald R. Matthews wrote in 1960, "a constituency as large as a state can be "represented' in many different ways."[30]

The fact that the period of active fund-raising on the part of senators has expanded or that senators now resort to "postal-patron" mass mailings or even that they go home more often does not necessarily mean that they are more timid or compliant or that they are trying to ape House members. Research on legislators at both the state and national levels shows that they make major adjustments as election time nears. They may bring their voting behavior more in line with the behavior of their legislative colleagues or they may establish a pattern of voting that is closer to the ideological middle.[31] They may also alter their pre-election voting habits to adjust to the characteristics of their likely challengers.[32] A dramatic example of this kind of anticipatory adjustment was the vote of liberal New Jersey Senator Frank Lautenberg against President Clinton's budget. Fearing a backlash from tax-phobic Jerseyans and a challenge from economy-minded state assembly speaker Garabed (Chuck) Haytaian, Lautenberg abandoned Clinton on the budget because it contained new taxes.

What does it mean when senators become cautious as re-election time nears? The most straightforward explanation is that they hope such modifications will enable them to win re-election. But it also means that they think that their preexisting behavior has not been entirely compliant with the wishes of the voters. To bring your votes or statements more in line with constituent views or likely opponents or to camouflage yourself by voting like the average of your colleagues suggests that senators believe themselves to have been too independent or to have shown maverick or even radical tendencies. Put more bluntly, "many senators spend the majority of their time consciously and deliberately behaving in a manner they realize will not please their constituents to the maximum extent possible."[33]

Senators also show no increased inclination to take on only uncontroversial issues or those that have a direct connection with the interests of their states. Senators continue to pursue issues that are of personal concern to them. This has led one researcher to conclude, "The common cynical view of senators that their legislative efforts reflect a mindless pursuit of electoral goals is not close to the mark." Indeed, he adds, "Most senators value their unique position in the political system and most use it to pursue issues that they consider important."[34]

Acts of conspicuous political bravery are not entirely absent even in the more treacherous waters of Senate politics. Locked in a tough reelection race in 2000, Virginia Democrat Chuck Robb cast a controversial vote to defeat a constitutional amendment that would have given Congress the power to make burning the American flag a crime.

It is, of course, not necessarily the case that all state issues are politically safe for senators and all national issues are politically risky. Most senators raise funds nationally, so their willingness to tackle less parochial issues may simply be a reflection of their new dependence on campaign money from outside their state rather than evidence of statesmanship. Nonetheless, "senators are inundated with requests [to take up causes]. . . . In contrast, many House members go begging for attention, are constantly on the prowl for some way to get more involved, and are envious of the ability of senators to steal their claim to the leading role on surfacing national issues."[35]

THE PERSISTENCE OF PATTERNS OF SPECIALIZATION AND GENERALITY

The fourth major area in which House-Senate convergence was detected in the early 1980s was in the degree of specialization and generalization that had hitherto been such a definitive difference between the two bodies. Accepted wisdom held that "it is the grand design of national public policy rather than the nitty-gritty details of legislation that is of prime concern to most senators."[36] The revisionist view was expressed by Norman Ornstein: "Committee and subcommittee assignments have proliferated, spreading House members much thinner. . . . The Senate has moved away from its focus on debate and deliberation towards a preoccupation with legislative nitty-gritty."[37]

The argument that the roles of the House and Senate on specialization have not merely converged but actually reversed receives little support from the senators interviewed. While the group does consist of both incumbents and former senators, the views of the ex-senators are valuable because all are still actively involved in lobbying and legal work associated with Congress. There was no difference, moreover, in the views of serving senators and former senators.

Texas Republican Phil Gramm asserted, "Senators are still by and large generalists. They are just involved in a lot more issues than House members. . . . They are people who are spread thin and on a short cord." Michigan Democrat Don Riegle made the case that there are simply practical limits to the amount of specializing a senator can do.

You have just so much waterfront to cover around here that the best you can hope for is to be knowledgeable on the subject matter of your committee.

You're expected to be an advocate for your entire state and the press expects you to be conversant on foreign policy matters. You're expected to be a knowledgeable person. I think that House members are just not under the same burden to the same degree; they really can concentrate on just a few things.

Pennsylvania Republican Richard Schweiker saw the senator's opportunities to diversify as a salient difference between the two chambers and also pointed to the difference in committee structures as the source of the difference: "There's more of an opportunity to work in the field of your choice in the Senate: to pick and choose. You really aren't in that kind of straitjacket they have in the House where the only chance you have to get a shot at something is through your committee. With only a hundred senators available for so many committees, there's no way in the world you're going to get the kind of special-ization they have in the House."

Recently, Steven S. Smith has argued that even with the greater variety of committee assignments available to senators, they are developing areas of concentration and leadership on issues that do not fit in neatly with the jurisdictions of the com-mittees on which they serve.[38]

All the senators agreed that if they were to seize all the op-portunities that come by, they would be overwhelmed. Even by picking and choosing, many senators feel that they are being pulled in a hundred different directions. All agreed with Mary-land Democrat Paul Sarbanes's verdict that "the job, to some degree, overwhelms you, whereas in the House you get much more of a sense of being in control of your job." There was, however, also a consensus around another Sarbanes observa-tion: "The Senate gives you a scope you just don't have in the House."

It is undeniably the case that many House members are tak-ing a much more expansive view of their roles than was the case traditionally. And it is also beyond dispute that there are senators who relish specialization. But there are simple, practi-cal limits to the degree to which senators can specialize.

There is, moreover, in the Senate, a kind of inexorable force that can elevate the sights of even the most locally minded "pothole senator." Indeed, it has happened in the case of the very man who coined the phrase, New York Republican Al-fonse D'Amato.

D'Amato's first public manifestation of concern about the drug policy in New York City was to don a battered army field jacket and visit the East Village of Manhattan as part of a me-dia event to publicize his concern. But the broader implications of the drug problem were not lost on the senator, and he be-came one of the harshest and most vocal critics of Panama's dictator General Manuel Noriega and of U.S. drug policy in general. In a like manner, his parochial concern about the effects of acid rain on the lakes in the Adirondack Mountains of New York State led to an interest in national environmental policy that often put him at odds with the Reagan administration. While D'Amato prided himself on his local focus, the implications of those parochial problems came to be drawn in broader strokes.[39]

REVERTING TO TYPE ON THE ROLE OF LEADERSHIP

Finally, there is the question of the dispersion of power in the House so that "hierarchical positions, whether in the formal party leadership or at the top of committees, mean much less today than they did in the 1960s; 'leadership on specific issues can come from any of 400 or more sources.' More and more, the House is an ad hoc institution, without firm control over its own schedule or priorities—much like the Senate."[40]

Here again, a snapshot of bicameralism taken in the early 1980s may well have produced an image that has faded over time. It is unquestionably true that the great dispersion of formal power that took place in the House in the 1970s continues to give representatives many forums for the raising of issues— forums that were once very few in number. The great power enjoyed by the chairmen of standing committees appeared to diminish. Moreover, in the early 1980s, with the Democrats holding only the most tenuous control of the House because of the practice of conservative "Boll Weevil" Democrats to vote with a highly cohesive Republican minority, the control of the Speaker was indeed problematical.

A contemporary view of the House, however, yields a picture much more in line with the classical view of this chamber as a place where real influence reposes in very few hands. As journalist Alan Ehrenhalt puts it, "The current House is democratic in the sense that all members, even the most junior ones, are part of the debate. But when it comes to making decisions, democracy is the wrong word to use."[41]

Representative Phil Sharp (D-Ind.), who served in the

House for more than a dozen years, observed, "The natural tendency of this institution is toward oligarchy. . . . What we have now is a technique for returning to a closed system where a few people make all the decisions."[42] The reassertion of the oligarchical nature of the House comes from two sources: the basic structural reality that a large and cumbersome body like the House simply cannot function with too many power sources, and the more short-run factor of a limited legislative agenda in which little is accomplished other than adopting a budget and passing the appropriations bills associated with it. So while membership in the traditional oligarchy came with the chairmanship of a standing committee, the new kings of the hill are those chairs whose committees either enjoy unusually broad jurisdiction (Commerce) or process "must-pass" legislation (Appropriations and its thirteen subcommittees, Ways and Means, and Budget). Other House committees such as International Relations may serve as excellent pulpits for individual members, but a high level of activity on the part of a few members should not be confused with influence.

There is no doubt that opportunities do exist for entrepreneurial House members and that, on occasion, individuals who are not assigned to the most active committees can have an important impact. The case of Representative, now Senator, Charles Schumer (D-N.Y.) and the role he played in passage of the 1986 immigration reform bill is one that is cited to support the assertion that there are opportunities for influence on the part of rank-and-file members who do not serve on prestige committees. This led Burdett Loomis to argue that "the oligarchy of the 1980s is a permeable one, subject to penetration by skilled, activist members."[43]

To acknowledge that House members are more free to pursue issues and causes and that some of them are successful tells us that the House has changed, but we cannot make a clear-cut case for convergence because it does not tell us that most House members now look like most senators.

The Persistence of House-Senate Differences

While the House and Senate have changed individually in many important respects and are different places from what they were fifty years ago, they have not converged to the point that an observer could say the differences between them are now trivial. Important distinctions persist and they are distinctions that define dramatically the differences between the two houses.

The average senator enjoys a degree of personal influence that the average House member cannot even dream of. While one could point to examples of influential House members and ineffective senators, that is not the norm. Indeed, a rank-and-file senator who had less of an impact on policy than a House back-bencher would be considered by most experts on Congress to be incompetent.

The importance of interpersonal relations and comity among colleagues is every bit as important in the Senate as it ever was. It could be seen in the obsessive concern with bipartisanship in the debate to confirm former senator John Tower as secretary of defense in 1989. In any organization in which so much business is expedited through the use of unanimous consent, agreements cannot trample cavalierly on collegial sensitivities. The House is not immune from such imperatives but the sensibilities of its least member are not a preoccupation of a leadership that is concerned with raw numbers, not concurrent majorities. The House can ignore the tantrums of the deviant or disaffected and may elevate to leadership posts disputatious figures such as Republican leader Newt Gingrich, chosen by his colleagues in 1995 for his fierce partisanship.

While leadership in the House is variable in its authoritativeness, it is almost always more despotic than Senate leadership. Senate leaders, however, are certainly not without instruments of chastisement. Many a senator during Robert C. Byrd's long reign as majority leader learned that, however limited the cudgels of party leadership, Byrd's position on the Appropriations Committee enabled him to reward and punish colleagues with some consistency. But not every Senate leader has the leverage of an important committee at his disposal, and even Byrd was known to call a colleague "Boss." Such a gesture by a House leader to a junior colleague would probably be thought of as condescending.

Senators appear, however, to have learned two important lessons from House members: the necessity to perform those dreary but necessary chores associated with constituent casework, and the need to raise money early and often. Senators have in recent years become somewhat more attentive to visits to the constituency although they apparently have not reached the heights of diligence found in the House. Town meetings have also become more common senatorial activities, even though the meetings are held in the senator's office in Washington for visitors from the state. It may well be that the high reelection success rate of House members in recent years has become so dazzling to the more vulnerable senators that they have followed the members' lead. In most states, however, there are practical limits to such a strategy.

A novel explanation of the more constituency-oriented senator is offered by Senator Chris Dodd of Connecticut, who lays the new emphasis to a generational change. Dodd points out that while many senators come from the House, where such ombudsmanship and social work are common, newer senators have had experience with the Peace Corps, VISTA, and other voluntary agencies and many came to political maturity during the 1960s when notions of participatory democracy were at their fullest flowering. The new service orientation, then, is not so much an act of emulation or even transference from the more casework-intensive House as it is a more complex phenomenon with its roots in the personal characteristics of younger senators.

Despite much complaining about everything from workload to the absence of up-to-date computer systems, no senator I interviewed expressed opinions that could, by any stretch of the imagination, be considered scornful of the Senate. In only one interview with an incumbent senator did I detect feelings of loss as the result of leaving the House, and that individual deplored only the diminished sense of intimacy with his smaller House constituency. Yet it is clear that at least some former House members fail to make the adjustment and look upon their period of service in the House as their Homeric age. George McGovern spoke of a few who, he thought, had suffered from the transition:

The late Lee Metcalf (D-Mont.) was never happy in the Senate. I think it was because he was totally overshadowed by his senior colleague, Mike Mansfield. In the House he had been a kind of leader of the young Turks consisting of maybe a hundred people.

The same thing is true of Gene McCarthy (D-Minn.). I don't know McCarthy well but my impression was that he loved his days in the House and never really enjoyed the Senate where he was overshadowed by Hubert Humphrey.

In the House we would talk about McCarthy's Marauders. He along with Metcalf had great influence with the younger and more liberal members of the House but I always felt that both McCarthy and Metcalf lapsed into a sort of cynical, almost apathetic, role in the Senate. They just didn't like the slow pace and the deferential business that went on over there.

Richard Fenno has focused some of his research on the dynamics of senatorial adjustment, and it is clear that some people have difficulty making the adjustment to the Senate and others probably never make it at all, even those with prior experience in the House. With their hopes so high for the more relaxed, influential, and visible senatorial career, it is not surprising that some former House members find it less glamorous than they had anticipated and become disillusioned.

Predictability has probably declined somewhat in both houses but the consensus of those interviewed is that the Senate is more apt to spring surprises for no other reason than the almost unlimited discretion that senators have in introducing nongermane amendments—acts obviated by House rules and the Argus-eyed vigilance of the Rules Committee. Scheduling seems more problematic in both places and there was much criticism of leaders who impose deadlines that usually cannot be met.

One indication of a coalescence of the House and Senate and a blurring of the lines of institutional distinction might be found in evidence that the Senate had slipped in general prestige and the House had gained. While none of those who made the case for convergence suggested that the prestige differential that had always favored the modern Senate had narrowed, evidence of a diminution of the prestige gap would be an important indicator of convergence. If, for example, there was evidence that the Senate was ceasing to act as a magnet for House members seeking political advancement, one might comfortably infer convergence. That is assuredly not the case. Currently, almost half the U.S. Senate (46 percent) has had previous service in the House. Since 1789, 600 House members have made the trek from the south side of the Capitol to the north; a mere handful of senators or former senators has made the trip south. In recent years only former senator Claude D. Pepper (D-Fla.) served in the House after having previously served in the Senate.

Another sign of institutional convergence might be seen in the equalization in the number of presidential aspirants coming out of each chamber. Historically, senators have always been among the most eligible group of officeholders lining up for presidential nominations. Since the Civil War, senators have constituted the largest group of contenders at national presidential nominating conventions. Over the period from 1868 to 1972, with 31 of 102 contenders, they outnumber all other groups of major officeholders such as governors, vice-presidents, members of the House, and federal appointees such as Cabinet members. The only other category of officeholders that comes close is governors with 29 contenders. In one period only—from 1892 until 1916—were House members more numerous than senators in the ranks of hopefuls at convention time. Between 1868 and 1972, however, House members constituted less than 10 percent of contenders, with only 10 of 102 hopefuls coming from the House.[44]

In the period from 1976 to the present, only four incumbent or recent House members were considered serious presidential hopefuls: Arizona Democrat Morris Udall in 1976; Illinois Republican John Anderson in 1980; and Representatives Richard Gephardt and Jack Kemp in 1988. During this same period nineteen senators (twenty-one, if former vice-presidents Humphrey and Mondale, who also served in the Senate, are counted) were contenders at some period in the course of the primary seasons. So the Senate continues to be the main source of presidential aspirants for both parties and the House only an occasional contributor. If serving as the nursery of presidential hopefuls adds luster to an institution, the Senate is still more brightly burnished than the House.

But the recent successes of Governors Carter, Reagan, Dukakis, Clinton, and Bush in securing nomination—and in three cases, election—suggest that for all their prominence as contenders, incumbent senators are not very good at winning nominations and are even less successful at gaining the presidency. Indeed, the last sitting senator to capture the White House was John F. Kennedy in 1960, and the only other twentieth-century incumbent senator was Warren G. Harding in 1920. As far as the national tickets of both parties are concerned, senators seem to be most useful as vice-presidential running mates who are chosen to act as insurance policies for good relations with Congress. Dan Quayle, Lloyd Bentsen, and Al Gore were picked with at least some weight given to their impact on congressional relations for a victorious presidential candidate.

More elusive but certainly influential as a factor differentiating the House and Senate is what Richard Fenno calls the "A Team–B Team" effect, whereby House members demonstrate symptoms of a kind of inferiority complex because they are forced into the shadow of senators and know that no senator ever aspires to a seat in the House.

The legislative career hierarchy was embellished upon by a man uniquely qualified to comment on House-Senate differences in prestige—former Indiana congressman Floyd Fithian, who made an unsuccessful try for the Senate and ended up serving as administrative assistant to Illinois senator Paul Simon. Fithian is the only former House member to serve as a staff member in the Senate.

My theory on American politics is that a person goes out and works their tail off to get elected to the state assembly for a two-year term and then an opportunity comes up because a state senator decides not to run again and they move up to that four-year state senate term as a normal path of progression. They have, quote unquote, advanced themselves.

Then, let's say the state senator gets elected to the U.S. House of Representatives, he has advanced himself. Now the next step higher on the rungs is the U.S. Senate. And you want to run for president. That is the progression.

There are, of course, some people in the House who have made a career of it—they've become Speaker or chairman or whatever. And these fellows wouldn't take a Senate seat if it were handed to them without competition. But those fellows are very, very few in number and the political graveyard is populated by all kinds of House members who wanted to become senators. And I'm one of them.

The status discrepancy between the two chambers was captured very vividly by Vicki Otten, a staff assistant to Senator Paul Simon (D-Ill.).

I remember several weeks into being here [in the Senate], Paul was meeting with a group of Illinois constituents and they raised an issue and he went over to the phone and called and immediately got through to a cabinet secretary. When he got through with the conversation he came back and explained what he learned in the conversation. Then, almost whimsically, he said to his constituents, 'You know, when I was on the House side and I called a cabinet secretary, my call was returned by an undersecretary or an assistant secretary. What I'm finding out over here is that there is no cabinet secretary who won't return my call.'

Virtually every senator who previously served in the House has a similar story. Timothy Wirth who spent twelve years in the House before being elected to the Senate in 1986 recalled,

A congressional liaison guy from the White House came by in 1981 right after Reagan's inauguration and introduced himself. Last week I got a call from the White House congressional liaison office asking me if I would help them on the INF Treaty. After I hung up the phone I realized that I had not talked to one of those guys at any time during the last seven years of my time in the House.

Differences so deeply rooted in the Constitution, in 200 years of custom and practice, and, above all, in the simple but stark difference in the size of the House and Senate, impose strict limits on the degree of convergence that could occur. There have been times that one chamber has taken on certain of the appearances of the other. There may even be a modest degree of emulation, but it usually does not generalize much beyond a very limited zone of imitation.

Most surprising, even for someone who has worked in both chambers, is the degree of isolation of the two bodies from each other. While one might hesitate to use the term "congressional apartheid," it would not be too wide of the mark. House and Senate occupy the same tiny island but the border between the two is well delineated. Border raids are repelled promptly and vigorously, as Senator Edward Kennedy learned when he attempted to get his nephew, Representative Joseph P. Kennedy II, a seat on the House Appropriations Committee. Cooperation beyond that which is dictated by the Constitution or by the specialized interests of members is limited. Partisan solidarity is a tiny hole in a fence and those periods of consistent bicameral cooperation between the institutional and party leaders of the House and Senate tend to develop at random. The most recent example of this was the period in the 1950s when Texas senator Lyndon B. Johnson and House Speaker Sam Rayburn, also a Texan and Democrat, worked closely together. Institutional differences always worked against this kind of cooperation, but party loyalty could mitigate the rigors of isolation. That bridge is now less sturdy, and when personal coolness prevails between the leaders of the two houses, the estrangement becomes more intense.

Even when both houses are under the control of the same party and have leaders pledged to cooperation, the essential differences between the chambers can precipitate harsh feelings. Indeed, one of the first issues to be tackled by the 100th Congress in which both houses were under Democratic control for the first time in six years proved to be one that inflamed feelings on both sides of the Capitol. It was a pay raise for Congress. While senators and House members earn the same salary, senators have a history of less enthusiasm for pay raises than do House members because senators are, on average, wealthier than House members and can usually earn more than House members as outside speakers because of their greater visibility. Other bicameral spats followed the pay-raise imbroglio. There was a late-1987 impasse on an omnibus spending bill that House members blamed on the leisurely procedures of the Senate. Failure to come to timely agreement on aid to Nicaraguan rebels was likewise laid by House members to dilatory tactics by senators. With great bitterness, Representative Mike Synar (D-Okla.) complained, "The Senate is a mess. It's worse than it's ever been. House members are being held accountable for a Congress that's broken that they did not break."[45]

House members, ever sensitive to the greater prestige of senators, rejoice in opportunities to put the upper house in its place. Even the most unlikely circumstance is seized upon to take the Senate down a peg or two. Take, for example, the case of the rice pudding served in the House of Representatives: Before each State of the Union address, the Secretary of the Senate, Gary Sisco, has a buffet supper prepared for the senators. At the 1999 buffet, one of the desserts on the table was rice pudding. Anticipating a delectable helping of the rice pudding he had savored in the House, Santorum filled his bowl only to discover to his dismay that the Senate version of the dessert was a pale imitation of the House version. He pulled Sisco aside and told him to get the recipe used by the chef in the House.[46]

Sisco assigned a deputy to track down the recipe, but she was unsuccessful in getting the House dining services to surrender it, and even when she offered to exchange some recipes from the Senate kitchen, they refused. Calling on higher authority, she appealed to Mike Marinaccio, director of Food Services in the Senate, to intervene with his House counterpart. When that failed, the hapless Senate aides purchased quantities of the House version and analyzed it for content and proportions, but when Senate chefs tried to duplicate the recipe, the results were disappointing.[47]

It turned out that the recipe was the personal property of "Ms. Janie" Galmon who works in the House kitchens. It was a recipe given to her by her grandmother in South Carolina, and she was not about to divulge it to anyone, including the U.S. Senate. Galmon, who was amused by the bicameral flap over her rice pudding, quipped, "Senators should be attending more to politics than to rice pudding." But the ultimate put down of the Senate came from Representative Bill Thomas (R-Cal.), chairman of the House Administration Committee that has jurisdiction over House restaurants. When told of the senators' plight, Thomas snapped, "Let them eat cake."[48]

While interviewing a former member of the House, now a Washington lobbyist, I mentioned the observation by now-Senator Donald Riegle that the longer a member serves in the U.S. House of Representatives the more he comes to detest the Senate.

The former House member turned his swivel chair and gazed out of his window, seeming to be engrossed in thought. Slowly, a malicious smile began to spread across his face.

"No," he said. "That certainly wasn't true in my case." Then he added, "I hated the Senate from the very first day I was in the House."

Senators, for their part, tend to be oblivious as to what the House members think of them. They do not deign to be angry. As Pennsylvania Republican Richard Schweiker recalled the relations between the two chambers,

There are these collective feelings but they run stronger one way than the other. The feeling in the House against the Senate is much stronger than the other way. If there was one term you had to keep using in the House it was 'the other body' when you talked about the Senate. Well, when you're a senator, you could care less whether you're called 'the other body' or not. You usually call the other place 'the House.' Now, you wouldn't rub it in and call it 'the lower house.' Senators don't believe in doing that.

I have attempted to build a case, thus far, that both the adversary and unitary forms of democracy are found in both houses of Congress but that the dominant expression in the House is adversary and the dominant manifestation in the Senate is unitary. David J. Vogler and Sidney R. Waldman, who applied Jane Mansbridge's framework of the two forms of democracy to Congress, stress the essential role of both forms. They state: "A policy decision, whether it is an adversary bargain struck among conflicting interests or a unitary agreement based on common interests, represents an end point of both types of democracy."[49]

But policy outcomes are only part of the picture, because "the democratic legitimacy of Congress rests on both the legislative process and the resulting policies."[50]

This process received one of its severest tests in 1998–99 when the House impeached and the Senate acquitted President Bill Clinton. The distinctive qualities of both houses were on display for a period of several months. The result of actions in both houses could be seen as merely a reflection of the partisan balance of power in both chambers against the background of a constitutional procedure that decrees that the House may impeach by a simple majority but the Senate can convict only by a two-thirds vote. Voting largely along party lines, the House, in which the Republicans enjoyed a majority, impeached the president, but he was not convicted in the Senate because there the Republicans enjoyed only a fifty-five to forty-five margin.

A story that is more interesting than the outcome itself is how the House and Senate did what they did. We will see that partisanship obviously played a major role in the outcomes in both houses but was expressed in dramatically different ways in each place. In an adversarial chamber where most members represent districts in which one party enjoys an overwhelming advantage, they may feel free to give full throat to their passions, savage their colleagues, and then go about their business. In the Senate, where the membership hears a broader variety of voices coming from their constituencies and has fewer places to hide, the incentive to keep even the most partisan impulses more tightly reined in its considerably stronger. It is not because senators are a higher order of being than House members that their work in the president's trial was concluded with a warm embrace on the part of the two floor leaders, but because, in their very essence, the House and Senate are, have been, and will likely always be, very different places.

NOTES

1. Bernard Mayo, *Henry Clay* (Boston: Houghton Mifflin, 1937), p. 271.
2. Ibid.
3. Nelson W. Polsby, "Strengthening Congress in National Policy-Making," *Yale Review,* 59 (June 1970), p. 487.
4. Alan Ehrenhalt, "Media, Power Shifts Dominate O'Neill's House," *Congressional Quarterly Weekly Report,* 44, September 13, 1986, p. 2135.
5. Ibid.
6. This encapsulated form of convergence theory is based on four important statements of the argument that are more elaborate and complex and deserve a thorough reading by anyone interested in exploring the question in detail: The four sources are Norman J. Ornstein, "The House and the Senate in a New Congress," in Thomas E. Mann and Norman J. Ornstein, eds., *The New Congress* (Washing-

ton, D.C.: American Enterprise Institute, 1981), pp. 363–371; David C. Kozak, "House-Senate Differences: A Test among Interview Data (or 16 U.S. Senators with House Experience Talk about the Differences)," in David C. Kozak and John D. Macartney, eds., *Congress and Public Policy,* 2d ed. (Chicago: Dorsey Press, 1987), pp. 79–84; Timothy E. Cook, "The Electoral Connection in the 99th Congress," *PS,* 19 (Winter 1986), pp. 15–22; and John R. Alford and John R. Hibbing, "Inverted Bicameralism: Electoral Sensitivity in the United States Congress," paper delivered at the annual meeting of the American Political Science Association, Washington, D.C., September 3–6, 1988.

7. Ornstein in Mann and Ornstein, eds., op. cit., p. 367.
8. Ibid., p. 368.
9. Alan Ehrenhalt, op cit., p. 2137.
10. Ornstein in Mann and Ornstein, eds., op. cit., p. 367.
11. Quoted in Tim Hackler, "What's Wrong with the U.S. Senate?" *American Politics,* 2 (January 1987), p. 7.
12. Quoted in Jacqueline Calmes, "'Trivialized' Filibuster Is Still a Potent Tool," *Congressional Quarterly Weekly Report,* 45 (September 5, 1987), p. 2115. See also Sarah A. Binder and Steven S. Smith, *Politics or Principle* (Washington, D.C.: The Brooking Institution, 1997).
13. For a fuller treatment of interpersonal relations among senators, see Ross K. Baker, *Friend and Foe in the U.S. Senate* (New York: The Free Press, 1980).
14. Ornstein in Mann and Ornstein, eds., op. cit., p. 368.
15. Kozak in Kozak and Macartney, eds., op. cit., p. 86.
16. Margaret Leech and Harry J. Brown, *The Garfield Orbit* (New York: Harper and Row, 1978), p. 198. Garfield won a Senate seat in January 1880 for a term beginning on March 4, 1881, but having won, in the interim, the presidency of the United States, declined to take his seat in the Senate. Inaugurated as president on March 4, 1881, he was shot on July 2, 1881, and died of gunshot wounds on September 19, 1881.
17. Evans C. Johnson, *Underwood: A Political Biography* (Baton Rouge, La.: Louisiana State University Press, 1980), p. 227.
18. Ibid.
19. Richard L. Neuberger and Stephen B. Kahn, *Integrity: The Life of George W. Norris* (New York: Vanguard Press, 1937), p. 48.
20. Charles L. Fontenay, *Estes Kefauver* (Knoxville, Tenn.: University of Tennessee Press, 1980), pp. 130–131.
21. Ibid., pp. 132–133.
22. Richard F. Fenno, Jr., *Homestyle* (Boston: Little, Brown, 1978), pp. 10–11.
23. Thomas E. Mann, *Unsafe at Any Margin* (Washington, D.C.: American Enterprise Institute, 1978), *passim.*
24. Richard L. Berke, "In Fight for Control of Congress, Tough Skirmishes within Parties," *New York Times,* September 12, 1999.
25. Richard F. Fenno, Jr., *The United States Senate: A Bicameral Perspective* (Washington, D.C.: The American Enterprise Institute, 1982), pp. 29–38.
26. "The Tin Cup Club," *Washington Post National Weekly Edition,* July 6, 1987.
27. Alford and Hibbing, op. cit., p. 30.
28. Glenn R. Parker, "Sources of Change in Congressional District Attentiveness," *American Journal of Political Science* (February 1980), pp. 115–124.
29. Clifford D. May, "Moynihan Working on Image," *New York Times,* Monday, April 20, 1987.
30. Donald R. Matthews, *U.S. Senators and Their World* (New York: Random House, 1960), p. 237.258

31. Richard C. Elling, "Ideological Change in the U.S. Senate: Time and Electoral Responsiveness," *Legislative Studies Quarterly,* 7 (February 1982), pp. 75–92.
32. Martin Thomas, "Election Proximity and Senatorial Roll Call Voting," *American Journal of Political Science,* 29 (February 1985), pp. 96–111.
33. Ibid., p. 111. See also Gerald C. Wright, Jr., and Michael B. Berkman, "Candidates and Policy in United States Senate Elections," *American Political Science Review,* 80 (June 1986), pp. 567–588, and Robert A. Bernstein and Michael B. Berkman, "Do Senators Moderate Strategically?" *American Political Science Review,* 82 (March 1988), pp. 237–245.
34. Steven S. Smith, "Informal Leadership in the Senate: Opportunities, Resources, and Motivations," paper prepared for the Project on Congressional Leadership of the Everett McKinley Dirksen Congressional Center and the Congressional Research Service, Washington, D.C., September 30, 1987, p. 10.
35. Ibid., p. 3.
36. Edward G. Carmines and Lawrence C. Dodd, "Bicameralism in Congress: The Changing Partnership," in Lawrence C. Dodd and Bruce I. Oppenheimer, eds., *Congress Reconsidered,* 3d ed. (Washington, D.C.: CQ Press, 1985), p. 425.
37. Ornstein in Mann and Ornstein, eds., op. cit., pp. 368, 371.
38. Steven S. Smith, op. cit., pp. 5–6.
39. Clifford D. May, "Image of a Senator: D'Amato Sticks to Local Issues," *New York Times,* Wednesday, May 11, 1988.
40. Ornstein in Mann and Ornstein, eds., op. cit., p. 367.
41. Ehrenhalt, op. cit., p. 2136.
42. Ibid.
43. For a fuller treatment of the new House activists see Burdett Loomis, *The New American Politician* (New York: Basic Books, 1988).
44. Robert L. Peabody, Norman J. Ornstein, and David W. Rohde, "The United States Senate as a Presidential Incubator: Many Are Called but Few Are Chosen," *Political Science Quarterly,* 91 (Summer 1976), pp. 237–258.
45. Janet Hook, "House-Senate Acrimony Bedevils Democrats," *Congressional Quarterly Weekly Report,* 46 (February 13, 1988), p. 296.
46. Ed Henry, "The Great Pudding Battle of '99: House Refuses to Share Secret Recipe for Rice Dish with Senate," *Roll Call,* June 24, 1999.
47. Ibid.
48. Ibid.
49. David J. Vogler and Sidney R. Waldman, *Congress and Democracy* (Washington, D.C.: Congressional Quarterly Press, 1985), p. 166.
50. Ibid.

7

The Impeachment and Trial of William Jefferson Clinton and the Persistence of Bicameral Differences

F EW FACTS ARE IN DISPUTE concerning the events that led up to the impeachment of President Bill Clinton by the U.S. House of Representatives on December 19, 1998, and his acquittal by the U.S. Senate on February 12, 1999. What concerns us in this chapter is less the outcome of the impeachment and trial than the manner in which the process was played out in the House and Senate and how very different these procedures were.

The impeachment grew out of an intimate encounter that took place in a Little Rock, Arkansas, hotel room in 1991 between then Governor Clinton and a young state employee named Paula Corbin. After Clinton became president, Ms. Corbin, who later married and was known now as Paula Corbin Jones, sued the president for sexual harassment under federal civil rights statutes.

Although the case would later be dismissed by federal judge Susan Weber Wright because Ms. Jones could produce no evidence that she had actually suffered any damage to her career from her apparent refusal to submit to Governor Clinton's sexual overtures, the plaintiff was permitted to introduce evidence that the man who was now sitting in the White House had a history of making sexual advances toward women. To strengthen her case, her lawyers attempted to track down such women and call them as witnesses against the president.

At roughly the same time, the former solicitor general of the United States, Kenneth Starr, was appointed under the 1978 Independent Counsel Act to investigate certain investments that had been made by Clinton and his wife Hillary Rodham Clinton in the Whitewater real estate development in Arkansas when he was governor.

Through an unusual set of circumstances, lawyers for Paula Jones learned of an intimate relationship that Clinton had been having since 1995 with a young White House intern named Monica Lewinsky, who had left her White House job in April 1996 for a post in the Department of Defense.

While at the Pentagon, Lewinsky was befriended by an older woman named Linda Tripp in whom she confided her relationship with the president. Tripp began secretly recording her conversations with Lewinsky. Such evidence of Clinton's involvement with another woman would obviously be of great value to Jones in her suit against the president. Unhappy about the loss of her access to the president and dissatisfied with the Pentagon, Lewinsky asked the president to find her a more suitable job in New York. To this end, the president enlisted the help of his close friend, an influential lawyer and former civil rights leader named Vernon Jordan.

On December 17, 1997, the president informed Lewinsky that she would be called as a witness in the Paula Jones case. Shortly thereafter, on January 12, 1998, Linda Tripp turned over the tapes of her conversations with Lewinsky to Independent Counsel Kenneth Starr, who quickly requested of the Attorney General Janet Reno and a panel of federal judges that he be permitted to widen the scope of his inquiry to include the president's relationship with Miss Lewinsky. The very next day the president gave evidence to Paula Jones's lawyers in a procedure known as a deposition. In this deposition, taken at the White House, Clinton denied a sexual relationship with Lewinsky.

When newspapers broke the story of the president's relationship with Miss Lewinsky on January 21, 1998, the president emphatically denied it. Starr's decision to pursue an inquiry was based on his belief that Clinton had concealed his relationship with other women in order to protect himself in the Jones case. When Paula Jones's case against Clinton was dismissed on April 1, 1998, it appeared that the president was out of trouble. Starr, however, had convened a grand jury in the District of Columbia to deal with the accusations surrounding Clinton's relationship with Monica Lewinsky and the possibility that he had lied about it to avoid having it exposed in the Jones case.

The president appeared before that grand jury on August 19, 1998, and admitted an "inappropriate relationship" with Monica Lewinsky but denied having sexual relations. Independent Counsel Starr continued to conduct an investigation for the purpose of recommending to the House of Representatives whether they should initiate impeachment proceedings against the president.

On September 9, 1998, Starr's 400-page report was presented to the House. October 8, the House, by a 257–176 vote, authorized the Judiciary Committee to conduct a formal investigation into whether there were grounds for impeachment. It was the last vote the House would take on this matter that was even remotely bipartisan.

After a stormy set of Judiciary Committee hearings in which all twenty-one Republicans voted to recommend impeachment to the whole House and all sixteen Democrats voted against, the House itself, on December 19, voted largely along party lines to impeach the president on two counts. The first accused Mr. Clinton of perjury before Starr's grand jury for denying a sexual relationship with Monica Lewinsky. The second charge alleged that Clinton had engaged in obstruction of justice through trying to buy Lewinsky's silence by concealing gifts he had given her and by attempting to find her a more prestigious job than the one she had at the Pentagon.

On January 7, 1999, the trial of the president opened in the Senate with the case against the president being presented by members of the House Judiciary Committee, known in the language of impeachment as "managers." The president was defended by his personal attorneys and lawyers from the White House legal staff.

After five weeks of testimony, the Senate acquitted President Clinton. With a constitutional minimum of two-thirds or sixty-seven votes needed for conviction, the president was found not guilty on both counts. Neither count gained even so much as a simple majority. On perjury he was acquitted by fifty-five to forty-five votes and on obstruction the vote was fifty-fifty.

Between the time the House members voted to authorize an impeachment inquiry on October 8 and voted to impeach Clinton on December 19, a congressional election had taken place that reduced the Republican majority in the House to a mere six seats and House Speaker Newt Gingrich had resigned. The fifty-five to forty-five Republican majority in the Senate that had prevailed since the 1996 elections remained the same. Accordingly, both House and Senate had Republican majorities, but very narrow ones.

The reasons that a Republican House impeached Bill Clinton and a Republican Senate acquitted him have much to do with some fundamental differences between the House and Senate.

The process also contained one major paradox. The House, which we might have expected to conform to the vision of the Framers of the Constitution and bow to public opinion, appeared to defy polls that consistently showed Americans strongly against impeachment. The Senate, invented by the Framers to be less susceptible to public pressure, seemed to sail with the wind of popular sentiment. Beneath this seeming paradox, however, is a reality that is entirely consistent with what we have encountered thus far in our exploration of House-Senate differences.

The House: The Triumph of Partisanship

Reflecting back on Chapter 3, do we find it unrealistic to believe that the House of Representatives might conduct a non-partisan impeachment? The most likely answer is that only a heroic effort by the leaders of the Republican majority and an equally Herculean restraint on the part of the Democratic minority might have produced a less fractious process. But it is important to recognize that even before the impeachment process began, relations between Democrats and Republicans were in tatters. After the House Judiciary Committee had taken its final party-line vote amid much partisan posturing and indignation, I observed to a staff member of a Committee Democrat that the hearings were so contentious the Democrats and Republicans were probably not speaking. She laughed and said, "They weren't speaking to each other before the hearings."

It is difficult to put a date of origin on the most precipitous phase of the House's slide into bitter partisanship, but it probably went into its steepest decline when Democratic Speaker Jim Wright was forced from office in 1989, largely as the result of charges of impropriety unearthed and publicized relentlessly by Representative Newt Gingrich of Georgia, then the second-ranking Republican in the House. When Wright was asked at a press conference how he felt about Gingrich, he replied, "I feel the same way a fire hydrant feels toward a dog."[1]

But many Republicans felt the same way during the forty unbroken years of Democratic dominance in the House. "Time and again, the internal politics of the House . . . [proved] a source of deep frustration for the Republicans who often [could] neither legislate nor score political points."[2]

The Republicans felt so oppressed that in a floor speech in 1990, Minority Leader Bob Michel likened the Democrats to the Communist Party in the Soviet Union in terms of the dictatorial measures used by both. Democratic attitudes toward the Republicans were summed up in Jim Wright's final address to the House before stepping down in 1989. He accused the Republicans of "mindless cannibalism." Bob Michel accused the Democrats of turning the House into a "den of iniquity."

Relations between the parties, if anything, became worse after the 1994 Republican takeover. Taking a cue from what the Republicans had done to them, the Democrats engaged in stalling tactics to frustrate the "Contract with America," the legislative program that had served as a platform for House Republicans in the 1994 election.

Newt Gingrich, the author of the contract, assumed the Speakership and asserted the powers of the office more aggressively than any Speaker in modern times. One of his boldest moves was to ignore the presumption of seniority in choosing committee chairmen and handpick more junior members to head major committees. Among these Gingrich choices was Representative Henry J. Hyde of Illinois to be chairman of the Judiciary Committee.

Toxic Turf: The Judiciary Committee

Representative Hyde, a widely respected member, was perhaps best known for his authorship of the 1993 Hyde Amendment that denied Medicaid payment for abortions except in limited circumstances. Despite his emphatic stand on abortion, Hyde was generally well liked by both Democrats and Republicans. But the membership of the committee consisted mostly of members who either sought out the committee or were placed there by their party leaders to do battle on the most contentious and least negotiable issues of the day: abortion, gun control, immigration, and school prayer.

One measure of just how polarized a committee this was on the eve of impeachment may be seen in the ratings posted by the most socially liberal and socially conservative interest groups, the Americans for Democratic Action (ADA) and the Christian Coalition, respectively.[3]

Based on their roll-call voting records for 1996, the ten

most senior Democrats on the committee received an average ADA rating of 89.5 out of a possible 100; their Christian Coalition score was 1.5 out of the same 100. On the Republican side, the ten most senior Judiciary Committee Republicans had a Christian Coalition Score of 85.1 out of 100; the same ten averaged an ADA score of 6.5.[4]

In 1974, the House Judiciary Committee had been given the responsibility for conducting the impeachment investigation and hearings into the conduct of President Nixon. The 1974 committee, however, was a very different body from the 1998 version. It contained a number of Republican members who kept an open mind about the possibility of impeaching a Republican president. Republicans such as Tom Railsback and Robert McClory of Illiniois, Charles Wiggins of California, and M. Caldwell Butler of Virginia made the vote on articles of impeachment in the Judiciary Committee bipartisan.

In contrast, the 1998 Judiciary Committee was composed largely of the most zealous members of each party.

House Republicans elected in 1992 [and] 1994 were the most dedicated conservatives to serve in the House in decades. . . . The Democrats [were] just as obviously reducing themselves to a core party of the left.[5]

Through a combination of retirements, redistricting, defeats, and switching of parties, the period of the 1994 congressional elections witnessed a dramatic reduction in the number of moderate (mostly Sunbelt) Democrats in the House. The number of moderate Republicans who mostly hailed from the Northeast and Midwest also declined. Of the seventy-three freshman Republicans elected in 1994, the overwhelming number were very conservative.

Within their own party caucuses in the House, conservative Democrats and liberal Republicans became an endangered species and not very popular with their more doctrinaire colleagues. So, while it is the case that "party leaders over the years have damned apostates in their ranks, . . . they have also depended upon some of them to act as bridges to the opposition. Members in the middle served as messengers, informants, agents of negotiation and brokers of compromise."[6]

The House Judiciary Committee was the very distillation of the parent body: diehard conservatives and passionate liberals. Yet there was a way in which the impeachment might have been steered away from a polarized committee and a likely polarized outcome.

House Speaker Newt Gingrich had entertained the idea of handing the impeachment inquiry to a select committee of House members rather than to the starkly partisan Judiciary Committee. Gingrich asked Representative James E. Rogan (R-Cal.) to study the impeachment process and make recommendations on which would be the best way to handle it. Rogan reported that "regular order" should be observed and that the Judiciary should take jurisdiction. That decision sealed the fate of impeachment and virtually insured that it would be starkly partisan.[7]

The Senate Trial: The Triumph of Bipartisanship

On the Saturday that the House voted to impeach the president, members of the Judiciary Committee led by Chairman Henry Hyde walked across the House side of the Capitol, under the dome, and into the North end of the Capitol that is the territory of the Senate to present the articles of impeachment to the Sergeant-at-Arms of the Senate. It was the first time since the impeachment trial of President Andrew Johnson in 1868 that House members had made such a trek.

The assumption from the very start of the impeachment process was that it was unlikely that the constitutionally required two-thirds of the U.S. Senate (sixty-seven votes if all senators were present) would vote to convict Clinton and turn him out of office. If all forty-five Democrats stuck with Clinton, the Republicans, with fifty-five members, would fall well short of the two-thirds majority.

The mathematics alone seemed to state the case eloquently that the Senate would be handling its part of impeachment differently from the House. The requirement of supermajorities of sixty votes in the Senate in order to process important legislation and invoke cloture against filibusters as well as the two-thirds requirement for convicting an impeached official argued for a bipartisan conclusion.

But suppose the Republicans had had sixty votes or even sixty-seven? Would the Senate have been as partisan as the House? That is a hypothetical question, of course, and we can never know the answer for certain. What is likely, however, is that there were enough Republican moderates in the Senate and their influence in the smaller Senate loomed so much larger than that of middle-of-the-road Republicans in the House that, even with a stronger GOP majority, the result might not have been different.

Half a dozen Republican senators simply could not be counted on to follow their leadership on all issues. In the Senate in 1999, that number included four New England senators: Olympia Snowe and Susan Collins of Maine, James Jeffords of Vermont, and John Chaffee of Rhode Island. Add to that number a scattering of independent-minded (or just quirky) Republicans, such as Arlen Specter of Pennsylvania and Slade Gorton of Washington, and the Republican margin shrinks to the vanishing point. As one observer noted on the day before the Senate voted to acquit Clinton, "In a process that has been marked so often by firm allegiance to party lines, the full or partial defection of a small brigade of Republicans was riveting."[8]

Whether it was simple math or chemistry—the peculiar chemistry of the Senate—the importance of proceeding in a bipartisan fashion was evident from the very earliest. The leader of the Republican majority in the Senate, Trent Lott of Mississippi, "wanted to escape the tar of partisanship. 'We could have rolled [Minority Leader Tom] Daschle,' the majority leader [said], but it would have hurt the overall atmosphere. For the sake of the Senate's reputation, both men decided to keep things relatively cordial."[9]

Even before the House had taken its vote on impeachment, the bipartisan wheels in the Senate were beginning to grind. Senator Slade Gorton (R-Wash.) was on his way to a resort in Hawaii on December 7, 1998, and placed a call from the plane to a Democratic colleague, Joseph Lieberman of Connecticut. Gorton and Lieberman, both political moderates, had become close when both served as attorneys general of their states and during their work on the V-chip legislation allowing parents greater control of their children's TV viewing habits. It is the kind of personal relationship that grows up readily in the more intimate confines of the Senate and often crosses party lines.

Believing the Senate was not facing up to the problems posed by the upcoming impeachment trial, Gorton sought out Lieberman to craft a plan to end the trial quickly by holding a series of test votes after only two days of presentations by House manager and the president's lawyers. If two-thirds of the Senate voted to accept the House managers' allegation as true, the trial would proceed. If the number fell below sixty-seven, the trial would be over and the president acquitted.[10]

Not receiving the unanimous consent required under Senate rules, the Gorton-Lieberman plan failed, and it appeared that a longer trial would be conducted. A number of senators had wished to avoid the appearance that the Senate was quickly and casually dismissing the work of the House. House managers were also asking the Senate to call as many as two dozen witnesses. The very issue of witnesses posed for the Senate the threat of a breakdown along partisan lines when it met on January 9, 1999.

If the Gorton-Lieberman initiative can be explained in terms of two moderate senators sharing common interests, the pairing of the names Kennedy and Gramm come very close to being a political oxymoron, yet it was a plan jointly sponsored by Senators Edward M. Kennedy (D-Mass.) and Phil Gramm (R-Tex.) that postponed the Senate's decision on witnesses and gave the institution time to resolve the thorny problem.

The agreement to defer the question of witnesses took place, not in the chamber where the Senate meets today, but in the old Senate chamber that was last used in 1859. The decision to meet in this ornate room with its red and gold appointments was made by Majority Leader Trent Lott. To further set the historical tone, Lott asked Democrat Robert C. Byrd, the Senate's unofficial historian and constitutional scholar, to deliver the opening remarks, which Byrd did by drawing on historical references ranging from *The Canterbury Tales* to the speeches of the great nineteenth-century senator Daniel Webster.

Gramm did little more than propose to his colleagues that the decision to call witnesses be put off, and Kennedy did nothing more than second Gramm's proposal. But it was perhaps that Kennedy, the staunch liberal, and Gramm, the strong conservative, had agreed on anything that caused some colleagues to proclaim it, somewhat hyperbolically, as "The Gramm-Kennedy Miracle."[11]

That such a minor point of agreement should have been the occasion for such great celebration underscores the climate of apprehension in the Senate that it would accompany the House in a descent into harsh partisanship.

In the aftermath of Gramm-Kennedy, there was an outpouring of self-congratulation among senators and a few not-so-sly digs at the House. Senator Patrick Leahy (D-Vt.) said, "If we went to the rancor of the House, we'd have totally failed. . . . I think that most of us, Republicans and Democrats, know the House failed miserably."[12]

But Republican House members saw the Senate—in effect, agreeing merely to disagree—as craven. Representative Bob Barr (R-Ga.), a member of the Judiciary Committee, observed, contemptuously of the senators, "How little interest, how little background they have to take on the tough issues."[13]

The senators had actually accomplished something quite important. As one observer put it, "[S]enators unanimous in the positive pleasure of letting the House, the White House, and the nation know today, at least, they had the backgone to go on record against partisanship in deciding the fate of the president."[14]

While the trial would continue for another five weeks, the tone set on January 8, 1999, prevailed; the Senate threatened on later occasions to abandon it but never did. The Senate, it appeared, had developed a kind of collective will that it would avoid the extremes of partisanship. And on the question of witnesses, which turned out to be the thorniest problem facing the Senate, six Republican senators confronting Republican impeachment managers from the House induced them to scale down the witness list to three people. The testimony they would give would be by disposition, not in live appearances in the Senate.

It is important to examine the elements of Senate bipartisanship and to identify those institutional features of the Senate that are either absent in the House or exist there in less concentrated form.

Intimacy, Power, and Restraint in the U.S. Senate

Less hierarchical and more individualistic than the House, the Senate has been very miserly in the power it gives to leaders. Each senator, with his power to filibuster or offer disruptive floor amendments, can delay Senate action in spite of the best efforts of the chamber's leaders. If a senator is pressed to the extreme, asserting his or her maximum rights and privileges would bring the institution to a screeching halt. But "because each senator's probability of attaining his goals . . . depends ultimately upon the Senate's power in the system, each has an interest in maintaining that power."[15]

Nonetheless, "each individual senator's behavior has little to no perceptible impact on the provision of the collective good."[16] This is a classic example of the problem of collective action in which individuals (U.S. senators, in this case) are disinclined to pay the price of acting in concert for the overall good of the institution because their personal payoff for doing so is so limited. If all senators pursue an independent course, however, the institution is crippled by the chaos of 100 members pursuing their self-interest. Individual senators, accordingly, are presented with objectives that seem basically irreconcilable.

But, as Barbara Sinclair has pointed out, "The Senate has been willing to coerce itself by giving leaders resources usable for institution-regarding behavior."[17] There is little doubt that Majority Leader Trent Lott played a pivotal role in developing a consensus in the Senate. One of the Senate's most passionate defenders of President Clinton, Senator Robert Torricelli (D-N.J.) praised the Republican from Mississippi: "I think Lott has proceeded professionally and in the best traditions of the Senate."[18]

Even as they recognized the critical role of leadership in the bipartisan solution, the senators' willingness to grant Lott this brokerage role arises from institutional characteristics that lie at the very core of the Senate.

The most fundamental institutional characteristic of the Senate and the one that sets it off most dramatically from the House is size. The Senate's very compactness in contrast to the sprawling House promotes and abets such things as filibustering, extensive floor amendments, holds in bills, and the use of senatorial courtesy—all prerogatives that if held by 435 House members would render that body unworkable. But does the Senate's compactness give rise to a restraint in the exercise of power so that both the goals of the individual senator and the maintenance of the Senate as an institution are served?

There is credible evidence that it does. The evidence of senators themselves—people of widely divergent philosophies—

attest to it. The paradox of power and restraint in the Senate was summed up by Senator Tom Harkin (D-Iowa). "The power of a senator to just throw sand in the gears is incredible. . . . In the House, one person can't do it. Maybe in some odd way that tends to make senators a little bit more cautious."[19]

Senator Robert Torricelli echoed his colleague's words:

Every senator is eventually dependent on every other senator to accomplish something. . . . Anyone can stop the institution, so no one can afford to be too divisive. So I think that keeps people closer.

I left the House of Representatives still not recognizing some members of my own party. The institution was so big and varied and people come and go with such frequency because of the electoral process. As a member of the Senate, I feel I live with these people. I ride on the same elevators. I eat lunch with them. We have caucuses together. I have social friends. I feel I know every member of the Senate. And I'm certainly not going to engage in some partisan and personal discord.[20]

From the other side of the political spectrum, Senator Phil Gramm (R-Tex.), co-sponsor of the Gramm-Kennedy compromise, used a colorful analogy to make the point that the considerable power vested in the individual senator promotes restraint: "You've got to get unanimous consent to do almost anything. I liken it to people wearing a gun in the Old West. People think of the Old West as being lawless, but in fact, the Old West was a place where people called each other 'Mister.' Because when everybody had a six-gun you were very careful with your manners. And basically under the rules around here, everybody's packin'."[21]

Bipartisanship in the Senate is a complex phenomenon. On the face of it, it might appear that the deference senators grant one another is simply a mutually assured destruction pact or a conclave of warlords, each of whom is armed to the teeth. Certainly there is some truth in these analogies, but there is also a positive dimension that cannot be ignored. Part of this dimension was summed up in a simple observation by Senator Byron Dorgan (D-N.D.): "In the Senate, someone sitting over there in the corner of the chamber someplace, [someone] you may not pay attention to, might hold the key to your legislative desire."[22] In a body of 100, it is simply easier to identify that person.

The opportunity to establish these ties over time, a strength reinforced by the six-year term, enables senators to build up a relationship of trust that can often be both mysterious and frustrating to members of the more partisan House, especially those who were part of the Republican class of 1994.

Reflecting on this in the months before his retirement from the Senate in 1996, Senator Alan Simpson (R-Wyo.) described an encounter with some newly elected House members of his own party. "They have a lack of trust. I know 'trust' is a corny word. If I tell people in Wyoming that I trust Ted Kennedy, they'll say, 'What kind of an idiot are you?' But it just means you work with him for seventeen years. And when you say, 'Ted, what are we going to do with legal immigration and the family preference system and chain migration?' he answers, 'You're right, and here's the furthest I can go.' . . . He's never once blindsided me, but his philosophy is different from mine."[23]

Impeachment and the Two Democracies

An important quesiton remains to be answered. If the design of the Framers of the Constitution was to establish a House of Representatives that was propelled by the winds of public opinion and a Senate that acted as a keel to give stability and moderation to legislation, how can this plan be reconciled with the realities of 1998 and 1999? Specifically, how is it that the House, in impeaching President Clinton, defied public opinion that consistently opposed impeachment and gave the president's performance in office high approval ratings, and the Senate, in acquitting him, comported with the apparent will of the public?

It is noteworthy that in the year between the revelation that the president may have had an intimate relationship with Monica Lewinsky and the end of the Senate trial, Clinton's job approval ratings never dropped below 55 percent and on two occasions were as high as 71 percent.[24]

On the face of it, the Republican majority that supported impeachment seemed to be ignoring public opinion, and if you believed the president guilty, it was acting with considerable courage in doing so. But recall the observation in the introduction that 180 of the Republicans represented safe Republican districts for whom there was little risk in casting a vote for impeachment. Indeed, as New York Republican Representative Peter T. King observed, "In those 180 districts, there's no damage in voting for impeachment. In fact, it would be very popular."[25]

Mass nationwide public opinion, then, can run strongly in one direction but in a single congressional district of less than 700,000 people that is dominated by one party or the other, the climate of opinion can be dramatically different.

The apparent willingness of the House Republicans to sail against the wind of public opinion, then, looks less impressive on closer examination, although there were House Republicans from competitive districts who did take a political risk voting with the majority of their party. But our examination of House-Senate differences is concerned less with the result than with the manner in which the two houses reached their decisions. In the House, the partisanship was open, bitter, enduring, and its effects were lasting. In the Senate, it was also partisan, but the partisanship was expressed more moderately (at least in public) and the fallout of personal ill will among senators was much less in evidence.

When we consider the reasons the House and Senate stories are so different, it is inescapable that those features of the Senate that derive from the smallness of its membership account for much of the difference. Rules that would be workable only in a small chamber are near the top of the list. Closely related are the powers enjoyed by individual senators which, if they were vested in 435 House members, would plunge that chamber into anarchy. The achievement of consensus through the routine use of unanimous consent agreements is at the very core of what makes the Senate such a distinctive institution, and it is this consensus-seeking imperative that enabled the Senate to escape the collateral damage suffered by the House while at the same time achieving a politically acceptable result.

Two Houses, Two Democracies

The consensus seeking found in the Senate and the apparent ability of senators to mute their partisan differences may appeal to that part of us that shuns conflict and embraces agreement, but conflict is as natural and necessary in human relationships as agreement. There are principles that need to be fought over. There are problems that do not yield easily to the soothing anodynes of conciliation. For this reason, the House, with its vigorous cut-and-thrust debate, its hard-edged partisanship, and even its extremist expressions, is no less a democratic place than the Senate.

Viewing the two chambers comparatively we see, in fact, two rather distinct expressions of democracy—what Jane J. Mansbridge refers to as "adversary" and "unitary" democracy.[26]

Simply stated, Mansbridge's argument is that the first of these forms of democracy, adversary democracy, sees the interests of citizens in perpetual conflict whereas democracy's unitary form is based on common interest and equal respect. It assumes that people have a common interest.

In adversary democracy, the majority rules. You take a vote and if you get 50 percent plus one, you win. Institutions in which unitary democracy is the rule arrive at their decisions by consensus, which is the end-product of face-to-face encounters.

The U.S. Congress, consisting of a House in which the issues of the day are aired and debated in a free-swinging fashion and a Senate in which the imperative of mutual respect and the terror of mutual destruction combine to promote consensus has served us reasonably well. The House may get carried away in the fiercest tides of partisanship, as it was during the impeachment, and senators may pull their punches in an effort to preserve an inflated notion of their own worth and dignity, but in the end, both the jagged edges and areas of convergence of public issues are exposed. In a world of imperfect institutions, Congress is less imperfect than most. In the words of E. M. Forster, "Two cheers for democracy."

NOTES

1. Quoted in John M. Barry, *The Ambition and the Power* (New York: Penguin Books, 1989), p. 632.
2. William F. Connelly, Jr., and John J. Pitney, Jr., "Congress' Permanent Majority?" (Lanham, Md.: Littlefield Adams, 1994), p. 91.
3. The choice of the ADA and Christian Coalition ratings as an indication of the philosophical polarization on the Judiciary Committee was made because some roll-call voting scores, such as those of the U.S. Chamber of Commerce or the AFL-CIO, tend to compile scores on economic issues. The jurisdiction of the Judiciary Committee deals more with the social issues of interest to the ADA and Christian Coalition, which are a better reflection of the split in the committee's membership.
4. Michael Barone and Grant Ujifusa, *The Almanac of American Politics, 1998* (Washington, D.C.: National Journal, 1997).
5. Ronald D. Elving, "Less Accommodation in a Partisan Era," *Congressional Quarterly Weekly Report*, April 15, 1995.
6. Ibid.
7. Peter Baker, Juliet Eilprin, Guy Gugliotta, John F. Harris, Dan Morgan, Eric Pianin, and David Van Drehle, "The Train That Wouldn't Stop," *Washington Post National Edition*, February 22, 1999, p. 6.
8. Frank Bruni, "More Senators Split from G.O.P. on Vote," *New York Times*, February 12, 1999.
9. Baker, Eilprin, et al., op. cit., p. 9.
10. Ibid.
11. Katherine Q. Seelye and Lizette Alvarez, "In a Rarely Used Venue, Rarely Seen Bipartisanship," *New York Times*, January 9, 1999.
12. Francis X. Clines, "One Senate, Indivisible (for Now)," *New York Times*, January 9, 1999.
13. Ibid.
14. Ibid.
15. Barbara Sinclair, *The Transformation of the U.S. Senate* (Baltimore, Md.: Johns Hopkins University Press, 1989), p. 210.
16. Ibid.
17. Sinclair, op. cit., p. 211.
18. Lizette Alvarez, "Lott in Spotlight on Impeachment's Center Stage," *New York Times*, January 3, 1999.

19. Alison Mitchell, "Signs of Moderation Emerge as Senate Anticipates Trial," *New York Times*, December 27, 1998.
20. Telephone interview, March 9, 1999.
21. Telephone interview, March 12, 1999.
22. Spencer S. Hsu, "Senators Partisan but Still Civil," *Washington Post*, January 31, 1999.
23. Claudia Dreifus, "Exit Reasonable Right," *New York Times Magazine*, June 2, 1996, p. 26.
24. "Public Satisfied with State of Nation, Clinton Accomplishments Outweigh Failures," News Release, The Pew Research Center (Washington, D.C.: The Pew Research Center for the People and the Press, January 18, 1999), p. 10.
25. Adam Nagourney, "Behind the Urge to Impeach," *New York Times Week in Review*, December 20, 1998.
26. Jane J. Mansbridge, *Beyond Adversary Democracy* (New York: Basic Books, 1980), passim.

Index

256